Welcome to

THE EVERYTHING® DOG BREED GUIDES

AS THE OWNER of a particular type of dog—or someone who is thinking about adopting one—you probably have some questions about that dog breed that can't be answered anywhere else. In particular, you want to know what breed-specific health issues and behavioral traits might arise as you plan for the future with your beloved canine family member.

THE EVERYTHING® DOG BREED GUIDES give you clear-cut answers to all your pressing questions. These authoritative books give you all you need to know about identifying common characteristics; choosing the right puppy or adult dog; coping with personality quirks; instilling obedience; and raising your pet in a healthy, positive environment.

THE EVERYTHING® DOG BREED GUIDES are an extension of the bestselling EVERYTHING® series in the pets category, which include *The Everything® Dog Book* and The *Everything® Dog Training and Tricks Book*. These authoritative, family-friendly books are specially designed to be one-stop guides for anyone looking to explore a specific breed in depth.

THE EVERYTHING® Poodle Book

Dear Reader:

As most poodle lovers will gladly tell you, poodles are the best! These loveable curly dogs have a way of worming themselves right into your heart. No matter what size you choose, you're bound to fall in love. They integrate themselves so well into the family, you might have to remind yourself that they're not human!

I can't imagine living without a poodle. While I have Standard Poodles now, I feel lucky that when I'm too frail to handle a fifty-pound dog, I'll still be able to have a poodle. I've had poodles I bought as puppies and poodles I adopted as adults. All are wonderful—and each has his or her unique personality.

My poodles have taught me the joy of positive training and the benefits of taking care of them holistically. Time and again, they've shown me the importance of trusting my instincts and intuition when it comes to doing the right thing for them. My goal for this book is to pass on some of these important lessons and to help you take the very best care of your poodle you can.

THE EVERYTHING® POODLE BOOK

A complete guide to raising, training, and caring for your poodle

Janine Adams

Adams Media
Avon, Massachusetts

To all my poodles, past, present, and future.

Publishing Director: Gary M. Krebs
Managing Editor: Kate McBride
Copy Chief: Laura MacLaughlin
Acquisitions Editors: Bethany Brown, Kate Burgo
Development Editor: Christina MacDonald
Production Editor: Jamie Wielgus

Production Director: Susan Beale
Production Manager: Michelle Roy Kelly
Series Designers: Daria Perreault and John Paulhus
Cover Design: Paul Beatrice, Frank Rivera
Layout and Graphics: Colleen Cunningham
Rachael Eiben, Michelle Roy Kelly, John Paulhus, Daria Perreault, Erin Ring

Published by Adams Media, an F+W Publications Company
57 Littlefield Street, Avon, MA 02322 U.S.A.
www.adamsmedia.com

ISBN 13: 978-1-59337-121-0
ISBN 10: 1-59337-121-7
Printed in United States of America.

J I H G F E D C

Library of Congress Cataloging-in-Publication Data
Adams, Janine.
The everything poodle book / Janine Adams.
p. cm.
(Everything series book)
ISBN 1-59337-121-7
1. Poodles. I. Title. II. Series: Everything series.

SF429.P85A34 2004
636.72'8—dc22

2004002192

BREED SPECIFICATIONS

UNLIKE MOST OTHER dog breeds, there are different sizes of poodle: Toy, Miniature, and Standard. Aside from height, weight, and other size-related criteria, the breed specification applies to all poodles, regardless of size.

Height:

Toy: 10 inches or under; **Miniature:** over 10 inches, but not over 15 inches; **Standard:** over 15 inches (with most measuring between 22 and 27 inches)

Weight:

Toy: under 10 pounds; **Miniature:** 12 to 20 pounds; **Standard:** 45 to 70 pounds

Head:

Skull should be moderately rounded with a slight but definite stop. (The stop is the indentation below the eyes where the muzzle meets the skull.)

Ears:

Should hang close to the head and be set at eye level, or slightly below. The ears should be long, wide, and thickly feathered, without excessive fringe.

Feet:

Should be rather small and oval, with arched toes and thick pads.

Tail:

Should be straight, set high, and carried up. The tail is docked to ensure a balanced outline. It shouldn't be set low, curled, or carried over the back.

Coat:

Curly and dense, with a natural harsh texture, or corded (coat hanging in long, tight curls, like dreadlocks). Poodles can be any solid color. Particolored poodles can be registered with the AKC, but they may not be shown in conformation.

Topline:

The back from the shoulders to the tail should be level.

Movement:

A straightforward trot with light, springy action and strong hindquarters drive. Head and tail should be carried up.

Temperament:

The poodle should carry himself proudly, with a very active and intelligent appearance and an air of distinction and dignity.

Acknowledgments

I'd like to thank Jacky Sach of Bookends for bringing this project to me, and Bethany Brown and Kate Burgo, this book's initial editors. Many thanks to the savvy poodle owners and breeders who helped me, including Marion Banta, Lynn Black, Steve Chin, Theresa Brandt, Judy Burch, Kathleen Cullen, Katharine Dokken, Debbie Edwards, Nancy Evans, Susan Fleischer, Gwen Gerow (my aunt), Mary Ann Giles, Caroline Hair, Marly Harvey, Else Leek, Grace Lossman, Patty McKnight, Kristi Murdock, Deb Phillips, Julie Borst Reed, Ellen Rivers, Lisa Runquist, Dott Smith, Kelly Lynn Smith, Irma Shanahan, Esther Underkofler, Gail Vinson, Diane Whitehouse, Linda Youmans, Janis Glick Zablocky, and Paula Zan. (Apologies to anyone I've inadvertently left out!)

Special thanks go to Shannon Wilkinson for keeping me on track and to Kim Thornton for her extremely generous help, both on this book and throughout my career. As always, many thanks to my husband, Barry Marcus.

• • •

Photo Credits

1. Photo on p. 69, Everdear's Ramsey owned by Sandra Nowlan
2. Photo on p. 39, poodle owned and photographed by Judith Winter of Rentiw Standards
3. Photo on p. 242, Seven owned by Liza Klosterman, photo by Bridget Anderson
4. Photo on p. 182, Seven owned by Liza Klosterman, photo by same
5. Photos on pp. 208, 30, 53, Lola owned by John Duquenne, photos by same
6. Photo on p. 222, Corbin My Man, CGC, TDI (left) and Leeloo the Supreme Poodle, NA, NAJ, OA owned by Jennifer Schraedel, photo by same
7. Photo on p. 124, Willie owned by Nancy Evans, photo by same
8. Photos on p. 166, 231, Kramer owned by Janine Adams, photos by Cliff Willis
9. Photo on p. 96, Scout owned by Janine Adams, photo by Cliff Willis
10. Photos on pp. 257, 138, Taz owned by Gilda Garcia, photos by Robert Avellan
11. Photo on p. 8, photo by Jean Fogle
12. Photos on pp. 81, 199, Fluffy owned by Esther Lind, photos by Theresa Mancuso
13. Photos on pp. 111, 151, 15, 263, Meiko owned by Enid Coel, photos by Theresa Mancuso

Contents

Introduction

▶WELCOME TO THE WONDERFUL WORLD OF POODLES! These fun-loving, beautiful dogs have legions of admirers. And it's no wonder—they're elegant, athletic, smart as whips, and great companions. All this in a package that doesn't shed!

One of the many great things about poodles is that there's a size for everyone. If you want a lap dog, you can get a Toy Poodle. If you're interested in a medium-sized family pet, the Miniature Poodle will fill the bill. And if you're a big-dog person, or perhaps someone who wants a dog you can hunt or run marathons with, the Standard Poodle is right up your alley. All three sizes excel in events like agility and obedience.

Poodles are glamorous, and that glamour has sometimes given them a bad rap. The unenlightened sometimes think they're sissy dogs, yappy dogs, or spoiled brats. While it is easy to spoil a dog as wonderful as a poodle (especially the tiny guys), a well-bred and well-socialized poodle is a joy to be around. These elegant creatures are so easily trained that with a just little effort they're an absolute delight to live with.

One thing that poodle owners often marvel about is the human quality of their poodles. While it's not fair to expect your poodle to act like a human—it's always a good idea to remember he's a dog, with a dog's motivations—sometimes poodles seem like small humans in furry coats. They seem to possess a capacity for reason that surpasses other breeds. And they're absolutely excellent at training their people. These dogs are so in-tune with their humans and so companionable that they easily become full-fledged family members.

You can take full advantage of these characteristics by involving your poodle in your activities and by focusing some of your family activities on your poodle. Get involved with agility (a sport that puts dogs through an obstacle course), obedience, freestyle (dancing with dogs), or any number of other great dog sports. Poodles tend to travel well, so you can take them along on family vacations, provided you choose pet-friendly destinations.

Poodles aren't for people who want to relegate their dog to the back yard. While they do need their exercise, they need to be with their human family members. And that wonderful, nonshedding coat does have some care requirements, so don't get a poodle if you're thinking you won't have to brush and trim his coat regularly (or have a professional groomer trim it, with regular brushing between trims). This requirement for regular grooming makes poodles one of the more expensive breeds to maintain.

Standard Poodles were originally bred to help hunters retrieve waterfowl. But poodles have filled a variety of roles through the centuries, including that of circus performer. Poodle lovers know what an appropriate job that is! These dogs love an audience. They learn tricks easily and love to perform. They enjoy being the center of attention, so the "Oohs" and "Ahs" of people admiring their tricks is music to their long, fluffy ears. Brains, beauty, and charm—poodles have it all.

Breed books are all about generalities. It's important to note that while generalizations can be made about a single breed, each dog is an individual. If you have more than one poodle in your family, you have more than one personality. Some personality traits might well match what you'll read in this book. Others might not. While it's important to learn about the breed, take all generalizations with a grain of salt, and don't fault your poodle for not conforming to everything you read. Rather, enjoy his individuality and revel in his quirks.

Poodles are a little like potato chips. Once you get one, you might want more and more. Provided your bank account will handle it, multiple poodles can be loads of fun!

CHAPTER 1

Meet the Poodle

POODLE LOVERS ARE PASSIONATE about their breed. And who can blame them? Poodles are glamorous, comical, elegant, athletic, and smart as smart can be. What you can train your poodle to do is limited only by your imagination. There's even a size to fit every taste. They're not low-maintenance dogs, however. The fact that they don't shed is wonderful, but that curly coat makes frequent grooming absolutely essential. And they require human companionship, but that's easy because they make excellent family members.

Poodle Popularity

In 2003, poodles ranked as the sixth most popular breed of dog in the United States, according to registration statistics from the American Kennel Club (AKC), the country's premiere registry for purebred dogs. Over the last ten years or so, American tastes have run toward the less fancy Labrador Retriever, but that wasn't the case in decades past. In 1960, poodles hit number one on the AKC's registry charts, and they held that top rank for twenty-three years!

The poodle was a cultural icon in the middle part of the twentieth century. What pops into mind when you think about 1950s fashions? Why, it's the poodle skirt, of course—*the* symbol of the carefree innocence and frivolity of that decade.

Fact

Gertrude Stein, John Steinbeck, and James Thurber are among the creative people of the twentieth century who have counted poodles among their muses. Indeed, Steinbeck's book about his journeys with his Standard Poodle, *Travels with Charley,* is a must-read for any poodle lover.

U.S. presidents, for the most part, haven't jumped on the poodle bandwagon. However, President Nixon's daughter Julie had a small silver poodle named Vicky, probably a Toy, when Nixon was in the White House. Vladimir Putin, the president of Russia, has a white Toy Poodle named Tosca.

A Brief History of the Poodle

The exact origins of the poodle are not clear. What we do know is that poodles are a very old breed—illustrations of poodles were carved on Roman tombs in 30 A.D., and clipped poodles appeared in French, Dutch, and Italian paintings as early as 1454.

While the name *poodle* was derived from the German word *pudel,* meaning to splash in the water, the breed has its origins in three countries: Germany, France, and Russia. An early English "Water Dog" similar to the poodle also existed. The Russian poodle was more like a greyhound in appearance, while the German poodle was sturdier and woollier.

In France, larger poodles became known as the *Caniche,* a variation on "*chien canard,*" or "duck dog." The smaller toy-like poodle in France was known as the *petit Barbet.*

Early poodles were large dogs used as water retrievers, and it is because of this serious occupation that the fanciful-looking Continental trim evolved. Poodles' coats were debilitatingly heavy when wet, so the dogs were shaved in the areas that didn't need protection from the cold water (like the hind end and the legs), with the ankles, chest, and head kept covered with hair. The Continental clip may appear silly to some (and has definitely given poodles an undeserved reputation as sissy dogs), but it has its origins in athleticism and hard work.

Essential

Although the poodle's origins can be traced back in part to Germany and Russia, these dogs are most often associated with France due to the breed's massive popularity there. The poodle is the national dog of France and indeed is erroneously called the French poodle by many.

Small poodles were also trained to be truffle dogs, used to sniff out and dig up truffles, the edible mushrooms that are considered a delicacy. These dogs, which became known as truffle poodles, were especially in demand in England in the late nineteenth century through the time of World War I. Truffle poodles were particolored, either black and white, brown and white, or lemon and white.

The AKC Breed Standard

Every breed has a written standard, established by that breed's national club, against which dogs are judged in conformation dog shows. In fact, the word "conformation" refers to how well the individual dog conforms to the breed standard. Dogs are judged not against one another, but against how well they match this written standard.

You can take a look at the following standard established by the Poodle Club of America (PCA) to see how well your poodle measures up to the standard. (The illustrated standard is available on the PCA's Web site, *www.poodleclubofamerica.org*.) If your poodle's appearance deviates from the standard, that doesn't make him an inferior or bad dog. It just means he's probably not going to win any dog shows. It also means that he's probably not a good candidate for breeding. In fact, dog shows were begun as a way to evaluate and identify excellent breeding stock. That is why spayed and neutered dogs aren't allowed to compete.

Fact

Whether a dog is a good candidate for breeding is determined in part by how well he or she conforms to the standard. That is why it's desirable to buy a poodle puppy whose parents are champions (and free of genetic diseases). It's an indication that dog-show judges have determined that these parent dogs are good examples of the breed.

The Overall Picture

That elegant air of distinction that surrounds most poodles—as well as the breed's legendary smarts—is written right into the breed standard. According to the PCA standard, the general appearance, carriage, and condition of the poodle is "[t]hat of a very active, intelligent and elegant-appearing dog, squarely built, well proportioned, moving soundly and carrying himself proudly. Properly clipped in the traditional fashion and carefully groomed, the Poodle has about him an air of distinction and dignity peculiar to himself."

Size and Variety

Poodles come in three sizes, Standard, Miniature, and Toy. The breed standard spells out the distinction:

- Standard Poodles are over 15 inches at the shoulder.
- Miniature Poodles are over 10 inches and up to 15 inches at the shoulder.
- Toy Poodles are 10 inches and under at the shoulder.

While it is technically the height of the dog that determines his variety, the type of poodle his parents are is also a factor. For example, an 11-inch dog born to a pair of Toy Poodles is usually considered an oversized Toy. Similarly, a 10-inch poodle born to Miniatures would be considered an undersized mini.

Size is the only thing that differentiates among the three classifications. In every other aspect, all three are measured against the same standard, though in reality poodles of each size tend to have a slightly different look.

Alert!

According to the breed standard, there's no such thing as "Teacup" Toy Poodles (extra-small Toys) or "Royal" Standard Poodles (extra-large standards). Such terms are used to make over- and undersized dogs seem special. Responsible breeders avoid this terminology.

Poodles should be squarely proportioned—they should be as long from the breastbone to the point of the rump as they are tall, from the ground to the top of the shoulders. The bone and muscle of both front and hind legs should be in proportion to the size of the dog, and that's why Toy Poodles are more delicate than Standard Poodles.

The Head and Body

According to the standard, poodle eyes should be "very dark, oval in shape and set far enough apart and positioned to create an alert intelligent expression." Those long, beautiful ears should hang close to the head and be set at eye level or slightly below.

The skull should be moderately rounded with a slight but definite stop. (The stop is the indentation below the eyes where the muzzle meets the skull.) The length of the muzzle should be about the same as the distance from the stop to the back of the head. Teeth should be white and strong and meet in a scissors bite, where the upper incisors slightly overlap and touch the lower incisors.

The poodle's neck should be long enough for him to carry his head high and with dignity. His back (known as the topline) should be level from the highest point of the shoulder to the base of the tail. The poodle's chest should be deep and moderately wide, with well-sprung ribs.

The poodle's front legs should be straight and parallel, and the feet should be small, oval in shape, with arched toes and thick pads. Hind legs should be straight and parallel when viewed from the rear.

The poodle's tail, with its signature pompom, is one of the most recognizable characteristics of the breed. According to the standard, the tail should be straight, set high, and carried up. It should be docked to a "sufficient length to ensure a balanced outline." Major faults are tails that are set low, curled, or carried over the back.

Fact

While most poodles seen in the show ring have long coats, the breed standard doesn't designate the length of hair. Some poodle owners keep their show dogs in a shorter Continental, with a shorter, cap-like topknot. This cut is called by some the "historically correct Continental," since it more closely mimics the cut that hunters originally gave their working poodles.

The Poodle Coat

According to the breed standard, the poodle's coat can be either curly or corded. A corded coat hangs in long, tight curls, like dreadlocks. Corded poodles aren't born with corded coats (though some are born with coats more amenable to cording); it's a hairstyle that the owner has to work to achieve. The cords—which are about the circumference of a pencil—are nothing more than matted curls carefully grown out and separated at the skin on a regular basis. Corded poodles were popular in Victorian England but are only rarely seen today, probably because of the work it takes to maintain the coat.

If you're going to show your poodle in AKC conformation, you must keep him in one of three cuts: a puppy clip for pups under a year old, or the Continental or English Saddle clip for adults. Dogs in the stud dog and brood bitch classes (where they're judged on the basis of their progeny), and those in a noncompetitive "Parade of Champions" can be shown in a sporting clip. See Chapter 10 for descriptions of these various clips.

Coloration

Poodles can be any solid color. An even tone within that color is desired, though in blues, grays, silvers, browns, café au laits, apricots, and creams, the coat may show varying shades of the same color. Poodles that aren't solid are known as particolored poodles, and these are disqualified from showing in AKC shows.

In order to conform to the breed standard, your poodle should have the appropriate color of nose, lips, eyes, eye rims, and nails. That color is black (with very dark eyes) for all coat colors except brown and café au lait, which should have liver-colored noses, lips, and eye rims, with dark amber eyes and dark nails. In apricots, it is preferred that these features be black, though amber eyes and liver-colored noses, eye rims, and lips are permitted.

Alert!

Though particolored poodles are not allowed in the AKC show ring, they can be registered in the AKC and can compete in obedience, agility, tracking, and any other AKC event. A particolored poodle can make a wonderful—and eye-catching—pet.

Gait and Movement

The standard calls for "a straightforward trot with light, springy action and strong hindquarters drive." When trotting, the legs should move on the diagonal–the front leg on one side goes forward at the same time as the hind leg on the other side. The head and tail are carried up. "Sound effortless movement is essential," according to the standard. In short, poodles should prance, with dignity.

The Work of the Poodle

Poodles are so clever and companionable they can make great working partners for people. If you can find a job for your poodle to do, he'll thank you for it. Working helps keep his brain occupied, and, depending upon the job, it might provide great exercise, too. As mentioned earlier, helping hunters is the original work of the poodle. If you don't enjoy the prospect of actually hunting, you can tap into your poodle's innate hunting skills by teaching him to retrieve a thrown toy. Poodles have also historically been performers, and they will love learning tricks to impress you and your friends.

▲ Poodles were originally bred as hunting dogs and most are natural retrievers.

Poodles can even work as assistance dogs. Standard Poodles are large enough to assist the physically disabled. Smaller poodles (as well as Standards) can perform other assistance jobs, like alerting hearing-impaired people to particular sounds.

Poodles make terrific therapy dogs because they don't tend to be intimidating, they don't shed, and they aren't marked by that strong "doggy" smell. If your poodle is friendly, loves people, and isn't afraid of strangers or strange situations, you might want to look into training him to become a therapy dog. There are a number of groups out there that will evaluate your poodle, help you train him, and place you in an appropriate therapy situation. See Appendix A for contact information.

Special Needs of the Poodle

As wonderful as poodles are, they do have some needs particular to the breed. The brains and beauty of the poodle must be maintained. But it's a small price to pay to have a smart, nonshedding, glamorous dog that is a great companion. If you're not able to meet the special needs of the poodles outlined below, you should seriously consider whether the poodle is the right breed for you after all.

Grooming Needs

One of the reasons people love having poodles as pets is that they don't shed. At least, the hair they do shed stays in their fur and doesn't go all over the house. But the price you pay for the convenience of a nonshedding dog is that they simply must be regularly groomed. If you don't groom your poodle regularly, you end up with a fuzzy, matted mess of a dog that is also very uncomfortable. Unlike some short-haired breeds, whose fur reaches a genetically predetermined length and then falls out, poodle hair doesn't stop growing. It's up to you to trim it (or have it trimmed) regularly. You'll find guidelines for basic grooming in Chapter 10.

Particularly if you start as soon as you get your dog, brushing and combing several times a week can be a pleasure for both of you, not a chore. The grooming process removes shed hair from the coat before it has a chance to form mats. And it makes life easier for you, your poodle, and your groomer.

Fact

Poodles will let you cut their hair however you want. Most don't mind being dressed up and in fact may enjoy the attention. They'll stand for just about any fashion statement you want them to make—that's one of the advantages to having a dog that has been handled for grooming from a very young age.

Attention and Companionship

If you're inclined to leave your dog alone all day in the yard, the poodle is not for you. One could argue that no dog should be an outdoor dog, but poodles in particular crave human companionship. They want to be full-fledged members of the family, and they'll do their part by being funny, protective, snuggly, and interactive. Don't leave your poodle in the yard. In fact, take him with you wherever you go, as much as possible. He's guaranteed to put a smile on the face of the people you encounter. If you train him (which is very easy to do), he'll comport himself beautifully. Your poodle wants to be with you, in the house, in the car, on errands. He doesn't want to hang out by himself in the yard.

Exercise for the Mind

Poodles are smart dogs. In Stanley Coren's 1995 book, *The Intelligence of Dogs,* the poodle ranked second (behind the Border collie) in terms of intelligence and trainability. A mind is a terrible thing to waste. Don't let your poodle's brain be understimulated. If you do, you might end up with a dog that creates his own diversions—and you might not like the activities he chooses.

There's plenty you can do to keep your poodle's mind occupied. You can train him (clicker training, in particular, is a great way to keep his mind working). You can give him puzzles to figure out, with interactive toys like the Buster Cube and Molecuball. You can make him work for his food by putting it in a Kong toy (a hollow rubber toy with a hole in the end) rather than in a bowl. He'll be forced to lick the food out (if it's wet and sticky) or toss the Kong around to get dry food to dribble out. If your puppy is very adept at this, freeze the food-filled Kong toy.

Essential

Your poodle might naturally be so well behaved that you don't feel the need to train her. But training her to do tricks is fun for both of you; plus, it strengthens the bond between you and provides important mental stimulation for your dog.

Exercise for the Body

It's important to exercise your poodle's physical body as well as his mind. It doesn't matter what size of poodle you have—your dog needs exercise. Exercise will keep your poodle fit. It will help keep his mind occupied. Regular walks allow him to see the world (or at least his neighborhood). Particularly if you have a young dog, giving him plenty of exercise will ensure that he sleeps, rather than getting into trouble when you leave him at home.

There are lots of ways to give your poodle exercise. If your dog is small, simply throwing the ball inside the house can provide a workout. Games of fetch in the yard, on-leash walks, off-leash romps (in a safe area, of course), and organized sports (described in Chapter 19) are all great ways to wear your dog out. Playing with other dogs is perhaps the best option. This will not only keep his body in good shape, it will broaden his horizons and expand his social skills.

Training Is the Foundation

Poodles are such social creatures, so smart and trainable, that it is both a pleasure and an obligation to provide them with some sort of training. Training provides that all-important mental stimulation for your clever dog. It's also a great way to open the lines of communication between the two of you. If your dog is well trained you can take him anywhere. That means you get to spend more time together, which will delight your poodle to no end.

Question?

Why should I bother training my Toy Poodle?
When you can scoop up your Toy dog to keep her out of trouble, or when you can barely feel it when she jumps on you, it's easy to think that training isn't necessary. But your Toy dog still deserves the mental stimulation and enjoyment that training provides.

The best part is that poodles make training easy and fun. They're so easy to train that harsh methods aren't necessary (and indeed can be counterproductive). So sign up for a positive training class, get yourself a clicker and some treats, and you and your poodle will be on the way.

CHAPTER 2

Looking for a Poodle

AS WONDERFUL AS POODLES ARE, you need to make sure the breed is right for you before you commit to getting one. And once you've decided on a poodle, where do you find the right one for you? With so many breeders, rescue programs, shelters, and pet stores offering dogs, it can be difficult to know the best place to get your poodle. But with a little research, you'll be able to find a healthy, happy dog to bring home, while avoiding the pitfalls some pet owners fall into.

Is the Poodle Right for You?

It's easy to extol the virtues of the poodle. They're good with kids, great companions, they don't leave shed hair around the house . . . the list goes on and on. These intelligent, friendly dogs aren't for everyone, though. Regardless of the size of poodle you select, the breed in general has certain needs that must be met. As explained in Chapter 1, all poodles need regular grooming (trims every couple of months and regular between-trim brushing and combing), human companionship, regular exercise, and games or training to keep their minds occupied.

Before you get a poodle, ask yourself some important questions:

- Are you able to devote the time necessary to raise your puppy and meet your adult dog's exercise and grooming needs?

- Can you afford the professional grooming and regular veterinary care your poodle requires?
- Will you keep your dog in the house, even when you're not at home?
- Can you keep a fairly consistent schedule so your poodle knows when to expect her walks, meals, and play times?
- Are you willing to make your dog a member of the family and take her needs and desires into consideration when making family decisions?
- Are you committed to caring for a poodle for her entire life—which may be fifteen years or more?

Don't bring a poodle home if you're hesitant about making any of these commitments or adjustments. You don't want to end up in a situation where neither you nor the dog is happy.

Poodles as Pets

If you want an athletic dog that can go running, hiking, or even hunting with you, a Standard or Miniature Poodle might be ideal. If you're looking for a lap dog to snuggle with while you're watching television, all three varieties of poodles can work well (though your lap has to be pretty big to accommodate a Standard Poodle). If you want a guard dog that will scare people away, the poodle might not be the most visually frightening breed, but she can be very good at alerting you to suspicious activity. The bark of the Standard and Miniature Poodle is probably enough to scare people away.

Getting Past the Stereotypes

One thing to bear in mind as a potential poodle owner is the anti-poodle bias that is all too prevalent in our culture. While poodles easily win over most people they meet, there are some folks who hold the relatively fancy appearance of the breed against them. The Toy Poodle, in particular, is subject to ridicule, though unfavorable comments are made about all three sizes. Some people may have mixed feelings about having the poodle as a pet rather than a tougher-looking breed. Poodle owners know what wonderful animals they're caring for and should turn a deaf ear to such comments.

▲ Poodle mixes can make adorable and delightful pets.

Poodles and Other Pets

Poodles can get along perfectly well with other pets in your family, particularly if they're brought up with them. Since poodles relate so well to the humans in the family (and often seem to consider themselves human), they may treat the other animal like their own pet, rather than as a peer. But there's no harm in that.

Your Cat: Friend or Foe?

Poodles and cats can certainly become the best of friends. To a great degree, the success in the relationship depends upon the cat. You also need to introduce the two animals carefully. See Chapter 6 for guidelines on this. Once the introductions are over and the two become accustomed to each other, poodles and cats can make very good interspecies companions.

Be sure to give your cat a high place where she can get away from the poodle. Escape routes are absolutely essential to keep your cat from feeling trapped. If she feels trapped, she may feel the need to swipe at the dog–if she makes contact, that might put a damper on their relationship.

Other Critters

Poodles are so intelligent and biddable that you can teach them to leave other pets, like rabbits, guinea pigs, and birds, alone. But use some common sense. Don't forget that poodles are dogs. And dogs are predators. So don't leave your poodle alone with loose fuzzy creatures your dog could view as prey. Keep your small pets out of your poodle's reach.

Poodles and Children

Poodles can make great companions for children. They're tolerant, easy to train, full of energy, and very smart. However, there are a few things parents should be aware of. As tolerant as poodles can be, you need to teach your kids to treat dogs with kindness and respect. Teach them to notice and obey any warning signals a dog might give that she's had enough attention (a curl of a lip or low growl, for instance).

Essential

Make sure everyone in your family wants a poodle before you get one. The sad truth is that there's an anti-poodle bias out there, and you want all family members to love your poodle and be proud to take him for a walk.

Small children should *always* be supervised around dogs. In fact, dogs and small children may need to be protected from each other. Toy Poodles are delicate and need to be supervised around rambunctious kids. If your child were to drop a Toy Poodle, the dog could break a leg. On the other hand, an exuberant Standard Poodle could knock over a small child in play. With proper supervision, however, a poodle could easily become your child's new best friend.

Who Will Care for Your Poodle?

Poodles make great family dogs. No matter which size you select, your new poodle will wiggle her way into the hearts of all your family members. If you're getting a dog because your kids want one, you can certainly involve them in the care of your new dog, but please be sure an adult takes the ultimate responsibility for your poodle's care. Being responsible for a living, feeling creature is a lot of responsibility for a child, and you owe it to your dog to see that her needs are fully met. A parent who thinks the children will take care of the dog will likely be disappointed, and the dog will be the one that suffers. That said, there are plenty of dog-related tasks that your children can take on, depending on their age.

Small children, for example, can help fill a food bowl and put it down for your dog. Older kids can exercise the dog—and even little ones can toss a toy for a poodle that has been trained to retrieve it. Poop pickup in the yard is a perennial favorite chore to assign to a kid. Particularly motivated older children can be the primary trainer in a dog-training class, provided the instructor allows it. Regular brushing can be part of a gentle child's routine responsibilities, though an adult must make sure that this important chore is done properly.

Where to Look for Your Poodle

There are a number of places you can buy a poodle, and some are clearly better than others. Since poodles, like all purebred dogs, are subject to genetic diseases, you're best off buying a puppy from a reputable breeder who has screened the parents to try to make sure they're not carrying any hereditary health problems. Unfortunately, many people who sell poodles don't fall into this category. If you can't find a breeder you like, adopting from a rescue group or shelter is another good option.

The Reputable Breeder

To find the ideal breeder from which to buy your poodle puppy (or an adult dog), look for someone who genuinely cares about the dogs he breeds. Such a person will provide health testing and certificates, spay or neuter all "pet-quality" puppies, supply a pedigree and health guarantee, and ask you questions about your lifestyle to make sure you'll be a suitable poodle owner. Stay away from breeders who advertise in the newspaper, breed without doing health screenings, or sell to pet stores or puppy brokers.

If you want to buy a poodle puppy, take the time to research breeders and find one who will sell you a healthy puppy. You can still love a poorly bred pup that suffers from health problems, but you and your poodle will be happier if you're not dealing with a lifetime of health concerns. Be prepared for these puppies to be expensive—whelping a litter responsibly is not cheap. See Chapter 4 for more information about reputable breeders.

Fact

> Price should not be a major factor in selecting a source for a poodle. The money that reputable breeders charge is spent on health tests and good care. It is paid back to you through fewer veterinary bills down the road. Purchase or adoption price is only a small fraction of the money you will spend on your poodle in his lifetime—make sure it is money well spent.

Breed Rescue Organizations

Another way to acquire a purebred poodle is by adopting a dog someone else no longer wants. Rescued poodles are by no means inferior. People often have to give up their dogs for a variety of reasons that have nothing to do with the health or personality of their pet, and some absolutely wonderful dogs are available through rescue organizations or shelters.

The main difference between adopting a rescue and buying a puppy is that, with a rescue, you don't have the health guarantees. You're throwing the dice a bit, but you're also taking the opportunity to help a homeless animal.

It's not always easy to find a purebred poodle puppy in need of rescue. But adult dogs, particularly of the standard variety, are available if you're willing to do a little searching and a little waiting. Contact the Poodle Club of America to find the poodle rescue person nearest you. Bear in mind that a needy poodle might be waiting for you in another state. If the rescue group allows out-of-state adoptions, you can apply long-distance and go pick your poodle up.

One advantage to adopting a poodle from a rescue group is that, typically, the dog will have been in a foster home. You can talk with the person who has been living with this poodle and get a sense of her personality, how she does with kids or other dogs or cats, and her likes or dislikes. This knowledge will help you select the right poodle to fit your family and lifestyle, and it also helps the rescue organization make the perfect match.

Alert!

Many poodle rescue people are responsible breeders who are so committed to the breed that they want to help all needy poodles. Expect to be grilled about your suitability as a poodle owner by a rescue group. Rescuers are as careful in matching a rescue poodle with his new family as they are in screening homes for the puppies they breed.

Animal Shelters

Many purebred dogs end up in animal shelters. According to research done by the National Council of Pet Population Study and Policy, 25 percent of shelter dogs are purebred. So if you're looking for a purebred poodle, don't rule out animal shelters as a place to find one. Bear in mind that if your area has an active poodle rescue group, the animal shelter may call the rescue group whenever a poodle shows up in the shelter. So if you don't see any poodles in shelters, it doesn't mean there aren't any available locally—they may just have already been sent to the rescue group.

If your local shelter doesn't have any poodles when you start your search, ask if they ever get any. They may refer you to a rescue group, or they may put your name on a waiting list so that you can be called should a poodle of the variety you seek become available for adoption.

Shelter animals make wonderful pets. It can be more difficult to tell their real personality when they're in a stressful shelter environment, but often you can take the dog to a get-acquainted room or take her for a walk. Many lifelong connections have been made in a single glance at a shelter.

The Internet

The Internet has revolutionized the way people find (and care for) their pets. If you're looking for a rescue poodle, you can find lists of poodles available for adoption. One site in particular, *www.petfinder.com*, is very helpful and user friendly. The database is searchable by breed, size, and location, making it easy to make a daily check to see if the poodle (or poodle mix) of your dreams has become available.

Essential

Once you find a reputable breeder, be prepared to wait for a puppy. Good breeders don't breed in great volume, and they usually have a list of people who want their puppies before the breeding has even taken place.

You can also buy a poodle from a breeder via the Internet, though you should use the same criteria for screening a breeder on the Internet as you would a local breeder. More scrutiny is in order, in fact, if you won't be able to see the breeder's facilities. Be sure to check references and get the necessary documentation with regard to health clearances for the parents. If at all possible, pick up your new poodle rather than putting her through the stress of being shipped.

Places to Avoid

Some people breed dogs in an effort to make money. And that often means cutting corners. Commercial breeders, in particular, do not generally screen dogs for health problems prior to breeding them. Nor do they take particularly good care of the dogs they own. Socialization can be seriously lacking. In short, a puppy that was bred by a commercial breeder often starts out in life with quite a few strikes against her.

But it's not just the so-called puppy mills that you want to avoid. Backyard breeders who don't take great care in screening their breeding dogs can produce unhealthy pups as well.

Pet Stores

Most pet stores get their puppies from commercial breeders. Some stores may get some dogs from backyard breeders, but reputable breeders will not sell puppies to pet stores. Commercial breeders don't breed with the genetic health of the puppy in mind. They tend to keep their breeding stock in less than ideal conditions. And, in order to get the puppies to the pet store when they're at their cutest, they often take them away from their mothers too early. The poor pups are often transferred in big, scary trucks. Unless they are sold right away, they languish in a cage at the age when they should be learning about life in their new home.

If you visit a pet store, you might be compelled to rescue an adorable, pitiful poodle pup from a cage. Resist that urge. While it would mean the world to that pup, it supports puppy mills and keeps the cycle going. It's much better to buy a healthy puppy from a reputable breeder or find a dog at a shelter or get one through poodle rescue. Many responsible dog owners refuse to even buy pet supplies from a store that sells puppies.

Alert!

Pet-store puppies are almost always of poor quality. Because profit is the driving motivation, they often cost as much as a puppy from a reputable breeder. Here's a case where you don't get what you pay for, so don't be fooled into thinking a high price tag at a pet store equates with a quality pup.

The Poodle Next Door

If your neighbors had a pretty poodle and decided to breed her, they might try to tempt you into buying a puppy. Heck, they might even give you the pup. If you take them up on their offer, however, you may be inviting trouble.

Chances are your neighbors won't have done any screening for genetic diseases, and they may not know how to properly socialize the young puppies from birth. Unless they carefully monitored the whelping, the puppy they'd intended for you might not even live through the birth. These people also won't have the knowledge of an experienced breeder to help you throughout the life of your poodle. If you have your heart set on a poodle puppy, you're better off finding a reputable breeder to sell you a healthy puppy.

The Newspaper

Don't make the newspaper classifieds the first place you look for a poodle puppy. They do have the advantage of instant gratification—you know the puppies in those ads are available. But reputable breeders don't advertise in the paper. It's an unwritten code among the best breeders. You're more likely to find ads posted by backyard breeders—the folks like your next-door neighbor who find themselves with a litter needing homes. These puppies probably aren't the offspring of dogs whose health status has been thoroughly checked. The parents probably aren't champions. They're not likely to have been born under the best conditions. They might be cute as can be, but they're not going to give you the very best chance for the healthiest puppy with the best temperament.

Essential

Don't pay a visit to a litter of puppies if you're not fully prepared to take one home. Before visiting a litter, check out the breeder thoroughly to make sure he's responsible and that you would feel comfortable buying a pup from him. Once you see them, those puppies are going to be very difficult to resist.

An Auction

Sometimes a charity will include a puppy in a fund-raising auction. This is a very bad idea, as the seller has no control over who buys the pup. Even if you would make a perfect poodle owner, don't encourage these auctions by bidding at one. The American Kennel Club officially considers auctions and raffles "not to be reasonable and appropriate methods to obtain or transfer dogs."

Similarly, an auction on the Internet is also to be avoided. These are worse, in fact, since they're usually conducted by commercial breeders (though occasionally a misguided pet owner will try to find a new home for his pet on an auction site). By buying a poodle at an Internet auction site, you're probably supporting commercial breeding, and you're taking a very big risk in terms of the health of the pup.

CHAPTER 3

Choosing a Poodle

ONCE YOU DECIDE THE POODLE is the right breed for you, and you know where to start looking, you've just scratched the tip of the iceberg in terms of the decisions you have to make before you choose your new dog. You'll need to decide on the variety you want—there's a poodle size to fit most people. Beyond that, you have to decide on gender, color, and whether you want an adult or a puppy. Once these choices are made, you can hone in on the right poodle for you.

Which Variety?

You can be a big-dog lover or a tiny-dog lover and still find a poodle that is just right for you. In fact, many people have more than one poodle variety in their family. While all three varieties are considered the same breed, there are certain differences to take into consideration in deciding whether you want a Toy, Miniature, or Standard Poodle.

Toy Poodles

Toys are poodles that are 10 inches or less at the shoulder. They typically weigh between 6 and 9 pounds, sometimes even less. These little guys are true lap dogs. Some fanciers say that the Toy variety is the clingiest of the three. If you'd like a sweet dog you can scoop up and carry around when you feel like it, one that makes himself comfortable on your lap, and one that travels easily, the Toy might be for you.

Fact

As tempting as it might be to carry around your Toy Poodle all the time, you need to let her be a dog and walk on her own four feet. It's the poodles that get carried everywhere that give the breed the reputation of being spoiled. Let your Toy be the canine that she is.

It's easier to exercise a Toy Poodle than it is a Miniature or Standard. You can play fetch in even a small yard and wear a Toy Poodle out. You can even throw a ball down the hall of your house for some major exercise.

Toys have the advantage over Miniatures and even more so over Standards in terms of being less expensive to keep. They do require veterinary care and grooming, of course, but their small stature means those services are usually less expensive. And, of course, they eat less.

Miniature Poodles

Miniature Poodles are between 10 and 15 inches at the shoulder and weigh approximately 12 to 20 pounds. These poodles are just right for those who find the Toys too small and the Standards too large.

They're hardy and athletic enough to play with kids and small enough to pick up when you need to. A smallish Mini can even fit under the seat in front of you if you choose to take him on an airplane. Their grooming is less expensive (and easier, if you do it at home) than a Standard's. They also tend to have fewer genetic health problems than Standards or Toys.

Standard Poodles

A poodle simply has to be over 15 inches at the shoulder to be considered a Standard Poodle, but most are much larger than that. Female Standard Poodles typically stand 22 to 25 inches at the shoulder, and males are usually 24 to 27 inches. Standards can range in weight from about 40 to 70 pounds (or even bigger), so they are ideal for those who prefer living with large dogs.

If you're looking for a jogging companion or a dog whose mere appearance can keep strangers at bay, the Standard might be the variety for you. Imagine having a poodle tall enough to stand on his hind legs and give you a big hug around your waist or shoulders!

However, it can take a little effort on your part to give a Standard Poodle the exercise he requires. Whereas a Toy Poodle can wear himself out running around the house, a Standard will need daily walks, games of fetch, or other focused activities. It's not enough to just leave your poodle out in your fenced yard and expect him to exercise himself, no matter how large your yard may be. Standards also eat more than their smaller counterparts, and professional grooming costs more. Be sure you're willing to provide for the extra needs of a Standard before making a final decision to get one.

Puppy or Adult?

When most people think about acquiring a dog, they imagine bringing home a cute little puppy. And certainly getting a dog as a puppy has its rewards. But it can also turn your life upside down. If you're not home during the day, or you want the new canine family member's introduction to your home to be less time-consuming and stressful, you should consider adopting an adult dog.

Benefits of Starting Young

It's a good thing puppies are so cute, because otherwise you'd want to kill them sometimes. They're just babies and need to be (gently) taught the rules of living with humans. It can be to your benefit to be the one teaching these rules from the time your dog is a puppy.

The puppy months are extremely important—things that happen when your dog is up to six months old can make a huge impression on him that can last the rest of his life. Being there for your puppy's formative months and helping make sure his experiences are positive can help you mold your poodle into the dog of your dreams. You have control over the training methods used, the disciplinary actions taken, and the things that your poodle is rewarded for doing. You carefully select his groomer so that grooming doesn't become a source of anxiety for him. You make sure he's exposed to all sorts of people and places, in a positive manner, so he grows up to be a happy, confident dog you can take anywhere. It's a great opportunity for your poodle to put his best paw forward.

Alert!

If you do choose to get a puppy, keep a camera handy from the very first time the two of you meet. You'll enjoy looking at these baby pictures (and growing-up shots) for years to come.

Puppies Need Extra Attention

The downside to buying a puppy is that it takes a real time commitment. Until your pup is housetrained, he needs to be supervised whenever he's loose in the house. He can't be confined for hours on end, which means you have to come home and let him out every so often. If your plan is to help mold him into an exemplary adult, you have to spend time socializing him. You have to teach him that cords aren't for chewing, cats aren't for chasing, and shoes aren't for eating. It's fun and rewarding—but it can be exhausting.

Adopting an Adult

If you choose to adopt an adult dog, he might seamlessly integrate himself into your family. In a best-case scenario, your adult poodle will already be housetrained, will know the rules of living nicely with humans, and will bond to you immediately. With poodles, this happens frequently.

Essential

Adult poodles do not have trouble bonding with a new owner. In fact, many people report that rescue dogs seem to be more grateful and loving than those that were acquired as puppies. Rescue dogs don't take you for granted!

If you adopt an adult from a rescue group, shelter, or previous owner, you may not be able to get a health guarantee or know with any certainty the poodle is well bred. But adopting a needy adult can have its own rewards and can be worth the risk of genetic diseases.

No matter what the source, even if your new adult dog has a few issues, that doesn't mean he won't be a great family member. Treat him with love and patience, and you'll know the special feeling of helping a dog blossom into a wonderful, happy companion.

What Color?

Poodles come in a variety of colors. The color you choose may simply depend on what color the breeder you select has available. You may, however, seek out a breeder who specializes in the color you prefer.

Color Generalizations

Theories (some say myths) abound about the effects the color of a poodle has on his personality. Generalizations—such as brown poodles are clowns, silvers are especially sweet, whites are sensitive, and blacks are especially smart—float around among poodle lovers. These generalizations are not factual or reliable. Perhaps because some poodles of the same color are related to one another, these theories sometimes can appear to be true. But the truth is that all dogs are individuals, and there are plenty of sedate browns, super-smart silvers, and sweet-as-pie blacks.

▲ Like all silver poodles, this puppy will eventually turn from black to silver as he grows up.

Your choice of color should be based on more practical considerations, like whether your poodle will be spending a lot of time around mud (in which case a white poodle might not be the best, though black poodles show off mud very well too), what color you find most visually appealing, and, perhaps most importantly, the color of the poodles available from the very best breeder you can find.

Particolored Poodles

The Poodle Club of America breed standard states that poodles must be solid in color. Those that are of more than one color may not be shown. But that doesn't mean that poodles of more than one color (known as particolored) don't exist. They certainly do—and in some people's eyes, they're even more striking than solid-colored poodles.

Starting in mid-2004, nonsolid poodles are eligible to be shown in United Kennel Club–licensed conformation shows. Solid and multicolored poodles are judged separately, with a best of breed chosen from both categories.

Although particolored poodles are still disqualified from being shown in the American Kennel Club's conformation ring, they are eligible for registration in the AKC. They can also compete in obedience and agility and all other events open to solid poodles.

Fact

The Standard Poodle that won Best of Variety at the poodle national specialty in 2003, Ch. JC Pioneer's Kaiser, is the son of a silver-and-white particolored poodle. Kaiser's breeders, Sarah Gessner and Julie Rossi, are leading an effort for inclusion of particolored poodles in the AKC conformation ring.

Reputable breeders do produce particolored poodles, as an accident of genetics. These dogs can make great pets. They can even be part of a responsible breeding program. However, a breeder who tries to charge you more for a "rare" parti poodle is probably not a reputable breeder.

Phantom Poodles

The phantom poodle is one with tan-pointed marks, like a Doberman. These are not as common as particolored poodles and are different genetically. They can come with black, brown, red, or silver base coat, with various color markings. The most common is the black and apricot. Like particolored poodles, phantom poodles would not be allowed in the AKC conformation ring, although they can make wonderful pets.

Male or Female?

Some people have strong opinions on whether it's better to have a male or a female dog. Some folks swear that males are more cuddly and that females are more independent. But poodles (like all dogs) are individuals, and certainly the generalizations don't hold true for all. There are no hard-and-fast rules about gender characteristics. Males do tend to be larger than females (though there's great variance in size in each of the varieties).

If you don't spay or neuter your poodle, gender can make a difference in terms of convenience. Females go into heat every six months or so, which can be messy and inconvenient, especially if you live with male dogs as well. Intact males tend to get into more confrontations with other dogs and to go crazy when females in heat are anywhere within sniffing range. Intact males are also more likely to lift their legs to pee in inappropriate places.

Alert!

If you are adopting a poodle to join another dog in your family, make sure the two dogs get along well. The general rule of thumb is that dogs of the opposite sex do best together—provided that both are spayed or neutered.

Try to keep an open mind about gender. Since both genders are great, try to choose a poodle based on personality and on whether he is a good match for your family. The gender of the poodle you adopt may be due to what the breeder or rescue group has available. Both male and female poodles make terrific pets.

Poodle Mixes

Perhaps it's because their curly hair is so cute, or maybe it's because they don't shed, but poodles have long been popular as an ingredient in cross breeding. People mix poodles with cockers, terriers—you name it. The progeny are cute as can be, but they're not purebred dogs. And as such, they don't have the predictability that you can expect from a purebred poodle. But if you're interested in owning a poodle cross, you have a variety to choose from:

- *Cockapoos*: Poodle/cocker spaniel mixes
- *Schnoodles*: Poodle/schnauzer mixes
- *Peke-a-poos*: Poodle/Pekingese mixes
- *Labradoodles*: Poodle/Labrador retriever mixes
- *Terri-poos*: Poodle/terrier mixes
- *Lhasa-poos*: Poodle/Lhasa apso mixes

The list can go on and on, since any breed can be mixed with a poodle. These mixes can be perfectly lovely dogs to adopt through a shelter or rescue, but don't buy one from a breeder. Anyone who intentionally breeds mixes and passes them off as a new breed is disreputable, and you won't be able to trust that they've done any health screening. Poodle mixes in pet stores more than likely come from puppy mills and should also be avoided.

Fact

Because poodles come in three sizes, the sizes of the mixes can vary, though they tend to be small or medium size. If you're adopting a young poodle mix, you probably have no way of knowing how big she'll grow up to be, unless you've seen both parents.

Picking a Poodle Puppy

It's a seemingly impossible task to choose a single puppy out of a whole, adorable litter. But if you're armed with an idea of the type of dog you're looking for and are buying from a knowledgeable breeder, you can get just the right puppy for you.

What's Your Ideal Poodle?

It's important to know what you're looking for in a poodle. Do you want an especially strong-willed or active dog? If you're planning to compete in performance activities, this might be the type of poodle that appeals to you most. A laid-back poodle might be better for a more sedate owner. The shy poodle takes a very patient, calm, and savvy owner to bring him out of his shell.

You should be very open with the breeder about your expectations for your poodle. Do you want to show him (a decision not to be taken lightly, because of the effort that goes into the coat and training), or do you aim to compete in agility or obedience? Or do you simply want a pet to take for regular walks and enjoy as a family member? The more information you can give the breeder about your intentions and lifestyle, the more successful she will be in making a good match.

Alert!

If your household contains small, active children, the Toy might not be the best size poodle for you. While they're sturdier than they look, these small dogs are more easily injured than the Minis or Standards.

Behavior and Temperament

Within any given litter, each puppy will be an individual. They may all have good poodle temperaments, but each will be a little different. To figure out which puppy might be best for you, watch the puppies at play. Is there one that is clearly the leader? Maybe he jumps on top of the others or steals their toys. He's the one you might want to avoid if you're a novice owner, since a natural-born leader can be somewhat challenging to own.

Is there one that stands away from the rest, watching? Maybe he's the one the other puppies pick on. He might not be the easiest pet either, since he might be somewhat fearful. Look for the pup that joins in the play but isn't necessarily the instigator.

Get on the floor, and call the puppies to you. Look for those that turn and approach you eagerly. The vulnerability of the shy poodle that avoids coming to you might make him appealing, but if you buy that poodle, you might have to expend a lot of effort helping him get comfortable with the world. If there are pups that don't rush to greet you but that do come with a little coaxing, they might just be a little cautious about life. This isn't necessarily a bad thing. It's the poodle that just wishes you'd go away you have to be careful about.

Breeder Knows Best

The most important part of choosing a puppy is listening to the breeder, who has been observing these puppies from the moment they took their first breath. She saw which was the first to find the best nipple and which one took a nap rather than competing to nurse. She's watched the puppies interact with one another through their whole lives.

Fact

Breeders can arrange for temperament testing for young puppies. This involves a two-minute test that grades each pup on a scale of one (the active, outgoing leader) to six (the shrinking violet). The easiest puppies to live with fall right in the middle of the scale. And, happily, most puppies are those middle-of-the-road puppies.

A good breeder has a great stake in making sure the right puppy goes to the right home. She's also very familiar with the breed and has the ability to identify which puppies will make the better show dogs, performance dogs, or pets. So when it comes to matching puppies with owners, your breeder should have the ultimate say.

Signs of Health

When you're looking at a litter of poodle pups, you want to make sure they're healthy. You don't want to buy from a litter of sick puppies, as this is a sign that the breeder isn't responsible. Moreover, if your puppy is sick, his development might be affected, and your bonding might be impeded.

Some signs of good health you can look for are great energy, pink gums (unless the gums are pigmented), and shiny coats. Watch out for signs of poor health: eye discharge, smelly ears, loose stools, or dull fur. A little beer belly could be the sign of a parasite infestation. If you see signs of poor health in the litter, or if your inner voice says that the litter or kennel isn't optimal, walk away without a puppy.

Choosing an Adult Poodle

To make sure that the adult poodle you're considering is the right one for you, walk into the meeting with an open heart, but be ready to walk away without the poodle if the match doesn't seem right.

Just as in choosing a puppy, you should have realistic expectations of what you plan to do with this poodle. An added consideration in adopting an adult dog is how much work you're willing to put into the relationship. If you adopt a dog with a little baggage, it may take some work on your part to help the dog realize his potential. It's extremely rewarding work, however, as long as you go into the relationship willing to do it. If you're an inexperienced poodle owner, you might require an adult that's already very well adjusted.

One advantage of getting an adult dog is that his personality has already emerged. When you meet the dog, pay attention to your gut instincts. Are there any warning signals that this might not be the best match? Does the dog respond to you? Does his energy level seem appropriate for your lifestyle? Listen to your heart, and you can adopt the perfect poodle.

CHAPTER 4

Reputable Breeders

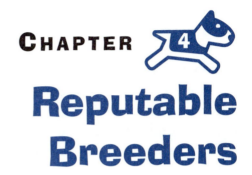

IF YOU'RE GOING TO BUY A POODLE PUPPY, and you want to make sure that your puppy will grow up to be of good health and sound temperament (and who doesn't?), you should buy her from a reputable breeder. It's that simple. Finding a breeder takes a little more work than walking into a pet store—and you need to learn how to recognize a reputable one—but the search is well worth the time and effort.

What Is a Reputable Breeder?

A reputable breeder, also known as a "hobby breeder," is a person who breeds dogs out of a love for the breed and a strong desire to better the breed. A reputable breeder is not in the dog-breeding game for the money.

A reputable breeder is extremely knowledgeable about the breed. Though everyone was a beginner at some point, an ideal breeder has had a great deal of breeding experience (at least five years). Reputable breeders are involved in conformation shows, and they only breed poodles that have achieved their championship.

The Health Connection

Reputable breeders get health clearances on all the dogs they breed and immediately stop breeding those they discover are carriers of inherited diseases. When a genetic test becomes available, a reputable breeder is quick to incorporate it into his breeding program.

Devoted Care

When a reputable breeder has a litter, the puppies become the focus of the breeder's life. He handles them frequently and makes sure they are familiar with the sights, sounds, and activities of a typical home. This makes the transition into a new home much easier.

Done properly, breeding is not a money-making proposition. It's expensive to do the genetic tests and health screens to ensure that a litter will be healthy. Veterinary bills and high-quality food add to the cost of whelping a litter. Even with a trouble-free whelping of healthy puppies, a breeder is lucky to break even.

Question?

Why is it so hard to find a puppy from a reputable breeder? Because frequent breeding is hard on the mother, responsible breeders breed litters only occasionally. Because of this, a puppy might not be available when you want one. It's important to be flexible when you start your puppy search. It's worth the wait.

Finding a Reputable Breeder

A good place to start in your search for a breeder is the PCA's Web site, at *www.poodleclubofamerica.org*. Another way to look (and learn a lot about poodles while you're at it) is to subscribe to one of the poodle Internet mailing lists, like the Poodle Support Group or Poodle-L. These groups are populated by breeders and pet owners alike. You can post an inquiry about breeders and can also read about and become acquainted with breeders you may be interested in buying a poodle from.

The Internet can be a valuable resource to get you started, but remember, just because a breeder is a member of the PCA, writes well on an Internet mailing list, or has a fancy Web site, it doesn't mean that he is necessarily reputable. You should check out the breeder thoroughly, just as you'd check out a breeder found through any other source.

Probably the best way to meet a group of breeders, and see some of their dogs, is to go to a dog show. Breeders will be happy to chat with you—but only after they've had their turn in the ring. Before that, they're busy grooming their poodles and getting ready to show. Puppies are not sold at dog shows, so come ready to learn, not to buy.

▲ Puppies learn important lessons from their mother and littermates, so most reputable breeders wait until the puppies are at least 8 weeks old before sending them to their new homes.

Questions to Ask the Breeder

When you start your search for a breeder, be prepared with a list of questions that will help you screen the breeder and convince you that this breeder is indeed reputable. Such questions should include the following:

- How long have you been involved with the breed?
- How did you become interested in poodles?
- How many litters do you breed in a year?

- Do you breed any other breeds?
- How old are the puppy's parents?
- May I come take a look at your kennel?
- What are the health problems in poodles?
- What health clearances do your dogs have?
- What health guarantees do you provide?
- Are there any negative aspects to owning a poodle?

If the breeder says that he breeds more than a couple of breeds, that's a big red flag (though breeding different varieties or colors of poodles isn't necessarily a problem). Remember, you're looking for an expert on poodles, not someone with a general knowledge of many kinds of dogs. Also bear in mind that a reputable breeder doesn't breed females before the age of two—and waits to breed until both parents are old enough to have all health clearances.

If the breeder won't allow you to come out to his facility, but suggests that he bring a puppy to you or that you meet in a neutral place, that's another red flag. You want to buy a puppy from a breeder who is proud to show you his entire kennel, so that you can judge for yourself its cleanliness and how he takes care of his dogs.

You should know before asking what the health problems in poodles are (from the information in this chapter and Chapter 13), so that you can judge whether the breeder is being completely honest with you.

Questions to Expect the Breeder to Ask You

The interview with the potential breeder is a two-way street. A reputable breeder will ask you a great number of questions in an effort to make sure you're a suitable owner for one of his puppies. A responsible breeder always screens buyers very carefully.

When you call potential breeders with your questions, expect to be asked questions such as these:

- Why do you want a [fill in the variety] poodle?
- Do you work outside the home, or will you be home during the day?
- Who will be the primary caregiver for the poodle?
- How will the poodle be exercised?
- Do you own your home?
- Do you have a fenced yard?
- Do you have children?
- Have you had a dog before? If so, what happened to him?
- What is the name and phone number of your veterinarian?

Don't be offended if the breeder grills you. In fact, you should welcome these questions, as they're an indication that the breeder really cares where his puppies are placed. If the breeder doesn't ask you any questions about yourself, be wary. That breeder is probably breeding just to make money.

Fact

The questions the breeder asks potential buyers (and the answers he receives) not only help him screen buyers to make sure they'll provide good homes, but they also help the breeder match the puppies in the litters to the most appropriate families.

Health Certifications

Like many dog breeds, poodles are prone to certain diseases they inherit from their parents. Because the gene pool is limited in purebred dogs, some diseases are passed on through the generations. Some diseases are recessive, meaning that the parent doesn't have to actually have the disease to pass it on to puppies. Those asymptomatic parents that pass on a disease are known as carriers. Happily, groups like the AKC Canine Health Foundation and the

Morris Animal Foundation are funding research to identify the genes responsible for heritable diseases in various breeds, with the ultimate goal of developing a genetic test that would identify carriers of these diseases.

Two DNA tests already exist to detect carriers of poodle-related diseases. One is for Von Willebrand's disease, a blood-clotting disease that affects all three varieties. The other is a test for Toys and Miniatures for a specific type of the eye disease called progressive retinal atrophy.

For those diseases for which genetic tests are not available, you can do your best to buy a healthy puppy by making sure that the parents have been properly screened to show they aren't afflicted with any of the diseases and that they haven't already produced offspring that are.

The following hereditary diseases can all be detected by screening tests. Most of these tests simply involve a specific physical exam, x-ray, or blood test. When you are looking for a poodle puppy, be sure to ask the breeder about the diseases listed here. If the parents haven't been screened for them, look elsewhere.

Hereditary Poodle Diseases

Disease	Description	Size(s) Affected*
Addison's disease	Poorly functioning adrenal glands	S
Hip dysplasia	Malformed hip sockets	S, M, T
Hypothyroidism	Poorly functioning thyroid	S, M, T
Juvenile renal disease	Fatal kidney disease	S
Legg-Calve-Perthe's disease	Hip disorder	M, T
Patellar luxation	Slipping kneecap	M, T
Progressive retinal atrophy (*prcd* type)	Eye disease	M, T
Sebaceous adenitis	Skin disease	S
Von Willebrand's disease	Blood disorder	S, M, T

***S = Standard, M = Miniature, T = Toy**

The results of these tests can be registered in various disease registries to help breeders decide which pairs of dogs to breed. The registry is also a good means of helping potential buyers check out the parents of puppies they're considering. These are the main disease registries to be aware of:

- **Orthopedic Foundation for Animals (OFA):** Provides x-ray evaluation as well as breeding advice. The OFA database holds information on seven diseases that commonly affect poodles, including hip dysplasia and Von Willebrand's disease.
- **Canine Eye Registry Foundation (CERF):** Registers dogs that are certified by board-certified veterinary ophthalmologists to be free of heritable eye diseases.
- **Canine Health Information Center (CHIC):** Certifies poodles that have received health certificates for a prescribed set of diseases recommended by the PCA.
- **The Poodle Health Registry (PHR):** A nonprofit association that has been formed to provide a centralized online database containing all available information about veterinarian-documented health problems in specific poodles of all sizes.

Be sure to ask your breeder for copies of the health certifications he has received from the appropriate registries. As trusting as you might like to be, this is too important to just take his word. Alternatively, you can confirm the certifications directly with the registries. See Appendix A for contact information and Web sites for each registry. (CHIC information can be found on the OFA site.)

Your Poodle's Papers

Some folks have the impression that if a poodle comes with "papers," it's an indication that she's a high-quality dog. (And some breeders try hard to make that impression.) In reality, the word "papers" simply refers to the AKC registration papers that a registered puppy will be sent home with (paperwork that has to be completed by you and mailed to the AKC). These papers are not a measure of quality, however. They simply indicate that the dog is purebred and that her parents were purebred and registered with the AKC.

Your poodle should be sent home with more paperwork than just an AKC registration. There's her pedigree, health records, the sales contract, and the health guarantee. Knowing what to expect in terms of paperwork will help you understand these documents when the breeder gives them to you.

Essential

Make the effort to pay a visit to the breeder in person. Along with seeing the living conditions and meeting the puppy's parents, you can get a feeling for how the breeder regards his poodles and (perhaps even more important) how the poodles regard him. Watch for casual signs of affection and adoring gazes on behalf of both dog and breeder.

Registration Papers

A breeder who says a particular pup comes with registration papers is probably talking about the American Kennel Club (AKC). The AKC is the largest and oldest purebred dog registry in the country (in Canada, the largest registry is the Canadian Kennel Club). If you'd like to participate in AKC activities, like conformation, obedience, agility, tracking, or hunt tests, your poodle will need to be AKC registered. The AKC requires you to register your dog within twelve months of her birth.

When you pick up your puppy, you should receive a blue form from the breeder, with all information about the dog properly filled in. You will need to complete this form and send it in to the AKC with the registration fee to register your pup. The breeder must register the litter before you can register the individual puppy.

If the breeder isn't able to supply the AKC form for registration, he should supply you with a signed bill of sale that includes the puppy's breed, sex and color, date of birth, litter number (when available), names and registration numbers of sire and dam, name of breeder, and date sold or delivered. When the breeder does eventually supply the AKC paperwork, compare the information on it to this identification information. If the breeder is not willing to supply you with that information, consider that a red flag.

Alert!

If a little voice inside you suggests that this is not the best breeder, don't buy the puppy. It can be hard to walk away from a poodle, but it's more important that the puppy come from an excellent breeder. Don't ignore red flags.

When you fill out the registration forms, you'll have to select a registered name for your poodle. The breeder may require you to include the kennel name in the registered name (or may require you not to), but after that, it's up to you. This is different than your poodle's call name (the name you will actually use every day), so you can have some fun with it. Bear in mind that your name choice is limited to twenty-five characters, including spaces and punctuation. If you're planning to compete in AKC events, the registered name is what your poodle will be known by, so select it carefully.

Limited Registration

If you are buying a pet-quality puppy (one whose physical characteristics don't make her a candidate for the show ring or for breeding), the breeder may designate a "limited registration," meaning that your poodle is registered, but any offspring she might bear cannot be registered with the AKC. This is designed to discourage the breeding of all but top-quality dogs. A breeder selling a pup with a limited registration will probably also have a clause in the sales contract requiring the spay or neuter of the dog. A dog with a limited registration cannot participate in conformation shows, though she can participate in other AKC activities.

If your poodle turns out to be a fabulous show-quality specimen whose breeding would further the breed, the poodle breeder can reverse his decision about the limited registration and give you a full registration. Only the person who owned the dog at birth may apply to the AKC for the removal of the limitation.

Alternatives to AKC Registration

Rescued poodles that don't come with an AKC registration may be eligible for an indefinite listing privilege (ILP) number that allows the dog to participate in AKC events. In order to get an ILP number, you must submit two color photos of your dog and a letter from your veterinarian stating that the dog has been spayed or neutered, along with an application and application fee (refundable if the dog is not issued an ILP number).

The United Kennel Club is another legitimate registry for poodles, though it recognizes Standard Poodles as a separate breed from other poodles (that is, Miniature and Toy). Like the AKC, the UKC also sponsors dog shows and events that poodles can participate in. It allows sporting clips on poodles in conformation competition, but UKC conformation events are less widely available than AKC events.

Essential

If the registration papers your breeder offers are from any registry other than the American Kennel Club, United Kennel Club, or the Canadian Kennel Club (provided you're in North America), walk away. Alternative registries, like the Continental Kennel Club and the World Wide Kennel Club, have much less stringent requirements.

The Pedigree

Anyone who has done any genealogical research is familiar with a pedigree. It's simply a chart that shows an individual, her parents, her parents' parents, and so on. Your poodle's pedigree will contain each of her forebears' registered names, often with prefixes before and suffixes after the name. As a general rule, the more dogs in the pedigree with the initials "Ch" before their name (an abbreviation for "Champion"), the better, since champions have been judged to meet the breed standard. Other titles, like agility and obedience titles, which appear after the name, sometimes also appear on pedigrees. A pedigree is not essential if you're not going to breed your poodle. But it's nice to have in your files. You might meet a poodle whose background you'd like to compare with your dog's. Sometimes researchers of genetic health problems in poodles will want blood or DNA samples and pedigrees from healthy poodles (as well as those affected by the disease in question). If you have a pedigree in your files, you can contribute to that research and help the breed.

Fact

Registration papers from the American Kennel Club have no bearing on the quality of the puppy. They simply signify that the dog is purebred and both his parents are purebred and AKC registered. They say nothing about the health or temperament of the puppy.

A reputable breeder will provide you with a copy of the pedigree, or you can request one from the AKC, provided your puppy has been registered.

The Sales Contract

Your breeder will supply you with a contract that outlines the terms of the sale. These terms might include a requirement for spaying and neutering a pet-quality pup on a limited registration. It may require you to return the puppy to the breeder if you end up needing to find a new home for her. It will spell out the purchase price and will include the terms of returning the pup within the first few days if a veterinarian finds a health problem.

The Health Guarantee

In addition, the breeder should provide some sort of health guarantee, which can be part of the sales contract or a separate document. This clause guarantees the poodle to be free of inherited health problems for a prescribed length of time. It will spell out the breeder's responsibility in the event of an inherited problem. He might offer a refund of all or part of the purchase price, a replacement poodle, or a discount on a poodle from another litter.

Even though a reputable breeder is willing to supply a guarantee against inherited conditions, please understand that it doesn't mean your poodle will never become ill. Many health issues aren't predictable, and even if you do your very best to select a breeder who tests his breeding stock and provides guarantees, your poodle might have a health problem. It's possible for a poodle to be a carrier of a genetic disease without the breeder's knowing it. If that should happen, look to your breeder as an ally, not a foe. He might be able to provide valuable information on dealing with the disorder because of his experience with the breed.

Essential

Always inform your breeder if your poodle becomes seriously ill. If the malady has a genetic component, this is information upon which he might base future breeding decisions. Approach the breeder without accusation. This news may be as devastating to him as it was to you.

Veterinary Records

Your breeder will have given the puppy some vaccinations and deworming medication. The breeder should supply you with a list of which vaccines and dewormers were administered and when. Take these veterinary records with you to your first veterinary appointment. They will help you make informed decisions about further vaccinations.

CHAPTER 5

Preparing for Your New Poodle

ONCE YOU'VE FOUND YOUR POODLE, it's time to think about the day he sets his four paws in your house. Before the big day arrives, you'll want to poodle-proof your home, purchase all the right equipment, and line up a veterinarian. If you expend a little effort in advance, your poodle's introduction into your household will be more relaxed, which will make the transition easier for all concerned.

Puppy (and Dog) Proofing Your Home

It's essential that you provide a safe environment for your new poodle. You don't want your puppy getting hurt–and you don't want your puppy hurting your things! Having a puppy around is not unlike having a toddler around. You need to take a look at your house, room by room, from a pup's-eye view. Think about the kind of trouble he might get into, and do your best to prevent it.

Living Areas

Start with the rooms where you spend a lot of time, like the living room, family room, and home office. If that's where you'll be, your poodle will want to spend time there too. Remember, until your pup is reliably housetrained, he needs to be supervised unless he's in his crate, exercise pen, or safe area. (More on those later in this chapter.)

Look at electrical cords. If any cords are accessible to a puppy, cover them with cord covers (made for childproofing) to prevent him from chewing on them. Or buy some aquarium tubing and cut it in half lengthwise to cover cords.

Fact

Poodle-proofing a house is important even if you're adding an adult dog to your family. While many adult poodles are angels—they wouldn't dream of taking something off the kitchen counter, for example—others can have a little bit of the devil in them. Until you know which type of poodle yours is, play it safe.

Put away all videocassette tapes and CD and DVD cases that a puppy could choose to chew on. The same goes for the remote controls—place them out of reach, and get into the habit of keeping them there. Unplug your paper shredder. As gruesome as it sounds, a dog's tongue can get caught in a shredder that turns on automatically.

Take an inventory of your houseplants, and make sure none of them would be dangerous if ingested by your dog. The Web site for the ASPCA Animal Poison Control Center (*www.napcc.aspca.org*) lists plants that are poisonous to dogs—complete with plant descriptions and photographs. If some of your houseplants are on the list, turn them into hanging plants so they're out of your dog's reach, or give them away.

Bedrooms

Your poodle will want to sleep in the same room with you. All dogs love human companionship—poodles especially love it. You can keep your puppy safe in your bedroom at night by putting him in a crate with the door closed.

But what about when your pup is loose (supervised, of course) in your bedroom? Pups are attracted like magnets to dirty laundry, particularly dirty underwear. They love to carry it around and chew on it. So pick up your laundry, particularly if you don't want to have to replace your entire wardrobe. Shoes are great chew toys in the eyes of a teething puppy. Put them away, or risk having them chewed up.

Essential

Puppies can get into trouble in the blink of an eye. In particular, Toy Poodle puppies are so close to the ground they can snatch up objects before you've had time to bend over to retrieve them. So pick up any small objects that you don't want to see in your poodle's mouth.

Again, look for electrical cords that need covering, and keep remotes out of your puppy's reach. You might want to put away any candles as well. Teach your kids to put away the toys in their bedrooms if they don't want to share them with the poodle. Toys that have small parts, like Legos, can be particularly dangerous if eaten by a dog, so make sure those are kept out of reach.

Kitchen and Bathrooms

When puppy-proofing the kitchen and bathroom, make sure cleaning supplies are kept out of reach. If you store them under the sink, put childproof latches on the cupboards to keep your inquisitive puppy from opening the door. Remember, poodles are smart—and some will enjoy the challenge of getting into forbidden places!

Trashcans should not be left out in the open. Kitchen trash is full of delicious-smelling, but dangerous, stuff. Bathroom wastebaskets contain tempting tissues and potentially dangerous items, like disposable razors and used dental floss. Keep your trash in a closet, or use covered cans (tie the lid on with a bungee cord if necessary).

You may find that your puppy likes to unroll the toilet paper. If so, just put it out of reach, if possible, until your pup grows out of that particular hobby.

Garage Safety

A poodle (or any other dog) can get into some real mischief in the garage. One of the most dangerous hazards of the garage is spilled antifreeze. Most antifreeze contains ethylene glycol, which is deadly to dogs—as little as a teaspoon can cause acute kidney failure, and even death, in a Toy Poodle. Unfortunately, it also tends to be very attractive to dogs, due to its sweet smell and taste. Make sure the garage is absolutely free of antifreeze. Remember that it is also contained in some windshield-wiper fluids. Change or add antifreeze away from the garage, and be careful not to spill it. Also clean up any oil leaks. You don't want your poodle walking through oil and then licking his paws.

Fact

Look for "pet-safe" brands of antifreeze like Sierra and Sta-Clean, which contain propylene glycol instead of ethylene glycol. These products aren't harmless, however, just less dangerous. So to be on the safe side, keep all antifreeze away from your poodle.

Fertilizers, lawn chemicals, and lawn equipment can be dangerous to your dog. Don't let your puppy eat any lawn products. And keep him away from the sharp equipment like scythes, shovels, and trowels. If you have a workbench in the garage, be sure to pick up any nails or screws that fall to the floor.

The Great Outdoors

The most important safety feature for your yard is a fence. The fence should be tall enough to keep your poodle in when he's full grown. Electronic (or "invisible") fences work via an underground cable that transmits a shock to the dog through a special collar he must wear. They are not 100-percent reliable. They allow other animals into your yard. And your smart poodle might soon figure out that once he passes over the barrier, the pain stops. And then he'd be hurt coming back into his yard. It's safer to fence your yard with a regular fence. If you're concerned about looks, you might look into the "virtually invisible" Friendly Fence offered by Benner's Gardens, Inc.

▲ **Your yard should be a safe haven for your poodle; secure fencing is a must.**

Tying out your poodle on a cable or chain is also not a good idea. Poodles want to be with you when you're home, and when you're not, your poodle is better off inside the house in his safe room or crate. Being tied out is very frustrating for dogs, since they can see other animals or people they want to get to, yet they're not able to reach them. Children can tease your poodle and drive him into a barking frenzy. That's not to say that your poodle shouldn't spend time in your yard. Provided you have a fence, your yard can be a wonderful playground for the two of you.

To keep your yard safe, pull up any mushrooms that you see. Stay on top of this one—your poodle might not be very discriminating about what he eats. Steer clear of lawn chemicals, which have been implicated in cancer—remember, your dog licks his paws–and either eliminate any toxic plants from your garden, or completely block access to those plants.

Alert!

If your puppy eats a houseplant (or any other potentially toxic item), and you're unsure whether she's been poisoned, call the ASPCA's Animal Poison Control Center at ✆888-426-4435. There's a $45 consultation fee, which can be charged to a credit card. The line is open twenty-four hours a day.

Choosing a "Safe Area"

Puppies get into trouble. That's part of their job description. Adult dogs that are new to your household can also get into trouble if given free reign in your home. So it's to your advantage to set up at least one room in your house that's completely poodle-proof. It should be a place where you can leave your puppy unsupervised without worrying he'll destroy your furniture or injure himself on something.

Kitchens and bathrooms make particularly good safe areas. The uncarpeted floor makes for easy cleanup. There's usually less furniture to destroy and fewer dangerous items. See Chapter 7 for more on preparing and using a safe long-term confinement area.

Where Will Your Poodle Sleep?

Decide in advance where your poodle will sleep. The precedent you set on the very first night is an important one. If your poodle puppy whines in the night out of loneliness–which he probably will, since he'll doubtless be missing his mom and littermates–and you bring him into your bed that first night to comfort him, he's going to expect to sleep in comfort with you from that moment on. As long as you don't mind the company, and you don't let leadership issues with your poodle develop as he grows up, that's just fine. You might want to think about the implications of having a yet-to-be-housetrained puppy in your bed, however!

At the beginning, you'd be wise to consider crating him at night with the crate right next to your bed. He'll have your comforting smell nearby, and you can put your fingers through the grid on the door while you lie in bed. While you can always invite him into your bed in the future, keep in mind that it's just very hard to uninvite him.

Essential

Some say it's a bad idea for your dog to sleep in your bed. That's not necessarily true, unless you have a dog that wants to dictate where you will sleep. If your poodle is easy-going, feel free to share your bed with her. But make sure you're certain before you invite her the first time.

Poodle Necessities

There are certain supplies you should have on hand that will make life easier when your poodle joins your family. This is the beginning of a lifetime of buying stuff for your poodle (an activity you'll enjoy for years to come), but these bare-bones necessities will get you through that first important week.

Collar and Tag

Buy a flat collar for your puppy, one that either buckles or uses a plastic quick-release fastener. Whichever type you get, be sure it's adjustable so you don't have to buy a new one every week as your puppy grows. You can choose leather, nylon, cotton, or even hemp. Martingale or limited slip collars can be a good option in situations where you're afraid your pup will slip out of his collar. They're typically made of nylon. When the dog pulls, the collar closes, but not so far that it chokes. These types of collars should be used on outings only, not as an around-the-house collar.

Alert!

Don't put a choke chain on your poodle. It isn't necessary. Poodles are so easy to train that you'll be able to use positive reinforcement–based training to teach your dog to walk on a loose leash without resorting to aversive methods like a choke chain. The same goes for prong or pinch collars.

Get a tag made with your name, address, and phone number, as well as your new dog's name (as soon as you know it), and attach it to the collar. Tags are available through pet-supply catalogs and Web sites in various shapes and in metal or plastic. In addition, many pet superstores have tag-making machines on the premises, so you can make a tag instantly. A collar tag is an essential piece of equipment, and your poodle's best ticket home should he ever become separated from you. There are more permanent means of identification (like the microchip and tattoo), but they should always be backed up with an ID tag.

Leashes

It's imperative to have a six-foot (or shorter) leash for outings to the veterinarian, groomer, and pet-supply store. They're also good for training. Leather is nice and probably the most comfortable to hold. Nylon can give you a nasty burn if it's pulled through your hand, though it has the advantage of being light. Chain leashes are difficult (and painful) to grab. If your new dog is a puppy, or even an adult Toy Poodle, buy a lightweight leash, with a small snap that fastens to the collar. A heavy snap can bonk your puppy in the face.

If you want a longer leash for walks, a retractable leash can be a good choice. These leashes, which extend to 16 or 26 feet, have a nylon cord that automatically rolls, fishing-reel style, into a plastic case with a handle, which you hold while walking your dog.

They give your poodle more freedom and more exercise on a walk. However, it is harder to control a dog on a retractable leash. And the nylon cord can burn your legs if it gets tangled around them.

Brush and Comb

Regularly brushing a poodle is essential. The sooner you start gently brushing your dog, the sooner he'll be acclimated to this important activity. Grooming is also a wonderful way to build your bond.

Buy a slicker brush (or a pin brush, if you're planning to show your poodle), as well as a "greyhound" comb (a metal comb with wider teeth at one end and more closely spaced teeth at the other). If you use these two tools regularly, always making sure you brush and comb all the way to the skin, you won't have to worry about mats and tangles.

Food and Water Dishes

Buy a bowl for your poodle to eat from and one for him to drink from. Stainless steel is a good choice because it's easy to clean. (Sturdy glass, like Pyrex, is good, too.) Plastic bowls aren't a great choice for food bowls. Because they're porous, they're hard to get really clean, and bacteria can easily become trapped. Plastic bowls have been linked to loss of pigment on dogs' noses, as well. Ceramic bowls have the advantage of being heavy and hard for the dog to move while he eats, but there is some concern about the toxicity of the glaze on those made outside the United States. Ceramics also can break when dropped.

Fact

You can buy special dishes intended for long-eared dogs that are narrower at the top and wider at the base, so those long ears don't fall in the food. (Or you can just pull your poodle's ears back with a scrunchie when she eats).

No matter what type of bowl you choose, you need to keep it clean. Make it a practice to wash your dog's bowls daily.

Nutritious Food

It should go without saying that you'll need food for your puppy or dog on hand when you first bring him home. Take time before you acquire your puppy to decide what you want to feed your poodle. (See Chapter 8 for information about diet.) You might not want to switch immediately to a new food, however. Ask your breeder what she's weaned the pups onto, and have a small supply of that food on hand. That way, you can make a gradual transition to avoid tummy upset.

Toys and Entertainment

Toys definitely spice up a puppy's life. You'll want some fleecy toys for your pup to curl up with (or destroy), some chew toys to give him when he tries to chew you, as well as balls or other toys to throw for him.

Essential

Be very choosy in the toys you give your poodle. Don't give her anything she can tear apart readily—she might choke on the pieces. And she shouldn't be given anything that will cause a blockage if ingested. Supervise your dog's interaction with any new toy until you can tell how safe she is with it.

An absolutely essential toy is the Kong. This hollow, virtually indestructible rubber toy can be filled with food (and plugged with cream cheese or peanut butter) to keep your dog occupied. Working on a Kong is a great way for him to amuse himself while he's in his crate, exercise pen, or safe area.

Your Poodle's Crate

One of the best investments you can make for your new poodle is to get him a crate (also called a cage or a kennel). Once he becomes accustomed to it, it'll be his own safe haven, a place he can go whenever he's stressed or wants to get away from it all. If you travel with it, he'll always feel at home.

Unless you want to buy more than one crate, buy one that will be large enough for your poodle when he's full grown. While your pup is small, use a concrete block or something similar to make the crate small enough to be effective as a housetraining tool.

Types of Crates

There are several types of crates from which you can choose. Plastic or fiberglass crates—the ones airlines accept for shipping a dog in the cargo hold—are preferred by dogs that enjoy a more den-like atmosphere. (One of the reasons dogs love crates so much is that they're descended from wolves, and wolves make dens.) These crates are especially sturdy, if not ultra-attractive. They come apart in the middle (the top and bottom halves are screwed together), and the two parts can nest for somewhat easier storage.

The wire crate has a more open feel to it. A poodle that is crated in a wire crate feels more a part of what's going on in the room around him. Many wire crates have the advantage of folding flat, making them easier to transport and store. They're typically quite sturdy.

A third type of crate is the travel crate or carrier. For Standard and Miniature Poodles, the Cabana Crate or a similar crate works well. They're made of mesh and nylon and fold quite flat. They're lightweight and perfect for travel. But they're not escape-proof. A determined dog can chew his way out or open the zipper. Nor are they crush-proof—they don't provide as much protection in the car as plastic or wire crates.

Toy Poodles can be carried in a Sherpa Bag or a SturdiBag, which are great for air travel if you carry your pet on the plane (but unsuitable if your dog and crate are checked as luggage). These bags, which can resemble duffle bags, are also lightweight and easily carried—even with a small dog in them.

If you're looking for a crate for confining your poodle for short periods of time when you're not at home, this third category is least appropriate. But once your dog is comfortable and reliable in his crate, travel crates are invaluable when you travel together.

Improper Crate Use

Crates are wonderful things. But you can't confine your puppy in one all day. If you leave him in his crate so long that he's forced to soil it, you lose the crate as a housetraining tool. And it's just not a nice thing to do to your poodle—dogs instinctively do not want to lie in their own waste (which is what makes crates so handy for housetraining). To keep your pup's crate from becoming a prison, you'll need to leave him in a safe area for long-term confinement.

Your Poodle's Exercise Pen

Another great piece of equipment for the new puppy is the exercise pen, also called an "ex-pen." These pens, which have no top or bottom, are made of wire panels that range in height from twenty-four to forty-eight inches. (Buy one tall enough to keep your poodle in when he's grown.) They're adjustable in size, depending on how many panels you use. You can form them in a circle or use a wall for a fourth side. One of the panels can be a door, allowing easy access.

Question?

How many ex-pens should I buy?
You might want to invest in more than one ex-pen. Then you can have one set up at the house and you can keep the other stored in the car to use on poodle outings.

The great thing about ex-pens is that they're portable and spacious. You can put newspaper or other absorbent material on the floor of the pen, put in a crate and some toys, and you've created a safe napping, resting, or chewing place for your puppy, and he can see everything going on around him.

If you travel to dog activities, like agility matches, the ex-pen is a great place to put your poodle when you're waiting for the next activity (with a shade cloth over top on those sunny days). An ex-pen, which may not be secure enough to keep your poodle in when you're away from home, can save your sanity when you are home with your puppy.

Choosing a Veterinarian

It's a very good idea to select a veterinarian before you need one. You'll want to take your new dog or puppy to the vet for an examination as soon as you get him, so having one selected in advance is a good plan. By asking your pet-loving friends for recommendations, visiting a Web site or two, and then actually visiting or talking to someone at the vet's office, you can select a vet who suits your needs.

One indication of quality is whether an animal hospital is accredited by the American Animal Hospital Association (AAHA). The 3,000 hospitals in the United States that are AAHA-accredited voluntarily undergo periodic onsite evaluations to ensure that they comply with the organization's standards for services and facilities.

Once you've narrowed down the field to a few choices, interview the veterinarians you're interested in, if possible, or at the very least call or go in and talk with the receptionist. Find out what the office hours are, the mechanism they have in place for emergencies, what the philosophies on vaccination are (avoid vets who maintain that annual vaccinations for all dogs are essential—they're probably not keeping up with the times), and try to get a sense of whether they actually listen to you. You want a veterinarian who treats you with respect, takes your concerns seriously, and considers you an integral part of your poodle's health-care team. Ⓔ

CHAPTER 6

Bringing Your Poodle Home

AS YOU CONTEMPLATE bringing your new poodle home, take the time now to make sure you're prepared. You should think about how you're going to introduce your poodle to her new family and get her settled in her new surroundings. You'll also want to take her to the veterinarian you've selected within the first day or two so that she can get a clean bill of health.

Planning Ahead

If you prepared for your poodle as outlined in the last chapter, the day you bring your poodle home should be relatively stress-free. Think ahead to determine the best time to bring your poodle home. Would that be on the weekend? During the week? Consider your family's schedule, and come up with a game plan for how you'll care for your poodle in the first few weeks.

Once you have your schedule worked out, you will need to make an appointment with your breeder to pick up the puppy. If you're getting your dog from a shelter or rescue group, you should still make advance arrangements so that both parties know when you'll arrive to pick up your new poodle.

Make an appointment with your veterinarian to give your new dog a once-over. Your breeder's contract will probably have a clause in it about the breeder taking the dog back within a certain period of time (usually twenty-four to seventy-two hours) if a veterinarian determines there is a problem. Schedule your appointment during that period, and keep it even if there appears to be absolutely nothing wrong with your poodle.

Essential

No matter whether you are getting a puppy or an adult, try to budget plenty of time in the first few weeks to spend with him. Take time off from work, if possible, so you can make the transition as easy as it can be for you, your family, and your new dog.

Avoid Bad Timing

If you're getting a puppy—or even an adult dog—your life will be temporarily turned upside down. Don't bring home a new dog during an already tumultuous time. That's hard on you and, perhaps even more important, hard on the dog.

A poodle may seem like a marvelous Christmas or birthday present for a family member. But giving a living being as a gift is fraught with problems. First, you must be sure that the recipient wants the dog and will be willing to care for her for a dozen or more years. Second, special occasions like Christmas or a birthday are typically full of celebrations. It is much better to bring your new dog into a calm household, where she can settle in at her own pace.

Another difficult time to bring in a new dog is when you have a new baby. It's hard enough to bring a baby into a household that already contains a dog—it takes special preparation for the dog, and you'll want to make sure your dog is secure in her role as a family member. If you have a new dog and a new baby at the same time, your baby will almost surely win out when they both need attention. And that's not fair to the new canine family member. If your new dog is a puppy, she'll require almost constant supervision until she's housetrained and has learned not to be destructive. How can you attend to her needs and a baby's at the same time?

If your work has busy cycles, don't bring in a new dog during the busiest season. For example, it's a bad idea for a tax accountant to buy a puppy at the beginning of April. Try to time it so that you have plenty of relaxed time to spend with your new charge.

Shipping Your Puppy Home

If you buy a puppy from a distant breeder, you may need to have her shipped to you. Breeders ship quite often, but before you make arrangements to have your puppy shipped, there are a few things to keep in mind.

Consider Personal Pickup

The early puppy months are impressionable times. The noise of being in the cargo hold and the stress of being carried around in her crate might be frightening for your poodle. The pup might handle it just fine, but if she has a fearful temperament, it might be very traumatic.

Alert!

If your breeder of choice is far enough away that you can't pay a personal visit, thoroughly check him out anyway. Ask for references from puppy purchasers. Ask to see pictures of the sire and dam and, ideally, the kennel. Ask for copies of all the health clearances and find out about the health history of other litters the breeder has bred.

Even if the breeder isn't within easy driving distance, you might be able to avoid shipping your puppy. A Toy or small adult Miniature Poodle can be carried on the plane in the cabin. A young puppy of any variety is probably small enough to fit under the seat in front of you in the cabin of the plane. Consider flying to your breeder's location (which gives you the advantage of being able to meet him in person and see his kennel) and bringing your poodle home with you.

If you're getting an adult Miniature or Standard that is too big to fly in the cabin, you can buy a one-way plane ticket to your breeder's location and rent a car and drive her home (or drive both directions). You'll have plenty of bonding time during this trip, and your pup will avoid the trauma flying in cargo.

Plan Every Detail

If you do decide to have your puppy shipped, try to arrange for a nonstop flight. The last thing you want is for your puppy to miss her connection and be stranded at a place where you have no contacts. Try to arrange for flights that are scheduled during the most temperate parts of the day. In the summer, that means early mornings and late evenings. In the winter, it's midday.

Be sure to contact the airline and find out exactly where you should pick up your puppy. If she's being shipped as cargo, that might mean you need to go to a special cargo terminal. Many airports have more than one; make sure you know the one where you'll find your puppy.

Fact

If shipping your puppy via air is impossible due to routes or weather (as there are federal requirements about shipping animals in extreme temperatures), at least two companies specialize in shipping pets via truck: Feathers and Fur Van Lines, and Pro-Pet Transports.

Visiting the Veterinarian

Shortly after you pick up your puppy, you should pay a visit to the veterinarian's office. The veterinary visit allows you to learn whether your pup has any infectious diseases or other problems. If a major problem is identified that prompts you to take the puppy back to the breeder, at least you've found out early enough that you can return the pup before you've had too much time to fall in love with her.

If you've selected your veterinarian carefully, this visit will allow your new poodle to develop positive associations with going to the vet. Your vet and all the staff should be gentle and caring, and you should do everything in your power to see that your pup isn't frightened.

Because the mother's immunity passes to the pups through her milk, your puppy may not be immune to infectious diseases, even if she has been vaccinated already. So when you're at the veterinarian's office this visit, carry her. A good vet follows sanitary procedures, so you shouldn't have to worry about her contact with the examination table. But it's wise to avoid contact with the ill dogs that might be at the vet's office.

Should You Vaccinate?

Don't give your puppy a vaccination at this vet visit. The painful shot might build a painful association with the veterinarian's office. Take a close look at the vaccination records your breeder will have given you. Talk with him in advance about his vaccination recommendations, and do some research so that you know whether a vaccination at this point is recommended. If so, schedule another appointment.

Vaccinations are not benign. Poodles, in particular, are prone to autoimmune problems, which can be triggered by vaccinations. (See Chapter 9 for more information.) Go to the vet prepared to discuss the issue, with a clear idea in mind of what you think is most appropriate for your pup. You can't take back a vaccination.

The New Adult

If your new poodle is an adult dog, a trip to the veterinarian to rule out any health concerns is still in order. If she's come from a rescue group or shelter, chances are good that she's been recently vaccinated. Don't vaccinate him again until you know for sure that she needs it. Again, you want to avoid overvaccinating your poodle.

Ask your vet to give your new dog a thorough exam and identify any potential problems you might want to keep your eye on. Make sure this first vet visit is a positive one, regardless of the age of your poodle. This is a chance to set some precedents and build positive associations for your dog.

Essential

If you're in doubt about your new poodle's vaccine history, you can ask the vet to run a blood test called an antibody titer to measure the antibodies for certain viruses that are circulating in the bloodstream at the time of the test. If the titer says that your dog is protected against parvo and distemper, for instance, he doesn't need those shots.

Arriving Home

Your puppy might be overwhelmed at having been removed from her mother and her litter, her trip to the veterinarian, and the trip home. Before you bring her into the house, give her the opportunity to go to the bathroom. If you have a yard and have selected a place in the yard where you'd like her to potty, take her to that spot. When she pees or poops, praise her sweetly but not too enthusiastically—you don't want to startle her. Then give her a treat.

Once in the house, chances are your tired puppy will need a nap. Bring her into the house and show her where to find her crate and her water bowl. She may settle right down. If not, let her explore, keeping a very close eye on her. Until she's reliably housetrained, she should not have full run of the house. If you see her squat to pee or poop, gently pick her up and take her outside. (See Chapter 7 for more information on housetraining.)

Try to keep your home calm this first day. If you have kids, they'll likely be excited and want to play with the new poodle, but explain to them that the puppy needs some quiet time. Don't let them bring their friends over to meet the puppy until she has had a chance to rest.

▲ Sometimes a coat or sweatshirt can help a poodle handle the elements.

Once your pup has napped, take her outside to potty. Then, when she's empty and raring to go, let your kids play with her (or play with her yourself), keeping everything happy and upbeat so you don't frighten the pup. You'll know soon enough whether your particular puppy is easily frightened. If your puppy chooses to chew on your hand or other body part (or your clothes) during play, calmly remove yourself and give her an appropriate chew toy.

Puppies are like babies. They wear out quickly. Be sure you give your puppy ample time to nap. When you can't supervise your poodle pup, put her in her crate for a little R&R. Be sure and take her out frequently to pee.

Naming Your Poodle

Some people have names for their dogs picked out before they've even met the dog. That can work just fine, provided the name fits the dog. But you might want to wait and meet your poodle before naming her. You don't want to waste much time, though, because you'll want your dog to start learning her name right away. As you get to know her this first day, try out some names for size. When you hit on the right one, you'll probably recognize it immediately.

Here are some things to keep in mind in naming your poodle:

- You'll be using this name thousands of times, so make sure it's one that is easy on the ear and not embarrassing.
- Your poodle's name can influence how she is treated by others, so think twice before naming her Killer, Butthead, or even FiFi.
- Short names can be convenient, especially in emergency situations–"Come, Rex!" is more efficient than "Come, Balthazar!" when you need your dog to come in a hurry.
- You can change your poodle's name if your original selection (or the name she came with) doesn't seem appropriate.

No matter what name you select, you're bound to have multiple nicknames for your poodle that may or may not have anything to do with the original name. Dogs can learn to respond to many names.

Introductions Among Pets

First impressions are important, so when you introduce your new poodle to your other pets, you want to do it right. That said, don't worry if they don't immediately take to one another–it doesn't mean the relationship is doomed. Some animals are just more sociable than others.

Acquainting Puppies with Dogs

Puppies can be rude, but they aren't particularly threatening to other dogs. If you can do so safely, introduce the poodle pup to your resident dog in neutral territory, off-leash or with the resident dog dragging a leash. Let them sniff, and praise them if they behave politely.

If the introduction doesn't go well–if your resident dog snarls at the puppy or scares her into vocalizing, or your puppy relentlessly bugs your resident dog so that he's forced to put her in her place, calmly attach the leashes (or pick them up if they're already attached) and walk both dogs toward home. Sometimes walking together, shoulder-to-shoulder, rather than meeting face-to-face can help dogs to tolerate each other better.

Fact

Leashes add tension to meeting. While they can be essential for safety (and safety is paramount), a dog that is leashed feels he has no recourse if threatened, except to get defensive. A loose dog has the option to walk away. If you must leash your dogs for their initial meetings, keep the leash slack.

If there isn't a safe, neutral place to introduce the dogs off-leash, try introducing them in your yard, again with no leashes or with slack leashes. If you don't have a yard, a third option is to have the dogs meet on-leash in a neutral area, like a park.

Introductions for Adult Dogs

If your new poodle is an adult, you can follow the same procedures in introducing her to your resident dog as you would a puppy, except you should let both dogs drag a leash. It's even more important to introduce the two on neutral territory, if possible. Ideally, you should make the introduction in an area where it's all right for them to be loose, and you don't have to hold their leashes.

Stay calm and upbeat, and think positively. If one dog warns the other dog off, don't yell or reprimand. Let the nongrowler heed the important warning of the growler or snarler. Keep your eye on body language. If either dog stiffens and shows her teeth, stay calm but be ready to grab leashes.

If the two dogs start to play, that's terrific. If they sniff, then ignore one another, that's fine too. If one dog tries to mount the other, don't worry about it. Let the mountee take care of it if she isn't happy about it.

Alert!

Keep the introductions upbeat. If you start to tense up or shout, you'll create bad associations for both dogs and potentially escalate any aggression. Even if the two don't seem to hit it off, give them plenty of positive, controlled opportunities to get to know each other.

When the two have finished their ritual greeting, pick up the leashes, and, in an upbeat manner, suggest that you all go for a walk together. In an ideal scenario, by the time you get home, the two should be friends, and your resident dog shouldn't mind the newcomer entering the house. When you go inside, keep your new poodle on leash so you'll maintain some control over her.

Meeting the Cat

When it comes to cats and dogs, cats tend to call the shots. For that first meeting, put your poodle on leash or in a crate and let the cat approach her. If the poodle wants to chase the cat, use the leash to restrain her. Praise both animals for calm behavior toward each other. Make sure your cat has access to a high place where he can escape from the dog. If your poodle corners your cat, the cat might scratch her. That may win your poodle's respect, but it's not an auspicious way to begin a relationship.

Supervise all interactions between the dog and the cat at the beginning, making sure the cat always has high places where he can get away from the dog. If your poodle doesn't calmly accept your cat (if she lunges and carries on in the cat's presence and it seems to bother the cat, for instance), start a program of gradual exposure for the two. Teach your poodle to give you eye contact when you request it (a clicker is a great tool for training this—see Chapter 14) and lavishly reward her when she does it in the presence of the cat.

Essential

Don't hold your cat in your arms when you introduce him to the new poodle. She might feel trapped and scramble to get away, injuring you in the process. Instead, keep the dog on leash and let the cat approach when she's comfortable.

Introducing Other Pets

If you have other pets in your family, like birds, hamsters, or reptiles, minimize the interaction between these pets and your new poodle until your poodle has settled in and you can anticipate what her reaction will be. Keep cages out of reach of the dog or in rooms that aren't accessible to her.

After you've gotten to know your poodle and are confident she won't try to hurt the little critters, expose her to the cages and let her sniff. Make your other pets' safety and security your most important priority. Never leave your poodle alone with an uncaged pocket pet or bird. Just like other dog breeds, most poodles have strong prey instincts, which could kick in at any time. It's entirely possible that your poodle will learn to ignore the other pets, or even become friends with them, but at the beginning you can't be too careful.

What to Do at Bedtime

After a busy day, your puppy will be more than happy to go to bed. Take her out to potty one last time before bed, and then put her in her crate in your bedroom. If she cries, and you're sure she doesn't need to go out, just ignore her. She'll eventually settle down.

Since she'll have been accustomed to sleeping with her mom and littermates, it can help to put a stuffed animal in with her, or, better yet, ask your breeder in advance to put a towel in the puppy's sleeping area that you can bring home with your puppy. That way she'll be able to snuggle with the familiar smell of her littermates.

CHAPTER 7

Housetraining

TEACHING YOUR POODLE where to eliminate is one of the most important things you can do for him. It can be frustrating if your poodle consistently has accidents in the house. Even worse, it can sour your relationship with your dog. With a combination of alert diligence, patience, rewards, and good management, you can teach your poodle where to go to the bathroom so that inappropriate elimination doesn't become an issue.

Management Is Key

If your new puppy makes a mistake in the house, it's really your mistake. You shouldn't give your pup the opportunity to pee or poop in the house. Always watch him carefully so if he does start to squat in the house, you can scoop him up and whisk him to the spot where you want him to eliminate (presumably outside). Better yet, learn to recognize the signs that indicate he's going to squat, and take him outside before he gets that far. For most puppies, those signs are sniffing and circling.

In the house, your pup should be either with you (perhaps even tethered to your belt or to a heavy piece of furniture), in his ex-pen or safe area, or in his crate. Under no circumstances should he be loose in another room while you're in the house. If he is, he can eliminate at will and miss out on the valuable lesson you give him by interrupting him and taking him outside.

When he eliminates outside, reward him immediately with a food treat. That makes him understand that peeing outside allows him to relieve his bladder and get something delicious, whereas peeing inside provides only relief.

Setting Schedules and Routines

The best way to make sure your pup learns to eliminate in the appropriate place is to put him on a schedule. Since what goes in must come out, if you schedule his food and water intake, you'll have a better idea of when he'll have to eliminate and can get him outside in advance.

You also need to know the times he'll almost always have to potty—for example, when he first wakes up, a half hour after eating, and following a big play session. These potty preferences are individual. You need to observe your particular puppy and figure out his unique schedule.

Feeding and Watering Schedule

Depending on the age and size of your puppy, you'll probably feed him three times a day (or perhaps four, if he's quite young). Try to make those times the same every day. Post the schedule on your refrigerator, if you have to. When you feed your pup, make sure you also put out water, but don't make water freely available during housetraining.

Question?

What if my puppy doesn't go the bathroom at the scheduled time?

Put her back in her crate or watch her like a hawk when you go back inside. Twenty minutes later, take her out again. Repeat as necessary, and be sure and reward her when she does go.

By sticking with a set pattern of feeding and elimination, your poodle's body will be in sync with your schedule. When you take him out at the same times every day, he'll know when it's okay to go to the bathroom.

Putting your dog on a feeding and potty schedule is just as important for a not-yet-housetrained adult dog as it is for a puppy. The only difference is that an adult will require fewer trips outside, since adults eat fewer meals a day and should be able to hold it longer.

Elimination Association

If your smart poodle puppy knows he gets to eat or play after he goes potty outside, he'll be more likely to do his business on the schedule. Take him out first thing in the morning, reward him for pottying, then bring him inside for breakfast. Let him rest for a half hour or so after he's eaten (or whatever his individual schedule is), take him out again, reward him with a treat for pottying, then bring him in. He'll be empty, so it's a good time to play with him. Once he figures out that there's no play or breakfast (or lunch or dinner) until after pottying, he'll be anxious to get the pottying out of the way so he can do something enjoyable.

Crate Training

When it comes to housetraining your dog, the crate is your best friend. Don't view it as a cage or a jail (though it can become one if you abuse it). View it as a tool for housetraining and a safe haven that your poodle can call his own.

Getting Him Used to the Crate

From his first day home, your poodle's new life with you should include his crate. But if your poodle isn't thrilled with the crate, you can take some steps to make him more comfortable with it.

Leave the crate door open when he isn't in it. Every now and then toss a treat inside, so that when he walks by he'll smell the treat, go in, and get rewarded. If that's not enough to make him feel better about the crate, feed him his meals in his crate to change his associations with it.

If your poodle won't get anywhere near the crate, use a clicker to shape him into entering it (see Chapter 14 for more about clicker training). Start with rewarding even a tiny step in the direction of the crate (starting as close to the crate as he's willing to be). If he steps toward the crate, click and treat. Do it again when he makes another step. If he actually sticks his head in there, click, then shower him with treats (trainers call this a jackpot). Keep gradually sensitizing your dog to the crate, in short training sessions, until he's willingly going in.

Once he's in the crate, close the door for a few seconds, click if he's quiet about it, then let him out. If he fusses in the crate, don't open the door until he's quiet. Click the moment of quiet, give him a treat, then let him out. You want to reward quiet behavior in the crate, not fussing. Gradually increase the amount of time you leave him in the crate with the door closed.

Alert!

Because of their natural den instinct, dogs do not want to soil where they sleep. This makes a crate is a great tool for housetraining, since your dog will do everything she can to keep from having an accident in the crate. That's why it's imperative that you not leave her in the crate so long she's forced to soil it.

How Long Is Too Long?

Don't crate your poodle puppy for more than a couple of hours if he's very young. A rule of thumb is that a dog can be crated for one hour per month of age.

Be sure to give him something to do when he's in his crate. This way you can turn the crate into Disneyland, rather than Folsom Prison. Give your pup a Kong toy stuffed with his food or with peanut butter. He'll spend a happy hour or so cleaning it out and then will settle in for a nap. If your poodle has a special toy he likes to sleep with, put it in there with him for security.

Fact

The biggest mistake people make with housetraining is to let their dog out in the yard alone. You must accompany your poodle to the yard, watch her eliminate, then reward her. The rewards help your poodle understand what you want and motivate her to do her business outdoors.

Bedtime Crating

Until your poodle is fully housetrained, keep him in his crate, in your bedroom, while you sleep. (Again, ignore any protestations on his part.) Be sure to take him out to potty right before bed. And take him out again the instant you get up in the morning. If your puppy cries in the night and you think he needs to go out, respond quickly. Carry him outside to potty, praise him if he does his duty, and bring him right back in to his crate. Nighttime breaks should be about going to the bathroom and nothing else. If he cries after you've just taken him out and you're sure that's not the reason for his crying, ignore him. He'll settle back down.

Essential

Most dogs can last through the night without having to potty long before they have bladder control during the day. If you get up to go to the bathroom in the night, however, be prepared to take your poodle out too. If you've awakened her, it's only fair to offer her the opportunity to relieve herself.

Beyond Housetraining

Once your poodle is reliably housetrained, don't put away his crate. The crate is more than a housetraining tool. It's a safe refuge your poodle can use his whole life. A side benefit to having your poodle accustomed to being in the crate is that you'll be able to crate him when workers come to the house or when you just need him not to be underfoot. You'll also be able to take your crate with you when you travel with your poodle and know he's comfortable in it.

If your poodle objects to being crated, ignore his objections. Don't yell at him or whack the top of the crate. (Can you imagine a better way to promote bad associations with the crate and destroy it as a safe haven?) And by no means should you let him out while he's complaining. Any of these reactions will promote future complaining. Only let him out of the crate when he's being quiet.

The Long-Term Confinement Area

If you must leave your poodle for more than a few hours, you'll need to put him in a long-term confinement area, rather than a crate. This area—your safe room—should be stocked with just a few basics: a water dish, some toys, and a place where your dog can eliminate if he feels the need. This is the only fair way to leave your puppy for hours at a stretch. If you crate him so long that he's forced to soil in his crate, you've ruined the crate for house-training. And you'll come home to a miserable, messy puppy. A comfortable bed that your puppy won't destroy is also a good choice. If he destroys everything you give him, try piling up some old towels for him to lie on. This way you won't be too upset if he chews them up. You might also want to see if he can be comfortable on the cool, bare floor—some dogs actually prefer this.

Fact

A device called Kong Time, from ProActive Pets, automatically dispenses five stuffed (or unstuffed) Kong toys at randomized intervals throughout the day. Selling for about $129 (including five Kong toys), it might be worth the investment to keep your poodle occupied all day.

Because your long-term confinement area is by necessity sparsely furnished and thereby boring to your pup, you must provide him with some diversion. A great way to do that is to provide at least one stuffed Kong toy. Leave other Kongs and safe chew toys in the room with him, so whenever he's awake he has something to do. Rotate the toys to keep things interesting for him.

Creating an Indoor Potty Spot

Ian Dunbar, veterinarian and renowned dog behavior specialist, recommends that the "toilet" area you leave for your pup in the long-term confinement area mimic what you want him to use outside. So if you're a city dweller who expects your dog to eliminate on the sidewalk or curb, bring in a paving square of concrete. If your poodle will be expected to eliminate on grass, bring in a patch of sod.

▲ Toy poodles can be trained to use a litter box if that is more convenient.

If you have a Toy Poodle, you can consider using a litter box designed for dogs, or special pee pads. Purina makes a litter box system for dogs called secondnature. It consists of coarse, absorbent, paper-based pellets, a litter box designed for small dogs, and a training booklet. (The training is similar to teaching your dog to eliminate outdoors.) Your dog can learn to use the box indoors, but it's up to you to keep it clean so it doesn't smell.

Returning to Your Puppy

When you come home, take your poodle outside to pee (and give him a treat when he does). If your dog has used the indoor area you set aside for elimination, just pick up any feces, but don't worry about trying to eliminate the urine odor. You want him to be attracted to that area. Try to monitor how much he eliminates while you're gone. You should find less and less mess as your dog gets bigger and begins to understand that eliminating outside earns him treats.

Now that you're home and your pup has had a chance to pee outside, it's time to play with him and spend some quality time interacting. Remember, don't leave him unsupervised anywhere in the house, besides his crate, long-term confinement area, or ex-pen.

Essential

Don't free-feed your poodle while you're housetraining. It may be easy for you, but if you allow your poodle to eat whenever she wants, you can't anticipate when she'll need to go out. Feed and water at set times, at least until housetraining is completed.

Establishing a Potty Spot

If you have a yard, picking a spot in the yard for your poodle to use as a toilet area has several advantages:

- When you take him there, he knows what to do.
- The area will smell (to him) like his past potty activity, triggering him to do his business.

- Urine stains on the grass are limited to one area.
- Cleaning up feces is easier–you don't have to make a treasure hunt of cleaning the whole yard.

If you've ever had to negotiate around a yard where a dog freely poops, you know how much more pleasant it can be if you isolate an area for the dog's bathroom business.

Choosing the Spot

Choose an area that's not too far from the door. If your pup has to go, he'll want to relieve himself immediately. The potty spot can be a grassy area (though if it's used throughout the life of your poodle, it'll probably be marked with urine stains) or you can use some sort of substance like wood bark or pea gravel. Another alternative is to plant the potty area with clover, which resists urine scalding.

Having a dog that has been taught to urinate on grass comes in handy when you travel, since you can almost always come up with a grassy patch to ask your dog to potty on. If you think you want your potty area to have a substrate other than grass, you might be wise to make that change after your dog has become accustomed to grass.

If you have a male dog that will eventually lift his leg, he might appreciate there being a tree or other vertical object for him to pee on. Some males don't lift their legs in their own yards if other dogs don't enter it–they don't consider it necessary to mark a vertical surface if there are no other dogs around to smell it.

Using the Potty Area

When you take your poodle to the potty spot, don't waste any time getting there, and take the most direct route possible. At the beginning, you might want to carry your puppy (it's unlikely he'll pee in your arms). After that, use a leash if your dog doesn't walk right with you to the area. Take the same route each time, so your pup knows what he's going to do when he enters the yard.

Put him down in the area; then prepare to be patient. Keep an eagle eye on him so you know exactly when he pees or poops. But don't talk to him—let him concentrate on the business at hand. As you see him about to squat, give him a cue that in the future will mean "Go to the bathroom now, please." That cue can be something direct like "Go potty," or something cuter or more cryptic like "Concentrate" or "Hurry up." In the future, particularly when you travel, you'll be grateful to have a cue so that your dog will understand when it's an appropriate time and place to go to the bathroom.

Be sure to exam your pup's stool after he poops. It can give you valuable information about his health. Any big change in stool, especially diarrhea, is worth noting. After you've examined it, clean it up. If you keep your potty area pristinely clean, your pup will be happier about using it. And you want your pup to be happy about using the potty area!

Dealing with Accidents

In an ideal housetraining situation, your puppy will never have an accident, because he'll never be unsupervised in the house, unless he's in his crate or ex-pen. And, in this ideal world, your schedule is such that your puppy never has to be alone in the house long enough that he has to eliminate inside, in his long-term confinement area. However, this is not an ideal world, and accidents do happen, so you need to know how to handle them.

Alert!

Don't be harsh with your poodle if you catch her in the act of eliminating in an inappropriate spot. If you are, she'll do everything in her power not to eliminate in front of you. You don't want her sneaking away and peeing in a hidden spot!

It's No Big Deal

If you find a mess in the house and you haven't observed it taking place, don't say a word about it. It does you no good to reprimand your puppy after the fact. Don't take your poodle to the spot or tell him how bad he is. Instead, silently clean it up.

If you catch your pup in the act, calmly and gently scoop him up, hustle him outside to the potty spot and put him down. With any luck, he'll finish the job there and you can give him a reward and bring him back in the house to play or chew or nap. If the interruption makes him forget that he had to go, just bring him inside and put him in his crate. Twenty minutes later, take him outside and try again.

The Big Cleanup

When you discover an indoor accident spot, you have to clean it up and clean it up well. Dogs are drawn to urinate in the same spot over and over again. So it's essential that you get rid of the faintest smell of urine.

The challenge lies in the fact that your dog's nose is much more sensitive than yours. So even if you can't smell urine, unless you completely eliminate the odor, your pup will probably be able to smell it.

To prevent your poodle from creating an indoor toilet area of his own, use a product designed for pet urine and feces that uses enzymes to completely eliminate the smell. Just deodorizing doesn't do the trick. Remember, the goal is to eliminate, not mask, the odor. Don't use ammonia to clean up after your dog, either. Urine actually has a slight ammonia odor, so using ammonia will actually encourage your dog to use the spot again. Liquid products like Petastic (formerly called Nature's Miracle) and Simple Solution, as well as a powder you mix with water called Odor-Mute, have been on the market for years and stood the test of time. Be sure to keep plenty of odor eliminator (and paper towels) on hand.

Using a paper towel, clean up the mess. Then use the odor-eliminating product, following the label directions. If your pup has gone on a rug or carpet (which they seem to be fond of doing), be sure to soak the carpet with the solution, following the directions on the product's label.

If you're not sure whether an area is clean, a black light will illuminate any urine spots you've missed. Pet-supply stores sell lights specifically for this purpose, but any black light will do.

Fact

Some people schedule vacation time around their puppy's arrival. If you can do that, keeping your pooch on a strict feeding and eliminating schedule, you can probably instill the housetraining ethic in a couple of weeks. However, it'd be best to keep that schedule up when you go back to work, hiring someone to come in during the day, if necessary.

Housetraining an Adult Dog

If you adopt an adult poodle, you might be lucky enough to get one that is already housetrained. All you'll have to do is show him where you want him to potty. You can do that by hanging out in the potty area for as long as it takes, then praising and rewarding him with treats when he eliminates outside.

If your new adult is a male (particularly if he's not neutered or was recently neutered), he might have the urge to lift his leg in your house to mark it as his own. If you catch him in the act, gently but firmly tell him "No," then take him outside. When he pees in the potty spot, praise him to high heaven and give him a treat. Be sure to remove the odor from the spot he marked in the house.

If your poodle seems to have never been taught that the house is not the place to go potty, treat him like a puppy. He won't require as many trips outside, but he should be crated or in his ex-pen when you can't supervise him, or in his long-term confinement area when you are away from home for a few hours. Take him out at regular intervals, and reward him for doing the right thing. He'll probably catch on quickly.

Alert!

Pet-store puppies can be more of a challenge to housetrain because they've been forced to eliminate in their cages. If you find yourself with a poodle that doesn't hesitate to soil his crate, stop depending on the crate as a housetraining tool. Instead, be extra vigilant with watching her and taking her outside on schedule. Don't take the crate away—it can still be her "safe haven."

Relapses in Housetraining

If your adult poodle is already housetrained but starts having accidents in the house, the first thing you should do is take him to the veterinarian to rule out a physical cause for the problem. He might have a urinary tract infection, or he might have an ailment, like diabetes, that causes him to drink more and therefore pee more. If he's on corticosteroids, like prednisone, they will make him drink (and pee) more. If your poodle is a female, she may have what's called spay incontinence, in which a lack of estrogen causes spayed females to leak urine. A gastrointestinal ailment might cause your dog to defecate indoors involuntarily.

Question?

How long does housetraining take?
Some especially easy-to-housetrain pups can be fairly reliable within just a few weeks. It might take several months for harder cases. If you find that housetraining is taking an inordinately long time, contact your veterinarian. There may be a medical explanation.

If a medical reason for the accidents is ruled out, look at the stressors in your dog's life. Is there an illness or some other problem that is stressing you or your family? If so, your poodle might be stressed as well. And he may show his stress—and make a bid for attention—by eliminating in the house. If you can, address the source of the stress; then give your poodle some extra time and attention.

If there are no identifiable reasons for relapses in housetraining, you should go back to square one and treat your poodle like he's an untrained puppy. Put him on a schedule, crate him when you can't keep an eye on him, and reward him like crazy when he does his business outdoors. If that doesn't work, talk with your veterinarian again or see a behaviorist for personalized help.

CHAPTER 8

Basic Nutrition

GOOD NUTRITION IS THE CORNERSTONE of good health. This is as true for your poodle as it is for you. If you want to achieve optimal health for your poodle, you need to feed her the highest quality food you can. Take the time to learn about nutrition, and weigh the various options carefully. And remember, the money you put into a high-quality diet might well be earned back many times over in reduced veterinary costs.

Essential Nutrients

Dogs' nutritional requirements aren't all that different from those of humans. Both species need these essentials: protein, fat, water, vitamins, and minerals. Some experts would also add carbohydrates to the list.

Protein for Energy

Dietary protein is an essential component of your dog's diet. High-quality proteins for dogs come from animal sources: meat, eggs, and cheese. Grains are a less expensive source of protein, but they're not as easy for your dog to digest and use. If your dog can't digest the protein source well, her body doesn't get as many nutrients from it. As a result, you have to feed bigger portions in order to get the same amount of nutrition.

Essential

Dogs are built to more easily digest protein from animal sources than from plant sources. Think of what your poodle's wild relatives, wolves, eat. Eating more meat and less grain is a more natural diet for your poodle.

Among the most important nutrients found in protein are amino acids. These building blocks of protein are vital for helping your dog create the specific compounds needed for her own tissues. Some amino acids can be synthesized within the body, but others, called essential amino acids, must be provided by food. Varying your dog's protein source allows her to get a variety of these essential amino acids. The higher the quality of the protein source, the more amino acids it offers.

Essential Fats

In human nutrition, fats are sometimes viewed as bad. But in fact, fats, like proteins and carbohydrates, provide energy. They also allow your poodle to absorb fat-soluble vitamins (A, E, D, and K). Essential fatty acids, found in fats, are necessary for a healthy brain and eyes, and they also help keep the coat and skin in good condition. Young dogs, working dogs, pregnant dogs, and nursing mothers require extra fat in their diet, as do those recovering from serious illness or injury or coping with cancer.

Carbohydrates

There is some debate over the issue of whether carbohydrates should be included in a dog's diet. Although most dogs seem to tolerate the high amounts of carbohydrates found in dry dog food, these grains can cause itchy skin and ear problems in some dogs, as well as gastrointestinal problems. (Fresh-food diets for dogs can also contain carbohydrates, in the form of grains and vegetables.)

Since dogs don't have an absolute need for carbohydrates, let your dog tell you whether she needs grains or not. Start with your choice of diet, either with or without grains. If she's having problems, try removing grains if you feed them, or adding small amounts if you don't.

Clean Water

Water is absolutely essential for your poodle's health—even for her survival. If she eats dry food, she'll need to drink even more water. You should make clean water available to her at all times. And you should think about the quality of the water. Depending on where you live, your tap water may not be perfectly clean. If you drink filtered or bottled water because your tap water tastes funny, don't offer tap water to your poodle. Allow her to drink the same high-quality water you do.

Vitamins and Minerals

Vitamins and minerals, most of which are derived from food, are absolutely essential to your dog's health. Vitamins from whole foods are more beneficial to dogs (and humans) than those added separately to the food.

Fact

Unlike humans, dogs are able to manufacture vitamin C within their bodies, so dietary supplementation of vitamin C isn't essential. However, some dog owners and veterinarians have seen benefits in supplementing this vitamin in ill or stressed dogs.

It's the delicate balance of vitamins and minerals that is so important. Most vitamins are water-soluble, so any excesses are flushed out with the urine. But excesses of fat-soluble vitamins (A, D, E, and K) are stored in the liver. This means that an overabundance of these vitamins can be toxic. Keep an eye out for these vitamins on the labels of the foods or supplements you give your dog to make sure she's not getting more than she needs.

Minerals make up a very small proportion of your dog's body weight, but they are still vital components of bones, teeth, and fluids. They're essential for proper growth and support enzyme and hormone functions.

Commercial Foods

While there's a growing trend toward fresh foods (see page 94), the vast majority of people buy commercial food for their dogs, and most dogs do fine on these. When it comes to commercial food, there's a dizzying array of choices. Most people feed dry kibble, but canned food is popular as well. In addition, there's semimoist and freeze-dried food, as well as commercially prepared frozen diets.

Even among the individual categories of food, especially dry and canned, the variety available is astounding. Choosing among them can be challenging, so take some time to learn what to look for, and then compare your options carefully.

Dry Food

The majority of dogs in this country are fed dry kibble. This food generally is made out of protein from meat and plant sources, extra vitamins and minerals, and maybe some dairy products. The source of the meat in commercial food is a concern for some dog owners. To avoid food made from diseased animals, buy kibble whose manufacturers say they use human-grade ingredients. To make the food more palatable, fats are sprayed on after the manufacturing process is complete.

The high-temperature processing that must take place when kibble is made means that the natural vitamins and enzymes in the foods are destroyed. Thus vitamins are added to commercial food. You can help make up for the destroyed enzymes by giving your dog digestive enzymes to supplement those her own body supplies.

Alert!

For a stomach-turning look at what goes into commercial pet food, read *Food Pets Die For: Shocking Facts about Pet Food,* by Ann N. Martin. This exposé of the pet-food industry explains how, among other things, road kill, zoo animals, and yes, pets, end up in pet food.

Canned Food

Canned pet food has a higher moisture content and a higher proportion of meat to grains than dry food. It's therefore more expensive to feed. As with dry food, the meat sources included in the food vary in quality from brand to brand. Learn to read the label and identify higher-quality protein sources. (See more about reading labels later in this chapter.)

Dogs tend to prefer canned food to dry, which isn't surprising. It's meatier and more aromatic. Since it contains fewer grains, it's more likely to be closer to a dog's natural diet.

Semimoist Food

Semimoist food has a moisture content between 25 and 40 percent, which is not as wet, or as messy, as canned food. It is also softer than dry food, so dogs tend to find it more palatable than kibble.

However, semimoist food is not a great option as far as nutrition is concerned. Take a look at the label, and you'll see that these foods are kept semimoist with preservatives and sugars, things you should avoid feeding your dog. If you're going to feed a commercial food, stick to high-quality dry or canned.

Commercially Prepared Raw Food

Raw diets are popular for their health benefits, but shopping for and preparing your dog's food is less convenient than measuring out kibble or opening a can. Because of this, a number of companies have made raw, frozen dog food available. Feeding this food is as simple as thawing and serving. You lose control over some of the ingredients by not preparing the food yourself, but if you buy from a trusted company you can be comfortable you're getting human-grade, or even organic, ingredients. See Appendix B for a listing of Web sites of raw-food manufacturers.

Freeze-dried food is a popular travel alternative for people who ordinarily feed a fresh diet. This type of food, which usually comes in patties, is a dehydrated version of a raw meat, bone, and vegetable diet. Since it doesn't require refrigeration, freeze-dried food is handy for traveling. It can be eaten dry (as long as your poodle has access to plenty of water) or rehydrated before serving.

Fact

Pet-food manufacturers and many veterinarians have done a good job of convincing dog owners that they're not capable of preparing a balanced diet for their dogs. Yet parents are trusted to feed their children properly. Do the necessary research before taking your dog's nutritional health into your own hands. But don't feel it's something you're not capable of.

Home-Prepared Diets

Many holistically minded poodle owners feel they are doing the very best for their dogs by feeding them a fresh-food diet, rather than kibble or canned. If you choose a fresh diet, you can provide great variety, thus maximizing the various nutrients your dog gets. You can reduce or completely eliminate the proportion of protein that comes from grains, a less natural component of a dog's diet. And raw food (as opposed to cooked or commercially processed food) has live enzymes, which have health benefits.

The Basic Ingredients

If you choose to prepare your dog's food, make sure you're meeting your dog's nutritional needs. The basic components usually include meat, bone, organ meat, and ground vegetables. You can also add grains, if you and your dog prefer.

You should buy the highest-quality ingredients you can afford. If you can't afford organic meat, you can buy meat from the supermarket and rest assured that you're still feeding meat that's healthier than that found in most commercial dog food. Organic vegetables aren't terribly expensive. If you can buy vegetables that haven't been grown with pesticides, your dog will be ahead of the game.

Essential

If you choose to feed a home-prepared diet, or even if you purchase a prepared frozen raw diet, you must do some research to make sure you're meeting your dog's dietary needs. See Appendix B for books about nutrition.

A grave mistake that some well-intentioned dog owners make when preparing a diet at home is to serve meat without raw bone or other calcium source. It's important that the phosphorous in the meat be balanced by calcium. Bone can be served whole or ground. If you cook, use bone meal or ground eggshell powder for added calcium.

Raw-feeding proponents stress that variety is very important in a home-prepared diet. Different meats and vegetables have different vitamins and other nutrients. If you feed a wide variety of foods, you'll be giving your poodle a broad spectrum of nourishment. Balance over time, rather than making sure that each meal is "complete and balanced," will serve your dog well.

Home-Cooked Food

Some people who feed a fresh diet prefer to cook their dog's food. Though most dogs are built to handle raw food, if you're not comfortable with the bacteria in the food, or if your dog is immune-compromised, you can cook her food before serving.

◀ Good nutrition is a key component to keeping your poodle healthy.

Do some research first to make sure cooking is necessary, and cook as lightly as possible. Cooking destroys many of the beneficial enzymes. It's also a lot more work than feeding raw. But done properly, it's a healthier alternative than kibble or canned.

Choosing a Food

What type of food should you choose? Dry foods are convenient. Canned foods are more palatable, typically, but more expensive. Fresh foods combine palatability and high-quality ingredients (and convenience if you buy a prepared frozen raw diet), but they also tend to be more expensive. The decision you make will depend on your lifestyle, budget, and how much time you can spend on researching the subject.

If you decide to feed a commercial food, feed the best food you can afford. In general, high-quality ingredients cost more. But there's an important caveat. If you buy the more heavily marketed food, some of the price is going into advertising, not ingredients.

No matter whether you choose to feed kibble, canned, or fresh food, it's important to give your dog variety. With kibble and canned, that means switching brands and protein sources every three months or so. This flies in the face of conventional advice that dogs don't need variety and they should eat the same food without variation. Feeding the same food year after year is a great way to develop a food allergy or sensitivity in your dog.

Understanding the Label

In order to compare dog-food ingredients and make sure you're getting the best food for your dog, you need to be able to read the label. The government makes it easier by placing certain requirements on labeling, so you know you're comparing apples with apples (or beef with beef).

What's in It?

The first thing you should look at on a dog-food label is the list of ingredients. They're listed by weight, in descending order. Look for the food with the greatest proportion of high-quality protein (meat, not grains).

Be on the lookout for tricks that might make one ingredient appear to be primary when it's not. One particular approach, called split-ingredient labeling, lists a particular ingredient in various components, to make it look like it's not the main ingredient in the food. For example, the main grain (wheat, corn, rice) might be listed separately as flour, bran, middlings, or flakes. Add them together, and they may outweigh the meat that's the first ingredient on the list.

Guaranteed Analysis

The guaranteed analysis, a required part of the label, lists the minimum amount of crude protein and fat in the food, as well as the maximum amount of fiber and water. The moisture content in canned food makes it hard to compare the crude protein between dry and canned. To even the playing field, subtract the percentage of water from 100, and divide the crude protein by the resulting number. This is called figuring out the dry-matter basis. So a dry food with 22 percent crude protein and 10 percent water would have 24 percent protein on a dry-matter basis. A canned food that is 7 percent crude protein and 78 percent water would have 32 percent protein on a dry-matter basis.

Question?

How can I learn more about commercial food?
An excellent primer on understanding dog-food labels is Liz Palika's *The Consumer's Guide to Dog Food*. It dissects the ingredient label, providing a detailed explanation of the labeling terms, including the definitions of each ingredient category, as mandated by the American Association of Feed Control Officials (AAFCO).

While the protein level is important, particularly when comparing foods, keep in mind that the guaranteed analysis says nothing about the quality of the protein source.

Feeding Guidelines

Each label contains suggestions on how much of the food to feed. You'll notice that less expensive food suggests a higher feeding amount than more expensive food. This is because the lower-quality ingredients are less nutrient-dense, and therefore more food is required to deliver proper nutrition.

If you feed a commercial food, take the feeding guidelines as just that—guidelines. You might start with the amount suggested, but keep an eye on your dog's weight (by feeling her ribs and watching her waist or simply weighing her), and adjust the amount you feed her accordingly.

How and When to Feed

When your poodle is a puppy, she'll need to be fed several times a day. After she gets to be about six months old (or slightly older, if she's a Toy), you can switch to a twice-a-day regimen. Some dog owners like to feed only once a day, but your poodle will probably enjoy eating more often.

Essential

Dogs have amazing internal clocks. Try to feed your poodle at roughly the same time every day. Keeping to a routine provides your dog with a sense of security. And probably no routine is more important to him than when he gets to eat!

Some people prefer to put down a bowl of food and let their dog work on it throughout the day. This only works for dry food, of course, which can stay out without going bad. If your poodle is an only dog, you can go this route. But if you have more than one pet, you risk one pet eating more than she should and depriving the other of his ration.

There are several benefits to feeding your dog a set portion of food at set mealtimes:

- You are in charge of when your poodle eats, which can be important in maintaining or establishing your position as her leader.
- You know how much your dog is eating and how enthusiastically she's greeting her food.
- You're able to know with certainty if she turns her nose up at her food, which can be a sign of illness.

- You're not restricted to feeding dry food.
- Your poodle has something to look forward to—mealtime!

Feed your dog before you leave for the day and again before you eat your own dinner. If you feed her before you eat your dinner, you'll minimize her begging at the table while you're trying to enjoy your meal.

What about Supplements?

If you're feeding commercial kibble or canned food, the bag or can will doubtless be labeled with a statement that the food is complete and balanced. Does that mean that supplements are unnecessary? Perhaps. But perhaps not. If your poodle has some health problems, supplements might be in order. However, too much of any nutrient can be a bad idea, so don't give supplements without doing research or consulting with your veterinarian. A holistic veterinarian is more likely to be well versed on the use of supplements than a conventional one.

If you're feeding a home-prepared diet, supplements will be part of the diet (just as commercial food has vitamins added before it gets to you). Do your research before you embark on a fresh-food diet, to make sure that you provide all the necessary nutrients, either from the ingredients themselves or through supplements. Some commercially prepared raw foods already include supplements, while others don't. Read the ingredients carefully.

One type of supplement that has gained favor among both conventional and holistic vets is essential fatty acids (EFAs), which can be helpful for dogs with itchy skin (and can help your dog avoid itchy skin). Talk with your vet about a product like DermCaps, or get advice on simply adding oils to your poodle's food.

Table Scraps

Should you share your food with your poodle? Sure, if your eating habits are healthy. In fact, if you feed dry food, supplementing it with a portion of your own dinner can be very beneficial. Avoid giving your dog added carbohydrates—she's getting plenty in her kibble. But extra fruits, vegetables, or lean meat can be a good addition to her diet. Limit extras to no more than 20 percent of your dog's food intake, or you risk upsetting the balance already established in the kibble.

This doesn't mean that you should scrape your plate into your dog's bowl when you're through eating. Don't feed her your rejects. Instead, prepare a little extra for her. Avoid foods that are potentially toxic for dogs, like chocolate, onions, raisins, grapes, and (of course) alcoholic beverages.

Alert!

If you're afraid that feeding your dog human food will make a beggar out of him, don't feed him from the table. Instead, top his food with some of yours, or just put it in his bowl as a snack.

Tempting Treats

Treats don't have to be unhealthy. They don't have to be expensive. And they don't have to come from the pet aisle of your grocery store. Try these healthy treats, which are easy for you to prepare:

Small pieces of cheese
Raw vegetables, like baby carrots
A lick of baby food
Croutons or pieces of crackers
Tiny pieces of liver dried in the oven
Strips of chicken or turkey breast dehydrated in a low oven

As you will see from the training chapters of this book, food treats are an important component of training. But you shouldn't restrict treats to official training sessions. Giving your dog a treat can help establish your role as a leader (provided you ask your poodle to do something to earn the treat) and make both of you feel good. It's a great bond builder.

Maintaining the Right Weight

Some poodles put on weight very easily, and it's a struggle to keep their weight down. Others have difficulty keeping weight on. Whichever camp your poodle falls into, it's up to you to feed the appropriate amount of food (and provide the appropriate amount of exercise) to keep her at a healthy weight.

Overweight Poodles

Being fat is no healthier for poodles than it is for humans. If you can't feel your poodle's ribs or see her waist, or if her belly isn't tucked up, you have a weight problem on your hands.

Essential

Talk with your veterinarian before embarking on a weight-loss program for your obese dog. You don't want to do anything drastic that might hurt your dog. The program should include reducing the amount of calories she takes in and increasing the amount of calorie-burning exercise she gets.

Dogs that are arthritic are caught in a vicious cycle. Excess weight exacerbates the problem and makes their joints more painful. And the pain makes them not want to exercise. One solution can be swimming. This provides a non–weight-bearing exercise, which is easy on the joints and shouldn't be painful. It helps the pounds (or ounces) fall off, which in turn makes the arthritis hurt less.

If you reduce the amount of food your poodle eats, she'll be hungry. She might also turn into a scavenger. To avoid this (and to keep her happier about her weight-loss regimen), try dividing her food into more frequent, smaller meals. This shouldn't affect the total amount she eats, but she'll feel fuller more of the time. If you feed a home-prepared diet, add extra vegetables and reduce the amount of meat and fat you serve. You can also add some low-calorie foods to her meal to make her feel more full. Try adding some canned pumpkin (not pumpkin pie mix) or green beans to her bowl. That might just take the edge off.

Being on a diet shouldn't mean that your dog doesn't get treats. Just make the treats very small. You can also use extremely low-cal treats. One idea is to use small pieces of rice cake as a treat. Store them with some powdered liver, and they should taste good to your dog.

Fact

If you have a dog that needs to lose a few pounds, you have lots of company. A 2003 study by the National Academy of Sciences determined that 25 percent of dogs and cats in the Western world are obese and need to lose weight.

The Underweight Poodle

If you can't keep weight on your poodle, perhaps you're feeding her the wrong food. Switch to a higher-density kibble, or increase the proportion of meat in your home-prepared food. Or simply feed your dog more. Reducing exercise isn't a great option for the underweight dog (unless she runs miles a day with you, in which case you could substitute another, less intense form of activity). Exercise is very important for dogs; it keeps them mentally and physically fit. Make sure that your poodle is getting enough calories to make up for the ones she's burning by exercising.

If your poodle loses weight despite eating well, that can be a sign of illness. Take her to the vet to try to pinpoint the source of the problem with blood tests. If no source is found, your veterinarian can advise you about a more appropriate diet for your poodle.

CHAPTER 9

Basic Health Care

TAKING CARE OF your poodle's health is similar to taking care of your own. Along with giving him good nutrition and regular exercise, it is important to monitor his health and pay close attention to how he's feeling. As in humans, it's important to perform regular at-home examinations as a means of detecting problems early. It's also a good idea to work with your veterinarian to prevent disease so that you aren't faced with treating it. Take the time to learn which preventive measures are appropriate for your poodle.

Spaying and Neutering

It's a sad fact that there are too many dogs and puppies in this world. Millions of adoptable dogs are euthanized in our nation's shelters every year. Unless you are a part of a responsible breeding program, as outlined in Chapter 4, you shouldn't breed your poodle. And if you don't plan to breed your poodle, you should spay her or neuter him.

When a female dog is spayed, her ovaries and uterus are removed. It's akin to a hysterectomy in a woman. The procedure is perfectly routine, and your poodle may or may not have to spend the night at the veterinarian's office.

When a male dog is neutered, his testicles are removed, though the scrotal sac is left in place. It's usually outpatient surgery—your dog won't have to spend the night at the hospital. He might be a little sore and have to be kept quiet for a day or two after surgery, but neutering is generally considered a routine and safe procedure.

Essential

Not only are there benefits to having your puppy spayed or neutered, you may actually be obligated to do so. If you buy a pet-quality poodle puppy from a reputable breeder, your contract may include a clause requiring you to spay or neuter your puppy by a certain age. If this is the case, be sure to uphold your end of the agreement.

Benefits of Spaying

A big benefit to spaying early is that it reduces the chance of your poodle developing mammary cancer later in life. Research shows that spaying a female dog prior to her first heat virtually eliminates her chance of getting breast cancer (her relative risk is reduced to only 0.05 percent). Spaying after the first heat, but before a second, leaves her with an 8-percent risk of breast cancer. If she goes through two or more heat cycles before being spayed, her chance of getting breast cancer rises to 26 percent.

Spaying also eliminates the risk of uterine and ovarian cancer (since those organs are removed), as well as uterine infection, which is not uncommon in unspayed females.

The other benefit to spaying your poodle is that you don't have to deal with your bitch going into season every six months or so, attracting the attention of all the male dogs in the neighborhood.

Benefits of Neutering

Neutering your male dog eliminates the possibility of testicular cancer. It also calms down the feisty male, since the testosterone in his system is greatly reduced. Unaltered males tend to get into more fights than their neutered counterparts. Even if they're not bullies themselves, they tend to be the target of negative attention. Intact males are also more likely to lift their legs in inappropriate places (though neutered males certainly do mark, too).

An intact male will go to great lengths to get to a female in heat. Your otherwise perfectly behaved male poodle might actually escape from your yard if tempted by a female in heat within sniffing range.

Fact

It's a good idea to spay and neuter while your poodle is young, but you might want to wait until your pup is at least six months old, so that he or she can have the growth and maturity benefits of the hormones. It's certainly an issue to discuss with your veterinarian and breeder before making a decision.

Vaccinations

The issue of vaccinations used to seem fairly simple. Vaccinations prevent diseases, therefore according to the conventional wisdom they were good and necessary. The label said they should be given every year, so responsible pet owners brought their dogs in every year for their shots.

Well, it's not really that simple. Veterinarians and pet owners are recognizing that annual vaccinations are not necessary and in fact can be harmful. In some dogs, vaccinations cause the immune system to overreact, creating autoimmune diseases, in which the body sees its own tissue as foreign and attacks it.

Unfortunately, poodles are among the breeds identified by prominent vaccine researcher Jean Dodds, DVM, as being particularly prone to problems caused by vaccinations. As a result, poodle owners should take care to educate themselves on the issue of vaccinations and see to it that their poodles are not overvaccinated.

Core Vaccines

The various vaccines given to dogs are divided into two groups: core and noncore. The core vaccines are given for the most serious illnesses. These include rabies, parvovirus (a gastrointestinal disease that can be fatal to puppies), distemper (a deadly airborne virus that affects the respiratory, gastrointestinal, and central nervous systems), and adenovirus 2 (which causes canine hepatitis, an infectious liver disease).

Annual revaccination is a practice based on tradition, as there is no scientific evidence to show that it is necessary. However, evidence does exist to show that it is *not* necessary. Duration-of-immunity research conducted by Ronald Schultz, Ph.D., a veterinary immunologist at the University of Wisconsin-Madison School of Veterinary Medicine, shows that the parvo, distemper, and adenovirus 2 vaccines last a minimum of seven years, probably longer. The rabies vaccine has been shown to last at least three years—no rabies duration of immunity studies have been conducted longer than that. According to Dr. Schultz's research, once immunity to a core disease has been attained, additional "booster" shots for that disease provide no benefit. And since these shots affect the immune system—as well as other systems in the body, such as the endocrine and the nervous system—they are not benign.

Essential

The rabies shot is the only vaccination required by law. Most states require that rabies vaccinations be given every three years. Yet some veterinarians continue to give the shot annually—and it's the same shot, no matter what interval it's given. If you live in a state with a three-year rabies law, do not vaccinate your poodle annually.

In 2003, the American Animal Hospital Association (AAHA) released guidelines for canine vaccines. These guidelines recommend revaccination for the core diseases no more frequently than every three years (unless a rabies vaccination is required more often by law). Many responsible poodle owners choose to vaccinate their poodles for the nonrabies core vaccinations even less often.

If you are unsure of whether your adult poodle needs a vaccination, ask your vet to run an antibody titer, which measures the antibodies for a particular disease circulating in your poodle's bloodstream at the time the blood is drawn. If the titer says he is protected against the core diseases you're testing for, don't give the shot!

When you have blood drawn for titers, ask that it be sent to a laboratory that has quality-assurance tests in place to ensure that the titers are actually protective. (Cornell, Colorado State, and Michigan State universities are among those that have these tests in place.) An alternative, if your vet has it, is an in-house titer-testing machine. Veterinarians can use these to test blood and get quick and simple "yes" or "no" answer in terms of whether the animal is protected.

While you can trust a titer that says your poodle is protected, it is possible to get a false negative—a titer that indicates your poodle is not protected when he actually is. However, 90 to 95 percent of dogs that have already been vaccinated will have titers saying they're protected.

Alert!

Vaccinations should be given to healthy dogs only. If you bring your poodle to the veterinarian because she's not feeling well, don't give her any shots while you're there, even if it would be more convenient. Also, don't stress her system by combining shots with surgery. In some states, it is possible to get a veterinary waiver in lieu of a rabies shot if your dog is not healthy.

Noncore Vaccines

Noncore vaccines are meant to prevent diseases that aren't that serious if contracted, like bordetella (also known as kennel cough, a self-limiting disease similar to colds that humans get), or are not considered completely effective, like the vaccines for leptospirosis and Lyme disease.

The lepto vaccine carries only a few of the many strains of leptospirosis out there, so its efficacy is very limited. In addition, it has caused more immediate adverse reactions than any other vaccine. The efficacy of the Lyme vaccine—the same vaccine that has been recalled for humans because of health concerns—has been called into question. Giving the Lyme vaccine complicates efforts to test whether your dog has contracted the disease.

The duration of immunity of noncore vaccines is a year or less, so titers for them are not a viable option. The AAHA recommends that veterinarians make individual decisions about these vaccines based on a particular animal's lifestyle and risk factors. For example, both Lyme and leptospirosis occur in only some parts of the country. If you live in an area that doesn't have these diseases, there's no reason to give the vaccines to your poodle. Even if these diseases do occur in your area, consider whether your poodle is actually at risk.

Think carefully before giving your poodle any noncore vaccines, weighing the risks of your dog contracting the disease against the risk of chronic illness caused by the vaccination itself.

Fact

While shots that combine as many as seven different vaccines are prevalent, you do not have to give your dog noncore vaccines in order to give them the core shots. Ask your veterinarian for single-disease shots, or shots that contain just the core vaccines. The fewer shots you give at the same time, the better.

Puppy Vaccinations

While annual revaccination has been called into question, not many veterinarians suggest that vaccinations be eliminated completely. It is to your poodle's advantage, however, for your vet to administer the minimum number of vaccines necessary to confer immunity against the core diseases.

▲ **Examining your poodle regularly can help you detect problems before they become serious.**

Puppy vaccinations are complicated by maternal immunity, which is passed on through the mother's milk. This immunity can prevent vaccinations from being effective. The problem is that no one knows exactly when maternal immunity ends—it's different for every litter. After maternal immunity is gone, the puppies are vulnerable to disease. In times past, breeders would vaccinate early and often, hoping to keep puppies protected. Since veterinarians today are recognizing that vaccinations are not benign, a more beneficial schedule for puppy vaccinations includes fewer shots.

Dr. Dodds has developed a modified schedule that some poodle breeders have adopted. It recommends that puppies be given a single shot that contains only the parvo and distemper vaccines at nine weeks, twelve weeks, and sixteen to twenty weeks. Rabies should be given at six months (or later, if the law will allow). Dr. Dodds recommends a booster at one year, to ensure that immunity was conferred, and also a rabies booster at a year but separated from the distemper/parvo shot by three to four weeks. Thereafter, her protocol calls for shots to be given no more frequently than every three years, with noncore vaccines given to at-risk dogs only.

Parasite Prevention

Fleas, ticks, heartworms, and other worms can be dangerous for your poodle and make him miserable. But parasites don't have to be a big problem. If your poodle is in optimal health, he'll be unattractive to parasites. If they do become a problem, your veterinarian can provide you with prescription pesticides to address them.

Treatments for Fleas

Fleas are nasty little bugs that feed off your poodle's blood, causing itchy bites and sometimes an allergic reaction to flea saliva (called fleabite allergic dermatitis) that can be very uncomfortable for your pet. But the adult biting stage is just part of the flea's life cycle, which can take from nine to two hundred days to complete, depending on conditions. After a female flea takes a blood meal, she lays eggs that fall off your poodle onto the floor, furniture, or bedding. They hatch into larvae, then turn into pupae, which mature in cocoons. Then they emerge as adults, ready to feed on an animal and start the cycle all over again.

You can break this cycle by treating your poodle with topical chemicals designed for use monthly (Advantage or K9 Advantix) or every three months (Frontline). These spot-ons kill the fleas before they can lay eggs, effectively stopping the cycle (unless the fleas have managed to drop their eggs before the topical is applied). Another product is Program, a pill taken monthly, which interrupts the reproduction cycle of the flea but doesn't kill the adult flea.

While the manufacturers say these products are safe, they are pesticides. Holistically minded pet owners who try to keep their animals as toxin-free as possible resist using chemicals when pest problems do not exist. Parasites tend to feed on weaker animals, so if your poodle is very healthy (particularly if you feed a raw diet), he might not be attractive to parasites, and therefore may be able to go without any chemical prevention methods.

Essential

If you live in a climate with cold winters, where fleas aren't a problem year-round, don't use flea preventives during the cold months. Give your dog a break from the chemicals.

Giving your poodle a bath with any type of shampoo will kill any fleas he might have on him. Shampoos or sprays with neem and/or citronella can also help repel fleas. Some home remedies for avoiding flea problems include feeding your poodle garlic, apple cider vinegar, and/or brewer's yeast, which are supposed to make dogs and cats less attractive to fleas. Garlic and brewer's yeast can be found in tablets sold for use in pets. Used in moderation, these remedies won't hurt and may help. This is true unless your poodle has a sensitivity to one of the ingredients; sensitivities to yeast aren't uncommon.

If you choose not to use monthly flea preventives, keep a close eye on the flea situation. If your poodle starts scratching himself, look carefully for fleas (they're easiest to see on the less hairy parts, like the belly). Comb your poodle over a white towel, and look for flea "dirt," a euphemism for flea feces, which look like brown specks. If you put water on the brown specks, they'll smear a reddish brown. That's your clue that you have a flea problem.

Attack at the first sign of fleas, before your house has a chance to become infested. You can apply Advantage for a couple of months, or Frontline for a single month. Avoid flea collars or over-the-counter spot-ons, which use more dangerous pesticides.

Dealing with Ticks

Ticks are a bit less insidious than fleas (you can see them and remove them), but they're more dangerous. Although fleas can cause problems—they may transmit tapeworms, and a severe infestation can cause anemia—ticks can transmit very serious diseases, like Rocky Mountain spotted fever, erlichia, babesiosis, Lyme disease, and tick paralysis.

Several medications exist for tick control. Frontline, applied topically, kills ticks for one month (though it works for fleas for three months). K9 Advantix, another topical, kills ticks (along with fleas and mosquitoes) for a month. The Preventic collar is also effective for fighting ticks.

Whether you need to apply regular tick preventives on your poodle depends upon your poodle's lifestyle. If you're in a heavy tick area, and your poodle spends time in the woods or tall grass, ticks might be a real problem. But even in a case like this you may be able to handle the problem through daily tick checks. It takes twenty-four to thirty-six hours for a tick bite to transmit disease. If you check your poodle for ticks each day and remove any you see, then pesticides may not be necessary.

Use latex gloves or tweezers when you remove ticks from your poodle. If you squeeze a tick with your bare fingers, it could transmit disease to you. Put your gloved fingers or tweezers as close to the skin as possible and pull the tick out in one straight motion. Then submerge the tick in rubbing alcohol to kill it. Don't put a match to the tick (you could singe your dog!) or smother the tick in petroleum jelly. Just get it out of your dog.

Preventing Heartworms

Heartworms are worms that can grow in a dog's heart. They're transmitted by mosquitoes and can be deadly. For this reason, many veterinarians recommend monthly heartworm "preventives." These pills or chewables don't actually prevent the transmission of heartworms. Rather, they kill the immature worms (called microfilariae) before they have a chance to mature inside your dog.

Giving their dogs a monthly heartworm pill is standard practice for most responsible pet owners. But some of the same holistically minded pet owners who choose not to give their dogs routine flea and tick pesticides also steer clear of monthly heartworm treatment, under the theory that these chemicals undermine the health of their dogs.

Like other medications, heartworm treatment becomes an issue of risk versus benefit. If you live in an area where heartworm isn't a big problem, or where mosquitoes aren't rampant, you may choose not to give your poodle heartworm pills. If your poodle spends very little time outdoors, he might not be exposed to mosquitoes and therefore not exposed to heartworm.

Alert!

To learn more about heartworm, check out the American Heartworm Society Web site (*www.heartwormsociety.org*). Here you'll find extensive information on heartworms, including the climate necessary for mosquitoes to transmit them. Depending on your location, a careful perusal of this Web site might make you reconsider giving monthly pills to a dog that spends most of her time indoors.

If you are treating your dog holistically, talk with your holistic veterinarian about alternatives to monthly heartworm chemicals, such as biannual blood testing for heartworm (if caught early, it's much easier to treat), heartworm nosodes, or natural mosquito repellents when your dog is outside.

While heartworm pills are labeled for monthly use, they're actually designed to last longer than that, on the assumption that pet owners won't be religious about giving the pill every month on the dot. Talk with your veterinarian about giving treatments less frequently.

Other Worms

Most heartworm products are designed to control other worms as well, like roundworms, hookworms, and whipworms. In the case of Heartgard Plus, this is accomplished by adding a pesticide to the mix. Interceptor tablets include a higher dose of the pesticide than would be necessary to kill just heartworm microfilariae. If you choose to address heartworms but don't care for these extra-strength precautions, talk with your veterinarian about prescribing a lower dose of Interceptor or giving Heartgard rather than Heartgard Plus.

If you don't worm your dogs regularly with souped-up heartworm pills, you should know the symptoms of worms so you can address them if they become an issue. If you see particles in your poodle's anal region that look like pieces of rice, you're looking at tapeworm. If your poodle has unexplained bouts of diarrhea, whipworm or hookworm might be the culprit. Roundworms look like pieces of spaghetti when vomited up. If you suspect your poodle has worms, see your veterinarian for treatment. It's also a good idea to bring a stool sample to your annual vet appointment.

Fact

A study done by Novartis Animal Health, makers of Interceptor (which kills heartworms and controls roundworms, hookworms, and whipworms) showed that the active ingredient of Interceptor, Milbemycin oxime, was effective in killing heartworm microfilariae when given at a dose just one-fifth the dose of regular Interceptor.

The Home Health Check

One of the best ways to monitor your poodle's health and identify any problems early on is to give your poodle regular, at-home health checks. Luckily, this is easy for you to do. It's also easy on your poodle, particularly if you start the monitoring while he's a puppy. Make it a habit to go through the following simple checks each day:

- **Body:** Rub your hands over your poodle's body and feel for any unusual lumps or bumps or areas of the body that are tender to the touch. Monitor for weight gain or loss by keeping track of how hard you need to press to feel the ribs.
- **Eyes:** Look for bright eyes surrounded by white whites, with little (if any) discharge.
- **Ears:** Pick up the ears and take a look inside. Look for any sign of redness or swelling. Also watch for brown, waxy gunk or bad odors, which can be signs of ear infection.
- **Mouth:** Your poodle's teeth should be pearly white and clear of tartar. Also take note of the color of his gums. Pale gums can be a sign of serious problems, so be sure and know what your poodle's normal gum color is.

If you encounter anything out of the ordinary when doing this check, contact your veterinarian to see if an exam is in order.

How to Give Your Poodle Medication

At some point, you'll probably have to give your poodle some sort of medication, even if it's just nutritional supplements. While it may sound like a daunting task, it needn't be traumatic for either of you.

Pills and Capsules

Before you jam a pill or capsule down your poodle's throat, try getting him to take it voluntarily. Some dogs will scarf a pill down with their food. If your dog simply eats around the pill and leaves it in the bowl, try coating the pill in something delicious (such as peanut butter, cream cheese, or pureed broiled liver) and offering it to him. Act like you're giving him a big treat. Many poodles will happily lick it off your finger and swallow the pill.

As a third option, you can try grinding the pill into a powder with one of those inexpensive pill grinders available at pharmacies and mixing it in with your dog's food. You can also empty capsules right into the food.

Essential

Before giving your poodle pills with food, check with your veterinarian to make sure it's okay. Some medications shouldn't be given with food, though many are less upsetting to the stomach if they are.

If your poodle won't eat medicine-laced food, you'll have to pill him. Ask him to sit, then open his mouth, pop the pill onto the back of his tongue, close his mouth, and rub his throat until he swallows. Make it one swift motion, with no fuss or fumbling. Be matter of fact and cheerful. Be sure to give him a treat when it's all over.

If you're going to be giving your poodle medication for an extended period of time, and he won't accept it in food, talk with your veterinarian about having a compounding pharmacist make up the prescription in a liver-flavored chewable or fish-flavored liquid that will be more palatable for your dog to take. This could save you the stress of having to pill him. And it might even be less expensive.

Dispensing Liquids

Liquid medications can be trickier to give your dog. If that's the only form the medicine comes in, look to your vet for the best advice in administering it. Generally, the easiest way to give a liquid is to put it into a syringe (with the needle removed) and squirt it into the side of your poodle's mouth. You want to avoid squirting it into the back of his mouth to keep it from going down his windpipe.

Holistic Care

More and more dog owners are seeking holistic care for their dogs. Holistic care emphasizes the whole animal. When health problems arise, the holistic veterinarian seeks to address the cause of the problem rather than the symptoms. For example, a poodle with recurrent ear infections that visits a conventional veterinarian will probably be prescribed antibiotics or steroidal ear ointment. This takes care of the infection, but the treatment doesn't address the reasons the dog is getting infections. If the same dog is taken to a holistic veterinarian, the cause of the infection will be sought. Perhaps it's related to diet or an immune imbalance. Perhaps the plucking of the poodle's ear hairs has caused irritation. The holistic veterinarian will seek to address the cause and help the dog achieve real health, thus avoiding future infections.

The holistic approach can take longer than treatment with antibiotics or steroids to make symptoms disappear. Yet advocates of holistic veterinary care feel that when the cause of illness is addressed, the dog will become healthier, and illness will arise less frequently.

Question?

What is homeopathic medicine?
The word "homeopathic" is often erroneously used interchangeably with "holistic." Homeopathy uses very specific methods and remedies, which are based on the symptom picture of the individual, to address the cause of disease. While a homeopathic vet should be holistic, not all holistic vets use homeopathy.

Key components of holistic care are feeding a natural diet and avoiding overvaccination and chemical pesticides. This is different from standard dog care, which usually involves feeding kibble, getting all available vaccinations, applying topical pesticides, and giving monthly heartworm pills. Holistic care requires the owner to educate herself, pay close attention to her dog, and have a certain amount of faith in the methods used, since gratification is not instant. A holistic veterinarian and her client become true partners in achieving the optimal health of the dog.

You can find a holistic vet who can guide you in this type of care by visiting the American Holistic Veterinary Medical Association's Web site (*www.ahvma.org*). Bear in mind that many holistic veterinarians do phone consultations.

It is not uncommon for dog owners only to seek alternative veterinary methods after their dogs become very ill and conventional care holds no hope. But using a holistic vet for preventive care makes even more sense. If you can keep your poodle healthy with the help of a holistic veterinarian and avoid chemicals and drugs, you may add to the number of years you get to spend together.

CHAPTER 10

Grooming Basics

GOOD GROOMING IS IMPORTANT for all dogs, but it's absolutely essential for poodles. In order to keep your poodle's wonderful, virtually nonshedding coat from becoming a matted mess, you must brush and comb her several times a week and have her groomed by a professional or trim her yourself every six to eight weeks. This isn't negotiable. But all the effort is worth it. A well-groomed poodle is beautiful to look at and a pleasure to live with.

Poodle Clips

One of the fun things about having a poodle is that you can change her hairstyle pretty much at your whim. If you pick a style you don't like, the hair will grow right back and you can try something else quite soon. While you'll find any number of clips to choose from, a few rise to the top in terms of popularity.

The Continental

In the Continental show clip—the one most familiar to people who watch dog shows on television—the poodle's face, throat, feet, and base of tail are shaved. The topknot is left long and is often pulled back with elastics. The hindquarters are shaved, with optional pompoms left on the hips. The legs are shaved, and the ankles are left with bracelets on the hind legs and puffs on the front legs. The rest of the body is left full and may be shaped with scissors.

The Working Continental

Some poodles sport a shorter, less extreme, version of the show Continental. This clip, known as the working Continental, is also allowable in the show ring (though it might be hard for a poodle in a working Continental to win). Owners who like the show cut often choose the working Continental if their dogs are doing fieldwork or other activities that a long coat would make more difficult.

The English Saddle Clip

The English Saddle clip, also allowed in the show ring, is similar to the Continental except that a short blanket of fur is allowed on the hindquarters. Into this blanket, a curved area is shaved on each flank and two bands are shaved on each hind leg.

The Puppy Clip

The puppy clip can be kept on a show poodle under the age of one year. The coat is kept long, and the face, feet, and base of tail are shaved. Some shaping of the coat is allowed, and there is a pompom on the end of the tail.

The Sporting Clip

The easy-to-care-for sporting clip (also called the kennel clip) involves a shaved face, throat, feet, and base of tail, with a short, scissored topknot and a pompom at the end of the tail. The body hair is clipped to follow the shape of the dog, and should be no more than an inch in length, though the leg hair can be slightly longer than hair on the torso. This clip is a popular one for pet poodles, but it is only allowed in the show ring in the stud dog and brood bitch classes or the noncompetitive "Parade of Champions." The lamb clip is similar to the sporting clip, only the legs are left longer. This clip is not allowed in the conformation ring, but can be an attractive, and relatively flashy, pet clip.

Pros and Cons of Home Grooming

Depending on the size of your poodle, doing a complete grooming at home can be quite a task, but if you have a do-it-yourself nature, you might want to learn how. Not only is home grooming less expensive, but people who enjoy grooming their poodles often build an even closer bond with them.

Essential

If you intend to show your poodle in conformation competition, you'll need the help of a professional. Keeping a poodle in a show coat is not a simple matter. Before you ever cut the hair of a poodle that is a show prospect, talk with someone who is experienced in grooming show poodles.

If you think you'd like to try your hand at grooming your own poodle, you should be aware of a few things:

- Grooming is time-consuming and requires patience.
- High-quality grooming equipment can be expensive.
- Your poodle may have some bad hair days as you learn the grooming techniques.
- No mistakes are permanent: Poodle hair always grows back.

A lot of work goes into making a poodle look like a poodle. At minimum, the face, feet, and base of tail are shaved close. The topknot is scissored, and often the legs are scissored as well. On a relatively short poodle cut, the torso might be shaved, with a blade that leaves more hair than the one used on the face.

If you want to do this yourself, you'll have to invest in good scissors and an electric trimmer. A grooming table with a nonslip surface is also helpful, so that you're not bending over your dog.

▲ Changing his hairdo is part of the fun of having a poodle; a moustache can be a handsome look.

Try to find a grooming mentor who can give you lessons on how to shave and scissor your poodle, and learn which blades will work for the clip you select. If you don't have friends who groom poodles, ask a professional groomer if he's willing to teach you. Offer to pay him a fee for sharing his knowledge. Alternatively, you can buy a video or two, study some books, or even enroll in an adult-education or correspondence course. It's wise to get your poodle professionally trimmed at the beginning, so that you can see how she ought to look. Your groomer may be able to give you some tips, if not actual lessons.

Selecting a Professional Groomer

For those without the time and energy to devote to home grooming, or those who have a show dog whose coat needs extra attention, finding a professional groomer is the way to go.

When it comes to selecting a groomer, word of mouth is very important. Familiarize yourself with the various poodle clips, and keep an eye out for well-groomed poodles in your area. When you see one, ask the owner who grooms that poodle. Keep a list of the names you hear, and take special note of any names that appear on your list more than once.

Fact

Even if you like the "natural" look of a poodle—fuzzy all over, with no shaved areas—you must keep up his coat. If you don't brush him, he'll become matted. Without periodic bathing and trimming, his coat will just keep growing, and he'll end up dirty and uncomfortable.

You should also check with your veterinarian or trainer for a groomer recommendation. If your breeder is local, she can probably give you some recommendations for good groomers as well.

When you have a short list of finalists, pay a visit to the shops. Take a look around and assess the cleanliness of the place. (Don't be alarmed by some dog hair on the floor.) Listen to the noise level–a very noisy shop might be the sign of unhappy dogs and may be stressful for your poodle. Find out whether the poodles must stay all day at the shop and, if so, whether they have to be in a cage when they're not being groomed. (Some shops allow dogs to play together.)

Essential

If possible, stay with your pup during the first few groomings. That way you'll get to see how your groomer interacts with your pup. If the groomer won't allow you to stay, ask why. He might say that in his experience, dogs don't stay still when their humans are around. This is a legitimate concern, but maybe he'll let you try.

Most importantly, pay attention to how the groomer interacts with the dogs. You want a gentle groomer who doesn't speak harshly and who seems to truly love the animals he grooms. Take notice of how your poodle reacts to going to the groomer. It's natural for her to be distressed about being left behind by you. But if she refuses even to walk in the door, that might be a sign that the shop is stressful for her.

Look for a groomer who seems to really like your particular dog and understands her good points. You also want a groomer who listens to what you have to say about your dog's haircut.

Brushing and Combing

Unlike the hair of short-haired dogs, which reaches a genetically programmed length and falls out, that wonderful curly coat on your poodle just grows and grows. When it does fall out, it stays in the coat—that's why poodles don't leave a lot of hair around the house. If you don't brush your poodle regularly, and the shed coat is allowed to remain there among the curls, it creates mats. Matted poodles are uncomfortable, and they can be very unattractive.

Brushing your poodle should be a regular part of your life together. Done properly and frequently, the task should be a pleasure, not a chore, for both you and your dog. If your poodle's coat isn't tangled, and you're gentle, there's no reason that brushing should hurt her.

Fact

Always brush and comb your poodle's coat before bathing him. If he has any mats, getting them wet and allowing them to dry will only make them tighten up. Brushing and combing also gets rid of some of the excess dirt.

Use a slicker brush (one with closely spaced pieces of wire mounted on a rectangular rubber base) or a pin brush to brush your poodle's coat. Make sure that you get the brush all the way down to the skin. Just raking it over the top of the coat won't get out tangles.

Start at the tail and brush out from the skin, working in small sections toward the head. You might find it's easier to work on one side at a time, with your poodle lying down. Once you finish the torso, move on to the legs, head, and tail.

After brushing, your poodle should be looking fluffy. Now you need to comb her. Use a metal comb with rather coarsely spaced teeth. This type of comb is often called a greyhound comb. By combing your poodle after you brush, you get out any small tangles that are left in her coat. Only after your comb has passed throughout your poodle's coat without resistance can you be sure there are no lingering mats.

Bathing and Drying

If you take your poodle to the groomer regularly, you may not need to bathe her between visits. But things happen—particularly if you have a puddle-loving poodle—and you might find that your poodle needs a bath at home.

Start by brushing and combing your poodle. Then put her in the tub (or sink) and wet her fur thoroughly, starting from her head and working back to her tail, then her chest, legs, and undercarriage. Make sure the water is pleasantly warm but not hot. Cold-water baths are unpleasant (which is a reason to have bath time inside rather than out back with the hose). Be upbeat, and act like this is the most fun either of you could possibly have.

Use dog shampoo to lather your poodle all over. Then rinse her thoroughly. Depending on how dirty she is, she might need a second lathering. Once you're sure she's thoroughly rinsed, rinse her one more time. You don't want to make your poodle itchy because of shampoo residue on her coat.

Once you're finished with the bath, blot your poodle with a towel so she's not dripping wet. Take her out of the tub (or sink) and put her on the floor. Be ready for her to shake and get you wet! Use a towel (or several) to dry her off some more. She may completely lose her mind after a bath and want to race around the house. Let her blow off some steam before you continue with the drying process.

Question?

How can I make bathing my poodle easier?
A hose attachment for your shower or sink is a huge help. Look for one with a head that can go right against your poodle's fur. The attachment should have a valve that allows you to turn off the flow of water without having to adjust your faucet controls.

If you don't mind your poodle's coat drying in ringlets, you can let it air dry from this point, and brush it out after it's dry. But if you want your clean poodle to have fluffy and straight hair, you should use a blow dryer and brush her as she dries. (Dry her in the same order you wet her hair in the tub.) If you're going to shave and scissor your poodle after her bath, then it's essential to use a blow dryer as you brush her out.

Trimming Nails

Keeping your poodle's nails short enough that their "click-click" on the wood or tile floor doesn't bother you is nice. What's really important is that you keep them short enough that your poodle can stand and walk comfortably.

Depending on how much walking on hard surfaces, like sidewalks, your poodle does, trimming may not even be necessary. But your groomer should evaluate your poodle's toenails at her regular visit and trim them if necessary.

If you have a poodle with fast-growing nails, you'll have to trim them yourself. It's not difficult, but may require a little patience on your (and your dog's) part.

Adjusting to the Toenail Clippers

Start trimming your poodle's nails when she's a pup, if possible, always keeping it a happy experience, full of treats, and with no force used. You might find it's helpful to work with an assistant who can distract your poodle from what you're doing by giving her treats. You might also find that it's easiest to trim nails while your poodle is lying down.

Your poodle might be so used to having her paws touched by you and the groomer that trimming is no big deal. But if she pulls away when you touch her paw for trimming, you need to start very slowly. A clicker can be helpful. Start by just touching her feet. Click and treat (or just treat, if you prefer) for calm behavior. Then handle her feet a little more, touching individual toes and holding her whole foot in your hand, again, treating for calm behavior. Then show her the nail clippers. Let her sniff them. Then just touch the clippers to her feet. Click and treat. If your dog is very nervous, end the session there. But come back to it soon.

Alert!

Don't lose your temper with your poodle if he resists when you try to trim his nails. If you do, you'll make the prospect of getting his nails trimmed even more onerous. Keep the process upbeat. If you find yourself losing patience, stop the session.

Cutting the Nails

Once your poodle is comfortable with the clippers around her nails, try cutting a nail. It's very important that you not cut into the quick, which could hurt your dog and forever change the way he feels about trimming nails. (It might also erode her trust in you.)

Unlike human fingernails, the dog's quick grows with the nail. If your poodle's nails are white, and therefore slightly translucent, you're in luck. You'll see the pink quick, and it'll be easy to avoid cutting it.

If your poodle's nails are black, you have to take a more cautious approach. It's safe to cut off the hook of the nail. But if your poodle's nails are short enough that there isn't a hook, you need to cut off just a little at a time. After each cut, look at the end of the nail. You'll see a small white spot just before you reach the quick. When you see that spot, stop clipping that nail. The clipping causes the quick to recede slightly, so in a few days you can cut a bit more off.

Essential

If your poodle's nails get very long, you might be tempted to have them cut short under sedation. Unless there's a compelling reason for the nails to get short very quickly, avoid this. It hurts! Your dog will probably have sore feet for a few days. It's not a nice thing to do to him.

Using a Grinder

Another way to trim your poodle's nails is to use a nail grinder, like a Dremel. You can buy one through a grooming supply store or at a hardware store. Use a sanding band of the appropriate size for your dog. (Your groomer might be able to advise you on equipment.) Because your poodle is accustomed to having her feet shaved with electric clippers, the nail grinder might not bother her. Introduce the grinder as you would the clippers, so your poodle's not scared by it. When it comes time to grind, gently hold your poodle's paw in your hand, supporting the toe you're working on, and hold the grinder straight up and down. Don't apply pressure to the nail with the grinder. Just touch it to the nail and let the spinning action trim the nail. As with traditional clippers, be careful not to touch the quick.

If your poodle has hairy feet, you can put a sock or stocking over her foot, with a hole cut in it to allow the nail you're working on to stick out. This will prevent your poodle's hair from getting caught in the spinning grinder.

Anal Sacs

Every dog has a pair of scent glands on either side of his anus (at about the four o'clock and eight o'clock positions). Normally, these glands empty when firm stool presses against them during defecation. (And sometimes they empty when your dog is really frightened.) In some dogs, however, the anal glands don't empty and get clogged. The clogging can even cause infection. This is more of a problem in Toys, but it can happen in Minis and Standards as well. A dog whose anal glands are clogged up might try scooting on the floor to empty them. Or she might lick at her anus.

Alert!

Be wary about having your poodle's anal sacs surgically removed, which is sometimes suggested when there are chronic anal sac problems. The surgery is delicate (a mistake can lead to fecal incontinence), and recovery is painful. Seek other solutions—including holistic ones—before resorting to surgery.

The anal glands can be emptied manually. Some groomers empty anal glands as part of their regular grooming procedure, and veterinarians usually empty the anal glands as part of a wellness exam. (If you don't want this done, be sure to mention it.)

When it comes to anal glands, if your dog isn't experiencing a problem, leave well enough alone. But if you find that she's uncomfortable in the anal area or scooting a lot, consult with your veterinarian about whether you should empty them for her. Perhaps an adjustment in diet will take care of the problem–sometimes adding fiber to the food will increase the bulk of the stool so the glands empty themselves.

Cleaning and Plucking Ears

Hair grows in the ear canals of many poodles. When this hair mixes with waxy discharge, a plug can form, which inhibits airflow and can lead to ear infections. Standard practice is that the ears are plucked free of hair each time the poodle is groomed. It is thought that this helps stave off ear infections.

Essential

If you pluck your dog's ears, they generally don't need to be plucked more often than your dog is groomed. Plucking the ears yourself between grooming sessions might cause irritation to the ear canal. Best to leave that task to the professional, or do it monthly, at most.

Some poodles have less hairy ear canals than others, however. And a very healthy poodle might not produce a lot of discharge, in which case hairy ears aren't a problem. If you already have a procedure in place for ear plucking, and your poodle does not suffer from ear infections, leave well enough alone. Just continue to do what you're doing.

If your poodle suffers from ear infections and you don't pluck, you might consider asking your groomer to start plucking and see if it helps. On the other hand, if your dog gets ear infections despite regular ear plucking, consider stopping. Dogs with recurrent ear infections would do well to see a holistic vet who can discover the source of the problem.

Dental Hygiene

Clean, white teeth are not only nice to look at, they're important for good health. When tartar accumulates on teeth, gum disease follows. Diseased gums can release bacteria into the bloodstream, which can potentially infect the heart, kidney, or liver.

In an ideal world, you'd brush your poodle's teeth daily. That's a lot to ask of many dog owners, who tend to have difficulty making the time for canine tooth brushing. But it's a goal to work toward, and it can be a major boost to your poodle's dental health. Luckily, it's not the only thing you can do to help your poodle's teeth.

Fact

Some dogs are born with better teeth than others. You might be lucky enough to have a poodle whose teeth seem to stay clean on their own. But more than likely, you'll have to give those teeth a little bit of help to keep them white and healthy.

Brushing Your Poodle's Teeth

Ideally, you'll start brushing your poodle's teeth when she's a puppy. But it's never too late to start. Begin by putting some toothpaste designed to be palatable to dogs on a toothbrush designed for use in a dog's mouth. Let your poodle sniff the toothpaste and take an experimental lick. If she seems to like it, put the brush against her teeth. When you do the outsides of the molars, she may try to chew the brush. That's no big deal. Canine toothpaste is enzymatic, so it works when it touches the teeth—the brushing action isn't as important as it is in humans. Try to brush the outside of the back teeth, as well as the front teeth. The insides of the teeth are harder to get to, so don't worry about them at the beginning.

Try to turn teeth brushing into a game. Act like you're giving your poodle an opportunity to do something really fun. Stay upbeat, and do it quickly. Try to get in the habit of brushing your poodle's teeth before or after you brush your own. (Your poodle follows you into the bathroom, doesn't she?) By starting a regular brushing routine, you'll reduce the need for cleanings under anesthesia.

Keeping the Teeth Clean

Raw bones can be great for keeping a dog's teeth clean. Find one in the appropriate size for your poodle. Knuckle bones are preferable to marrow bones, because they force the dog to keep moving her mouth around and seem less likely to cause fractured teeth.

Some people who feed their dogs a raw diet composed of meat and ground bone find that the enzymes in the food keep their dogs' teeth sparkling clean without brushing.

Essential

Any bones you feed your dog should be raw, not cooked. Raw bones don't splinter, while cooked bones (particularly cooked poultry bones) can. Raw bones contain enzymes that help clean teeth.

Greenies are chewable, manmade, toothbrush-shaped "bones" designed to keep a dog's teeth clean, particularly as maintenance after a dental cleaning. They're made of natural ingredients, and are highly palatable to dogs, who appear to just love chewing and consuming them. Because Greenies contain wheat gluten, which many dogs are sensitive to, you might want to limit your poodle's consumption to once a week.

Teeth Cleaning at the Vet's Office

If tartar builds up long enough on your poodle's teeth, you might have to have it removed by the vet. Most humans have their teeth cleaned a couple of times a year. But the difference with dogs is that most dogs need to be anesthetized in order for a dental cleaning to be performed. Anesthesia is not without risk. So keeping your dog's teeth clean at home can be very beneficial.

If you do have your poodle's teeth cleaned, ask for preanesthesia blood work to be performed, to pinpoint any problems that might make anesthesia unadvisable. After the dental procedure, do your best to embark on a program of dental hygiene so your poodle won't have to have another one any time soon.

CHAPTER 11

Common Illnesses and Injuries

EVEN WHEN YOU TAKE the very best care of your poodle that you can, he will get sick or hurt at some point. Some common illnesses and injuries can be taken care of with home care, while others require a trip to the vet. As a responsible pet owner, it's important for you to be aware of common problems that may develop and to know what to do about them. A good relationship with your veterinarian is also very important.

What's Normal?

In order for you to judge whether your poodle is ill, you need to have some sense of what normal is. If you observe your poodle carefully on a daily basis, you'll be able to identify when something is "off." Sometimes it's just a feeling you have. Listen to it. If the problem doesn't seem serious enough to involve the veterinarian, make a note of it in your calendar. This way, if symptoms do worsen, you'll know when you first started noticing that something was up.

Body Temperature

Normal body temperature is between 100.5 and 102.5°F for dogs, with 101.3°F being the average. To take your dog's temperature, lubricate the end of a thermometer with some petroleum jelly, KY Jelly, or butter, then lift his tail and insert the thermometer into his rectum until the silver end is covered. Hold it there for a minute or two. (If you're using a digital thermometer, wait for it to beep.) Make sure your dog doesn't sit down so you don't risk breaking the thermometer while it's still inside him.

If your dog's temperature is below 99°F or above 104°F, contact your veterinarian immediately, or visit the nearest emergency facility.

Fact

Don't like the idea of taking your dog's temperature rectally? An ear thermometer, called Pet Temp, has now been developed for dogs. (A human child's thermometer won't work because the dog's ear canal is shaped differently.) If you're willing to spend the money, temperature-taking can become a little easier.

Respiratory Rate

A dog's rate of breathing varies according to his level of exertion, but at rest the average dog breathes twenty-four breaths per minute. Normal resting breath ranges from ten to thirty breaths per minute, with Toy Poodles generally breathing more rapidly than Miniatures or Standards.

Dogs pant to cool themselves down. This is normal. But rapid breathing (not panting) can be a sign of pain, fever, or distress. Difficult or labored breathing is also a sign of something serious, including heart or lung problems.

To measure your poodle's respiration rate, watch his side or chest and count how many times he breathes in fifteen seconds. Then multiply that by four to calculate breaths per minute.

When Do You Need to Visit a Vet?

You and your veterinarian should be a team dedicated to keeping your poodle healthy. If you have a good relationship, you might be able to call and ask questions about problems that crop up, rather than taking your poodle in to the clinic. But there are times your vet needs to see him, no matter how healthy he is.

Question?

When should blood work be done?
Blood tests can provide a look into what's going on inside your dog. If your dog is eight or older, an annual—or even twice yearly—blood chemistry test is a good idea for early detection of disease or organ failure.

The Annual Exam

Every dog should visit the veterinarian at least once a year for a wellness checkup. At that exam, your vet will give your dog a thorough looking-over, examining his eyes, ears, teeth, skin, and coat. She'll palpate him, feeling for lumps or signs of pain. She'll also probably want a stool sample to check for worms and a blood sample for a heartworm test. This annual appointment is important for early detection of disease and for allowing your vet to see your dog when he's feeling well.

Problem Visits

In an ideal world, your poodle wouldn't need to see the vet any more often than his annual wellness appointment. But there's a real possibility that you'll need to take your poodle in because of some illness or injury. Don't be afraid to set up an appointment if you feel a problem is serious or if it is not clearing up with your home remedies.

When it comes to deciding whether to pay a visit to the vet, listen to your intuition. If it tells you that something serious is going on, it's worth it (if only for your peace of mind) to visit or call your vet.

◀ Your poodle depends on you to figure out when he's feeling poorly and seek veterinary care for him.

Relieving Poodle Allergies

Allergies to food or pollens are not uncommon in poodles, or dogs in general. An allergic reaction is an immune response to something to which the body is overly sensitive. Generally, allergies in dogs manifest themselves in itchiness. Your poodle might lick his paws or scratch his ears or the back of his front legs. Allergies can also lead to red, goopy eyes or gastrointestinal problems.

Inhalant Allergies

Inhalant allergens such as grasses, pollens, mold, or dust tend to make a dog very itchy and can lead to miserable skin problems. However, it is very difficult to avoid allergens in the air. Since allergies are essentially caused by an imbalance in the immune system, there are two approaches to take: suppressing the immune system so that it won't react, or balancing the immune system.

Fact

If your poodle is suffering from allergies, don't vaccinate him. Vaccinations introduce foreign proteins into your dog's system and give an already out-of-balance immune system an unpleasant jolt. Vaccinations should be given only to healthy dogs; allergic dogs are not healthy.

Conventional therapy for severe allergies is to use corticosteroids like prednisone to suppress the immune system. Unfortunately, long-term steroid use is hard on your dog's body and can potentially lead to serious problems. While cortisone can provide your poodle relief—which can be very important—it can also shorten his life. Another conventional approach is allergy shots, which contain small amounts of the allergen that your poodle is sensitive to. These allergens are injected into your dog, in hopes of slowly reducing his sensitivity to the allergens.

An alternative approach is to consult with a holistic vet about nutritional therapy to help balance the immune system. Other holistic modalities, like homeopathy, glandular therapy, herbs, acupressure, and acupuncture, can also be helpful. Once the immune system is balanced, it will stop overreacting to the allergens.

Alert!

If your dog is on cortisone (prednisone) therapy for allergies, you may be able to wean her off with holistic support. But never cut her off abruptly, which can lead to shock (and even death). You must always gradually wean a dog off steroids.

No matter how you deal with the problem, avoiding the allergens—to the extent possible—can give your poodle some relief. Use HEPA air filters or air deionizers (like the Ionic Breeze from Sharper Image) to help clear the air of allergens. Vacuum frequently using a vacuum cleaner with a HEPA filter. Once your dog's immune system is balanced, you may be able to expose him to those allergens and not get a reaction.

Food Allergies

Food allergies, which happen when a dog becomes overly sensitive to an ingredient in his diet, can lead to itchiness, inflamed ears, and gastrointestinal problems. Dogs become hypersensitive to ingredients they eat day in and day out. Grains are often a source of allergies. If your poodle develops a food allergy, you can switch diets to avoid the offending ingredient and seek to increase your dog's overall health with holistic support.

You may want to consider switching to a home-prepared diet (as described in Chapter 8). This will give you more control over what goes into your dog's body. Also, the fresh ingredients in the home diet can lead to increased health, which can, in turn, reduce the allergic reaction.

Fact

Lamb and rice foods aren't any more "hypoallergenic" than other foods. You can feed your dog any food that is totally new to her if she develops an allergy to her regular food. Foods made from lamb, duck, even kangaroo are helpful only if your dog has never eaten them before.

Diagnosing Allergies

Food allergies are often diagnosed through an elimination diet. This means you feed your dog a very limited diet of ingredients he's never eaten before. Then you slowly add the ingredients of his old food to determine what is causing the reaction.

This type of strategy doesn't work with environmental or inhalant allergies since you don't have control over the environment the same way you do over food. But two types of tests are available to determine the allergens. One is the intradermal skin test, done under sedation, in which antigens are injected into the skin so the sites can be examined for reaction. A less invasive option is blood testing. Some veterinarians say that blood tests aren't reliable for allergies, but many holistic vets have used them with great success. They're easy to do and provide detailed results.

Alert!

If your poodle has itchy skin or a poor coat, and you suspect allergies, ask your veterinarian to draw blood for a complete thyroid panel. An underactive thyroid can cause these symptoms. Your vet should run a full panel, not just a T4 test, which is an unreliable indicator on its own.

Cuts and Scrapes

If your rough-and-tumble poodle gets a few cuts or scrapes, you can treat them like you would a kid's scraped knee. Wash the area with some soap and water and apply some Neosporin or calendula ointment (a natural antibiotic available at the health food store). For deeper cuts that may need stitches, take him in to see the vet. Watch for signs of infection as the wound heals (redness, swelling, or tenderness). If you think you have an infection on your hands, call your vet.

Dealing with Foxtails

Foxtails are small grasses with brush-like spikes full of seeds. The seeds have barbed sides and sharp ends, and when they're dry (as they are in the summer and fall) they can attach themselves to your dog. If you don't remove them, they can get entangled deeper and deeper into the fur and can even go through the skin and enter the body. Foxtails can also get caught in the nose, eyes, and ears. They cause pain and discomfort for your poodle and, if they enter the body, can be dangerous and hard to detect.

If your poodle has been running through tall grass, inspect him thoroughly when he's finished and remove any foxtails or burrs that you find. If your poodle is sneezing repetitively, shaking his head or pawing at his ears, do a close inspection for foxtails. If he's squinting or licking a paw, it might be due to foxtails. If you find one that's become imbedded, particularly if it's in the eye, ear, or nose, take him to the vet for immediate removal.

Relief from Hot Spots

Raw, weepy spots on your poodle's skin, known as hot spots, are usually caused by the poodle himself. He gets an itch from something, like an allergic reaction to a fleabite, and licks it and chews on it until it's raw. A healthy, natural way to provide him some relief and help make the hot spot go away is to make a paste from water and powdered bovine colostrum (available in powder and capsules at health food stores) and apply it directly on the hot spot. It will soothe and also help heal. Aloe gel (either from the health food store or directly from the plant) can also be soothing and healing. Clipping the fur around the hot spot can help it air out and stay dry.

Fact

A cone-shaped Elizabethan collar might stop your poodle from licking his hot spots, but in the long term, you should really concern yourself not with stopping her from licking, but rather with finding out why your poodle is getting hot spots. Then address the underlying problem.

Lumps and Bumps

Feeling for lumps should be part of your routine at-home examination of your poodle. Dogs can get all sorts of lumps, ranging from benign fatty lipomas to abscesses to cancerous tumors. If you find a lump on your dog, contact your veterinarian so you can get an expert's opinion. Your vet may want to remove it or aspirate it with a needle to look for cancerous cells.

It's scary to find a lump on your poodle. As he ages, they will crop up more and more often, and you'll probably become an expert about knowing when to worry. Make sure your vet feels them, and ask her to keep a map of your poodle's lumps and bumps in his chart, so it's easy to monitor them.

Gastrointestinal Problems

Loose, watery stools and vomiting can be caused by all sorts of things, ranging from the relatively innocuous (dietary indiscretion) to the serious (metabolic problems). Sometimes it's nothing to fret about, but if it's happening frequently, a vet visit is usually in order.

Diarrhea

If your poodle has occasional diarrhea and you can figure out a relatively harmless cause (stress or excitement or a snack of spicy food, for example), it's not something to worry about. In general, it's a good idea to let diarrhea run its course, since the body uses diarrhea to flush out toxins.

When your dog has diarrhea, withhold food for twelve to twenty-four hours, keeping water available so he doesn't become dehydrated. Then feed bland food, like boiled chicken or hamburger (with fat rinsed off after boiling), or scrambled or soft-boiled eggs accompanied by cottage cheese or white rice. Slowly ease him back to his regular food.

However, if the diarrhea occurs frequently, lasts more than two days, is bloody or black, or is accompanied by vomiting, weakness, or fever, give your vet a call. Together, you should try to find the source of the problem and address it.

Vomiting

Vomiting can also be caused by a number of factors. Something as simple as stress or drinking water too fast might make your poodle vomit. If he regurgitates his food right after eating, then tries to eat it again, he may have just eaten too fast.

If your dog vomits just once and seems to feel well otherwise, don't worry too much about it (though it's a good idea to mark it on your calendar). If your dog vomits a couple of times but is otherwise healthy, withhold food for twelve hours, then feed him a small amount of bland food.

Alert!

If your Standard Poodle is uncomfortable and tries to vomit but is unable to do so, feel her belly. If it's hard or distended at all, she may be bloating. Bloat is a medical emergency in which the stomach fills with air or gas and twists. If you think your poodle might be bloating, rush her to the emergency vet.

If your dog is vomiting violently and frequently, or if the vomit smells like feces or contains blood, contact your veterinarian. If the vomiting is accompanied by severe diarrhea, a vet visit is also in order.

Lack of Appetite

If your poodle normally scarfs down everything you put in front of him, lack of appetite can be an important indicator that something is up. Not wanting to eat is a sign of a number of illnesses, including Addison's disease and cancer. It can also be a sign of poor dental health or infectious disease. Of course, it can also just be a message that your poodle doesn't like what you're feeding him! If your poodle refuses to eat, first try offering him something else. If he won't eat anything and he seems to be feeling poorly, take him to the vet.

Ear Infections

Thanks to their dogs' long, heavy ears, most poodle owners are very familiar with ear infections. They're not hard to detect. You might notice your poodle shaking his head a lot or scratching his ears. When you smell the ears during your regular at-home exam, they might stink. If the infection is quite bad, your poodle might cry out or flinch when you try to handle his ears.

Essential

If your poodle shakes her head a lot because her ears itch, she could break blood vessels in the ear and a painful, fluid-filled hematoma could form on the ear flap. Severe hematomas sometimes have to be surgically removed. To keep this from happening to your dog, address ear problems at the first shake of the head.

Treating Ear Infections

If your poodle has an infection, your veterinarian might prescribe antibiotics to fight it. If the infection is particularly severe, your poodle may need to be anesthetized so that the ears can be flushed out.

One product that can help clear up ear infections without antibiotics or steroids is called Zymox Otic, made by Pet King Brands, Inc. It uses four types of enzymes to fight bacterial, viral, and fungal infections. It works quickly and painlessly and comes with or without hydrocortisone, which can help reduce pain and inflammation. Ask your veterinarian if she can order some if she doesn't already carry it.

Antibiotics may sometimes be necessary, but if your poodle has recurrent infections, you'll need to do more than give your dog course after course of antibiotics. Chronic ear problems don't happen just because airflow to the ear canal is inhibited by your poodle's long, heavy ears. Frequently, they're a byproduct of other health problems, like allergies and yeast overgrowth. Pesticides, in the form of flea and tick control products or residue on food ingredients, have been blamed for chronic ear problems, as have vaccinations. If your poodle suffers from one ear infection after another, and antibiotics and steroidal ointments aren't addressing the cause, consider seeking advice from a holistic veterinarian. This way you can try to find the source of the problem, rather than just addressing the symptoms.

Ear Cleaning

If your poodle's ears have a lot of brown, waxy discharge, you may need to clean them to keep him comfortable. You can buy a lot of veterinary preparations for cleaning out the ear, but an easier method is simply to warm some olive oil, dip a cotton ball in it, and gently wipe the underside of your poodle's ear flap.

Don't become a zealot about keeping your poodle's ears clean and plucked. In a healthy dog, frequent cleaning should not be necessary. Putting too much liquid in the ear can cause ear problems, and plucking the hair in the ear canal can irritate it. If your poodle's ears look good and smell sweet, don't rock the boat by cleaning and plucking.

Lameness or Limping

An active dog can get an occasional limp that's nothing to worry about. He might have something as simple as a pulled muscle, an abrasion on his paw, or a charley horse. However, if it goes on for a while or the pain seems extreme, it might be something more serious.

Toe Problems

A torn toenail can cause your poodle to limp. If your dog tears a nail off, apply pressure with a cloth to stop the bleeding. If the nail isn't torn completely off, take him to the veterinarian, who can finish the job, sedating him if necessary.

Fact

Although a nail can be torn if your dog is playing hard in the grass, this damage can also be a sign of an autoimmune problem called lupoid onchodystrophy. If your poodle tears more than one nail, talk to your vet about the possibility of an underlying issue.

If a lump develops under your black Standard Poodle's toenail, consult your vet. She might suspect toe cancer (squamous cell carcinoma, or SCC). SCC has a genetic basis, and black, large-breed dogs, including Standard Poodles, appear to be predisposed to develop it. More than one toe may be involved over a period of time. Treatment involves amputating the toe to stop spreading of the cancer.

Other Causes of Limping

Whether or not you can find an obvious cause for it, don't ignore a persistent limp. Not only is it an indication that your poodle is in pain, a chronic limp can also be a sign of a potentially serious problem. Particularly if he's older, a limp might indicate that your poodle has the beginning of degenerative joint disease (arthritis). See Chapter 21 for more on what this is and how to treat it.

Probably the scariest source of a limp is bone cancer (osteosarcoma). A limp that shifts from leg to leg can be a sign of polyarthritis, an autoimmune condition. In addition, a limp might mean a strained or torn cruciate ligament, a condition that seems increasingly common in dogs. Surgery is usually required to repair the torn knee ligament.

If your dog is limping but is using the leg and doesn't seem to be in much pain, you can take a wait-and-see approach. Make a note of it in your calendar. If the limp goes away within a day or two, chalk it up to something minor. But if the limp persists, or your poodle is refusing to put weight on the leg, take him to the vet immediately.

CHAPTER 12

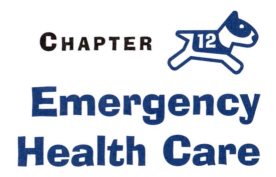

Emergency Health Care

YOU CAN BE THE MOST CAREFUL person in the world and do everything in your power to keep your poodle safe and healthy and still be faced with an emergency. As with so many things in life, being prepared is the key. The best thing you can do for your poodle is to recognize an emergency when you see it and have the proper first-aid materials on hand. You also need to know how to perform first aid on your poodle until you can get professional help.

Being Prepared for an Emergency

Even if your poodle is living a normal, active lifestyle, you never know when an emergency will crop up. It might come in the form of an injury. It might be a sudden illness. Stuff happens. And you need to be ready for it.

When an accident happens, it's sometimes hard to know how serious it is. If you're unsure whether your poodle needs veterinary assistance, it's certainly better to err on the side of caution. In the event of an injury or sudden illness, look out for signs of a serious condition, such as stopped or difficult breathing; loss of consciousness; shock (signs include pale gums, rapid breathing, cold skin, and a weak, but rapid, pulse); gaping wounds; severe bleeding; and abnormal body temperature.

If your poodle is involved in severe trauma (from a fall or being hit by a car) and she can't put any weight on her leg, can't move at all, or you see bone sticking out of the skin, suspect a fracture. Don't try to set the bone yourself or even diagnose a fracture. Instead, prepare her for transfer to your nearest emergency clinic.

The First-Aid Kit

Having a first-aid kit on hand—and knowing what to do with its contents—can save your poodle's life. It's best to keep one in your home and one in the car. You can buy a fully equipped first-aid kit from a pet-supply store or catalog, or you can create one of your own. A basic kit includes the following items:

- Ace bandage
- Activated charcoal (ToxiBan)
- Antihistamine (Benadryl)
- Antiseptic cleanser (Betadine or Novalsan)
- Blunt-tipped scissors
- Commercial cold/hot packs
- Cotton balls
- Gauze bandages and rolls
- Hydrogen peroxide
- Karo syrup or honey
- Muzzle
- Petroleum jelly
- Rectal thermometer (bulb or digital)
- Sterile saline solution
- Tweezers

Other items to keep in or near your first-aid kit include a clean blanket, towels, and a washcloth. The blanket will keep your dog warm if she goes into shock and can also act as a stretcher. You can use the towels or washcloth to apply pressure to stop bleeding.

Essential

Vetrap bandaging tape, a stretchable gauze that sticks to itself, is a valuable addition to your first-aid kit. If you need to apply a bandage, it does a great job without sticking to your dog's fur. It also comes in fun colors.

Important Phone Numbers

Keep emergency numbers posted by your home phone, programmed into the speed dial of your cell phone, and on a card in your first-aid kits. These should include the telephone numbers of your veterinary clinic, the local emergency animal hospital, the ASPCA's Animal Poison Control Center (888-426-4435), and your veterinarian's pager number or home phone, if he supplies you with one.

When you're faced with an emergency, you don't want to have to find a telephone book or your personal address book. Having the telephone numbers handy could save you precious minutes.

▲ Learn in advance what to do in case of emergency so you can act quickly to protect your precious poodle when time is of the essence.

How to Muzzle Your Poodle

Your poodle is probably extremely gentle, and you couldn't imagine her ever biting you. If she's been injured, though, and your efforts to help her cause more pain, her instinct will be to bite. She won't pause to think about it first, and she might not even realize whom she's biting. To avoid this, the very first thing you should do–for the sake of you both–is to muzzle her.

You can buy an appropriate-sized muzzle and keep it in your first-aid kit. A soft cloth one with strong Velcro fasteners is probably easiest to use in an emergency. Practice putting it on your poodle when you get it, so that you know how to use it and are sure it fits.

Question?

Is there a safe way to fashion a muzzle in an emergency?
Take a piece of cloth (the proper size will vary depending on the size of your poodle—a necktie may work, or even a leash), then circle your poodle's muzzle with it and tie a half knot at the top. Cross the ends, and make another knot under her chin. Pull the ends back behind her neck (go under her ears) and tie a knot or a bow.

Restraining Your Injured Poodle

In addition to muzzling your poodle if she's injured, you need to know how to safely hold her while someone else gives her first aid. The proper restraining position will keep your dog from injuring herself further by struggling.

There are several ways to restrain your poodle, depending on where her injury is and how big she is. For the reclining restraint, which works well for Standard Poodles, put her on her side with the injured side up. Put your hand on her bottom foreleg and your arm across her shoulder. With your other hand, take hold of the ankle on the bottom hind leg and press your forearm against her hips.

For the stretch restraint, which works best for small poodles, hold your dog by the scruff of the neck with one hand, and hold both her hind legs with the other. Gently stretch her out on her side on a table.

To use the hugging restraint, for dogs that weigh over twenty pounds, hug your standing poodle to your chest, with one arm under her head and around her neck. (Think of a wrestler doing a half nelson.) Put the other arm under her belly and up across her outer side, resting your hand at her shoulder. You can also reach over her side and grasp her underside, if that's easier.

How to Move an Injured Dog

Moving your poodle when she's injured or unconscious can be difficult, even dangerous, for your dog, depending on the injury. Be extremely careful–you don't want to cause your poodle any additional pain, and you certainly don't want to make the injuries worse.

If your poodle is small enough, take her to the vet in her carrier. If she can walk, let her. If you suspect a back injury, carefully slide your poodle, on her side, onto something stiff. For a Toy Poodle, you can use a cutting board, a cookie sheet, or even a large book. For larger poodles, an ironing board or a piece of plywood might work. Cover her with a towel, and tie her onto the board so she stays on. Use tape, if that's more convenient, since it's the towel, not the dog, that the tape will be touching. Tape or tie the towel behind the front legs and in front of the back legs. Gently place the board, with your poodle on it, into the car.

If a stiff surface isn't available, gently place your poodle on a blanket or towel and lift it like a stretcher. You'll need helpers for this. One person can take each end for a small dog, but you might need a person at each corner for a large Standard.

Essential

Don't hold your injured dog in your lap in the car. It's less stable, it might impede his breathing, and he'll more easily pick up on your emotions if you're upset. Instead, put him on the seat and bolster him, if you can, with pillows or towels. Cover him up with a blanket to help ward off shock.

Performing CPR on Your Poodle

Many people are familiar with cardiopulmonary resuscitation (CPR) for people, but they may not know it can also be done on dogs. It combines artificial respiration with heart compressions and can help dogs whose hearts have stopped beating and that have stopped breathing. If a dog in distress has stopped breathing, but her heart is still pumping, artificial respiration alone can be used.

Artificial Respiration

To breathe for your dog, first check to see that the airway is clear. If you see a foreign object, take hold of her tongue and pull it, using a washcloth to get better traction. That might dislodge the object. If not, try to remove it with your fingers or tongs. If you can't reach it, perform the Heimlich maneuver (page 156). If that doesn't restart the breathing, you'll need to start breathing for your poodle. Do this while someone drives you to the vet:

1. Place your poodle on her right side. If she's small, you can cradle her in your lap. Straighten her neck by lifting her chin.
2. Hold her mouth closed and put your mouth completely over her nose and mouth (or just the nose, if your poodle is a Standard). Blow two breaths into her, and watch for her chest to rise, a sign that her lungs are expanding.
3. Blow just hard enough to move her sides (but no harder). Let the air escape between breaths. Do fifteen to twenty breaths per minute, watching to see if she starts breathing on her own.

Be absolutely sure that your poodle isn't breathing before starting artificial respiration. Watch her side to see if it's rising and falling, or put your hand or mirror under her nose to detect breath. Look at her gums—they'll turn blue if she's not breathing.

Chest Compressions

If your poodle stops breathing and her heart stops beating, you'll need to combine chest compressions with the artificial respiration.

Feel for a heartbeat with the palm of your hand directly behind the left front elbow (or put your ear there and listen). Alternatively, use three fingers to check the femoral artery, located on the inside of the thigh at the groin. Be absolutely certain that the heart has stopped beating before you start chest compressions. Doing CPR on an animal that is breathing and/or whose heart is beating can damage her heart and lungs.

Fact

It's easier for two people to perform CPR on a dog. One handles the artificial respiration while the other handles the chest compression. If you're faced with doing CPR on a dog, see if you can quickly find a helper.

If your poodle weighs in at under twenty pounds, you'll do chest compressions using the cardiac pump technique, in which you squeeze the heart (through the skin) to pump blood. To find the heart, gently flex her left front leg backward. Her heart is located where her elbow touches her side.

To start the compressions, place your small poodle on her right side, cup your hand over her heart and squeeze firmly, pressing in about half an inch, with your thumb on one side and your fingers on the other. Try to do a squeeze each second, or more frequently if you can (up to two squeezes a second). If your dog is a puppy, you can hold her in the palm of your hand and use your thumb and one finger to help the heart pump.

Directly compressing the heart of dogs over twenty pounds is ineffective because the space between the ribs and heart is so large. Instead, do compressions at the highest part of the chest. Lay your poodle on her side and kneel behind her, with her back against your knees. Place your hand flat on the highest part of the rib cage (which is also the widest part), place the other hand over it, straighten your arms, and push down firmly. The smaller the dog, the less pressure you should use. Press for one count and release for one count. Try to compress sixty to eighty times per minute.

Alternate between one breath and five compressions for any size dog. Continue until your poodle starts breathing on her own and her heart starts pumping, or until you arrive at the animal hospital.

Essential

See if you can find an animal CPR class being offered locally. Your local branch of the American Red Cross is a good place to start a search. In this class, you can learn from an expert and practice CPR on a dummy dog.

The Heimlich Maneuver

If your poodle tries to eat something that gets lodged in her airway, you might be able to save her life with a modified version of the famed Heimlich maneuver. If she starts coughing, gagging, or retching, or if she has difficulty breathing, suspect that something is caught in her windpipe. If she's conscious, take her to the vet. If she loses consciousness or completely stops breathing, and you're fairly sure something is caught in her throat, start the Heimlich maneuver.

For a poodle small enough to be easily carried, pick her up and hold her, face out, so that her head is at your chest and her feet are dangling. Put your fist in the soft hollow underneath her rib cage and push in and up, toward your belly and your chin at the same time. Use a strong, thrusting action.

For a larger poodle, place her on her side and kneel behind her so that your knees are touching her back. Her head should point toward your left. Lean over her and fit your right fist just below her rib cage. Press sharply upward and inward toward her back.

Do the maneuver three times, then check her mouth to see if the offending item has become dislodged. If it hasn't, rush her to the emergency vet. Get someone else to drive so you can continue trying the Heimlich maneuver in the car to extricate the item.

If you're successful in dislodging the item, but your poodle still isn't breathing, do artificial respiration, as described earlier.

Dealing with Emergencies

An emergency is a life-or-death situation. By knowing some basic first aid and acting quickly, you might be able to save your dog's life, stabilize her, and get her to the veterinarian as quickly as possible. You need to be calm and reassuring in an emergency in order to keep your poodle as calm as possible. Here are some common emergencies and what to do about them.

Cuts or Lacerations

If your poodle is injured and starts bleeding, your first course of action should be to try to stop the bleeding. If the wound isn't deep, and you are able to stop the bleeding, a visit to the veterinarian may not be necessary. (See the following sections on cuts and puncture wounds.)

Alert!

If your poodle is bleeding from his nose, mouth, or anus, and there is no apparent injury, take him to the veterinarian immediately. This is a sign of internal bleeding, which can be caused by poisoning or internal injury.

The best way to stop bleeding is to apply direct pressure. Take a clean cloth or gauze pad, put it over the wound, and press down. (A sanitary napkin works well, too.) If your cloth or pad soaks through, don't remove it. Rather, put another over the first. If you remove the cloth, you may also remove any clots that have formed. If direct pressure isn't doing the trick, make a pressure bandage.

Keep the pad over the wound in place and cover it with roll gauze or an Ace bandage wrapped around your poodle's body several times. The pressure bandage should be firm, but not so tight that it cuts off circulation. If your poodle is small, clear plastic wrap can be used. Bleeding should stop within five to ten minutes. If it doesn't, head straight for the veterinarian's office.

Loss of blood can lead to shock, which can be fatal. Keep your poodle warm and watch for signs of shock: weakness, disorientation, and pale gums. If you suspect shock, wrap her in a blanket, give her a couple of drops of Karo syrup or honey, and rush her to the vet.

If you are successful in stopping the bleeding following the above procedure, carefully trim the fur around the wound, with a border an inch wide all around the wound—now's not the time to worry about appearances! Flush out the wound with water so that you can remove debris and get an idea of how serious it is.

Essential

Homeopathic arnica, available at health-food stores, can be very helpful in reducing swelling and pain when there's a trauma. Give your poodle (regardless of size) a dose of the 30c potency every couple of hours while she's in pain.

Bandage a gaping wound by putting gauze or more absorbent material like a sanitary napkin or even a disposable diaper over the wound and wrapping with an Ace bandage or Vetrap.

If you suspect that your poodle's cut might require stitches, don't delay in taking her to the vet. In order to best help the wound heal, stitches should be put in place within two to four hours of the injury.

Puncture Wounds and Animal Bites

Animal bites are serious because they can become so easily infected. If you can provide first aid within an hour of the bite, you can help ward off bacterial infection. Try to stop the bleeding with pressure and seek veterinary care if the bleeding doesn't stop within five minutes. If the bleeding does stop, an ice pack can help numb the pain and reduce swelling and bruising. It's a good idea to have your veterinarian look at any bite. Antibiotics might well be called for.

You might not see an animal bite, however, and the first sign could be swelling and infection. If you find a painful swelling on your poodle, and she's running a fever, take her to the vet, who will probably open the abscess and clean it out. He'll probably also prescribe antibiotics to help stop the infection.

Insect Bites and Stings

If your poodle is bitten by an insect or stung by a bee, she may start to swell. If the swelling is mild, a simple paste of baking soda or Ac'cent Flavor Enhancer (containing MSG) and water applied to the bite can provide some relief from the discomfort.

If the bite or sting is on your poodle's face, the swelling could cut off breathing. In that case, give her an antihistamine, like Benadryl, to stop the reaction. The dosage is one milligram per pound of body weight. For Toy Poodles, you can buy the liquid sold for children; it's easier to get a smaller dosage. Repeat the dosage every six to eight hours as needed.

If your poodle's reaction to the bite or sting is severe—pale gums, weakness, vomiting, diarrhea, wheezing, or collapse—take her to the vet for immediate help. This could be an anaphylactic reaction to the sting or bite, which can be deadly.

Alert!

If your poodle has ever had an anaphylactic reaction to a sting, his risk for an even more severe reaction is high. Ask your veterinarian for an epinephrine pen that you can use to give your poodle immediate care in the event of a future sting.

Electrocution

Some dogs—even poodles—chew on electrical cords, a very dangerous practice. If you find your poodle unconscious near a cord, turn off the main power switch to your house, then unplug the cord. If you touch your dog before turning off the power, you may get shocked. Administer CPR immediately. Once he regains consciousness, rush him to the vet.

If the shock is minor, and your poodle doesn't lose consciousness, she might be coughing, drooling, or have a strange-smelling mouth. Keep her quiet and offer her some cold water, which might soothe her mouth. Take her to the vet for an examination.

Overheating and Heatstroke

Dogs can suffer serious heatstroke when left in a car in the sun or exercising vigorously in the heat. Like so many emergencies, prevention is the best course of action. But if you feel your poodle has overheated—she's been exposed to warm weather, is panting rapidly, seems depressed, and has thick saliva and a bright red tongue—act immediately.

Take your dog's temperature to assess the severity of the heat stroke. (Here's a great reason to have a first-aid kit in the car.) If her body temperature is between 104°F and 106°F, she is suffering from moderate heatstroke. In that case, get her into the air conditioning and wrap her in cold, wet towels or put her in a tub of cool water or in a cool shower. Put ice packs in her groin and armpits. Give her cold water to drink and monitor her temperature until it reaches 103°F. At that point, stop cooling her down.

If your poodle's body temperature is above 106°F, she's suffering from severe heatstroke, which is very dangerous. If she's lost consciousness and you can get her to a vet within five minutes, going to the vet should be your first course of action. If possible, use rubbing alcohol and ice to cool her armpits and groin, and place her in front of the air-conditioning vent on your way to the hospital.

If your poodle is conscious, or if you're more than five minutes away from the vet, try to cool her off as described above before taking her to the vet. Be prepared to give artificial respiration or

CPR if she stops breathing or her heart stops beating. Monitor her temperature every five minutes, and when it's down to 106°F, take her to the vet.

Fact

An excellent reference to keep on your shelf in the event of an emergency (and to read before you need it) is *The First Aid Companion for Dogs and Cats* by Amy D. Shojai. It's an A-to-Z compendium of potential emergencies and what to do when faced with one. It also includes a symptom-finder to help identify what the emergency might be.

Hypothermia and Frostbite

The flip side of heat stroke is hypothermia, when a dog's body cools below 95°F. Dogs are less prone to hypothermia than people, given that they're covered in fur and that they're programmed to shiver to help stay warm. But if your poodle gets wet in cold weather, or there's a lot of wind with the cold temperatures, her body temperature could drop. Dogs who are suffering from hypothermia shiver, are cold to the touch, and are sleepy.

If your poodle has been out in the elements, and you suspect hypothermia, take her temperature. If it's between 90 and 95°F, put hot-water bottles (or plastic soda bottles filled with hot water) wrapped in towels on your poodle's groin, armpits, and the sides of her neck. If your efforts don't result in increased body temperature within thirty to forty-five minutes, go to the emergency clinic. If her body does start to warm, take her to the vet after it reaches 99°F.

If your poodle's body temperature is 90°F or below, do not take the time to try to warm her. Instead, rush her to the vet for treatment of severe hypothermia. Her temperature might be so low that it doesn't register on your thermometer. If that's the case she may even not be shivering, as the shiver reflex stops when the body temperature drops below 90°F.

If it's cold enough for your poodle to suffer from hypothermia, it's probably cold enough for her to get frostbite, which happens when extremities freeze. Look for discoloration of the skin on the toes and the tail. If you suspect frostbite, seek immediate veterinary care.

Toxic Substances and Poison

Unfortunately, dogs aren't always sensible about what they choose to eat. There are many substances out there that can be poisonous to your poodle, including antifreeze, rat poison (or mice or rats who have eaten poison), household medications, snail bait, insecticides, some plants and mushrooms, putrefied animal carcasses, and even chocolate.

Essential

If you can, take the bottle or packaging from the item that your dog ate with you to the veterinarian. Try to figure out how much was ingested. Also, collect anything your dog vomits for the vet to examine.

If you discover that your poodle's eaten something that you suspect is toxic, the first thing you should do is call the ASPCA Animal Poison Control Center. This service, which charges a $45 fee, is open twenty-four hours a day, seven days a week. The experts there can guide you on what to do for the particular substance your poodle has ingested. Carefully follow their directions. And get her to the vet's office.

CHAPTER 13

Congenital and Hereditary Diseases

POODLES AS A BREED SUFFER from a number of inherited diseases. If you buy a puppy from a reputable breeder who does health testing on all breeding stock, you reduce the chances of your poodle being affected. But because definitive tests are not available for all diseases, there's a chance your poodle may come down with one of the following ailments. It's in your best interests to familiarize yourself with these diseases, so you'll recognize them early.

Bloat and Torsion

Bloat, also known as gastric dilatation-volvulus (GDV), occurs when the stomach swells with air or gas to the point where the gas and air is unable to escape. The stomach may flip over on its axis (think of twisting a balloon), which cuts off the blood supply. This is called torsion. This condition, untreated, can be deadly in a matter of minutes.

Risk Factors

While the genetic connection to GDV is not entirely clear, researchers at Purdue University determined that a dog with a first-degree relative (parent, littermate, or offspring) who has bloated has a 63 percent higher risk of GDV than a dog without an affected relative. The researchers therefore recommend that dogs having a first-degree relative with a history of GDV should not be bred.

This research also determined that dogs with an especially deep and narrow chest (compared with dogs of the same breed) are at higher risk of bloating. Large-breed dogs that eat quickly have a higher risk of bloat than their slower-eating counterparts. Surprisingly, the Purdue researchers found that raising the bowl when feeding (a common practice to try to avoid bloat) actually increases the risk of bloat by 110 percent. The risk of bloat also increases with age.

Fact

According to a study done by Purdue University's Center for Veterinary Medicine, among the eleven large and giant breeds studied, Standard Poodles are fifth highest in terms of their risk for bloat (after Great Danes, Akitas, Bloodhounds, and Weimeraners).

Treatment for Bloat

A dog that bloats needs emergency veterinary assistance. The vet will try to pass a tube down his throat to the stomach to let the gas and air out. An x-ray will be taken, and if the stomach has twisted, emergency surgery will be performed to untwist it. At that time, the stomach will be tacked to the abdominal wall (a procedure known as gastropexy).

If your poodle bloats but his stomach doesn't twist, emergency surgery won't be necessary, but your vet might ask you to consider having gastropexy done anyway, to stop it from twisting in the future. Dogs who have bloated once are highly likely to again bloat with torsion, so veterinary researchers consider gastropexy a prudent action.

Blood Problems

Poodles are prone to two blood diseases that could be fatal. One involves the destruction of red blood cells, while the other affects the body's blood-clotting ability.

Autoimmune Hemolitic Anemia (AIHA)

Autoimmune (or immune-mediated) hemolytic anemia is a blood disease in which the body's own immune system destroys red blood cells. This destruction happens when antibodies stick to the red blood cells, and the immune system attacks those antibodies. AIHA is a life-threatening disease, because without red blood cells, tissues aren't able to receive necessary oxygen. It may be triggered by toxins, cancers, drugs, a blood parasite, virus, or even vaccinations, but exactly why it happens is not understood.

Essential

Routine vaccinations have been implicated as a trigger for autoimmune hemolytic anemia. If your poodle ever suffers from AIHA or any other autoimmune disease, forgo future vaccinations. They could prompt another bout of AIHA or other autoimmune disease.

Symptoms of AIHA include weakness, lethargy, pale gums, unusually dark urine, and yellow-tinged whites of the eye. A complete blood count (CBC) will show anemia. A blood chemistry panel might pinpoint other problems associated with the anemia, and a further blood test called a Coombs test can tell whether the anemia is autoimmune in origin.

Treatment of AIHA typically involves use of steroids. Corticosteroids, like prednisone, are usually given in high doses to suppress the immune system's reaction to the antibodies. If steroids aren't enough, more powerful chemotherapeutic drugs, like Imuran or Cytoxan, can be used. If your poodle has AIHA, he might be hospitalized until he stabilizes. Once home, you'll probably have to bring him to the vet for frequent blood tests to monitor the anemia, which should improve with treatment. After the red blood cell count is at normal levels, you'll be able to start slowly weaning him off the immune-suppressing drugs.

Von Willebrand's Disease (vWD)

The von Willebrand factor is a blood factor that plays an important role in blood clotting. Dogs with vWD lack the von Willebrand factor, which makes them subject to prolonged bleeding. You should suspect vWD if your dog has excessive and prolonged bleeding after injury or surgery, has visible blood in his urine, or is bleeding from the nose or gums. The disease is diagnosed through blood work.

◀ The distinguished appearance of a poodle can come with a price if breeding healthy puppies isn't the primary goal of the breeder.

Dogs with Type I vWD (which is inherited in poodles) often have only mild symptoms and can lead very normal lives, but if they need surgery or are injured, the difficulty in clotting will come into play. You'll need to be especially careful that your poodle doesn't get injured. Poodle-proofing your house by padding sharp corners and any other hazards can help prevent injury and excessive bleeding. In case of injury, applying direct pressure on wounds might stop bleeding (though you should seek veterinary assistance if it doesn't help immediately). Take extra care when trimming your poodle's toenails, and inform your groomer and any new vet about the condition.

Von Willebrand's disease is one of only two diseases in poodles for which a genetic test has been developed so far. It is now possible to identify carriers and avoid breeding them. Each parent must be either affected or a carrier in order to have affected offspring. Puppy buyers should ask breeders if they've tested their dogs for vWD before breeding.

Endocrine Diseases

Along with the immune system and the nervous system, the endocrine system performs some of the most important functions of the body. Poodles are prone to two serious endocrine problems, one involving the thyroid, and one involving the adrenal glands.

Hypothyroidism

Low thyroid function (hypothyroidism) is the most common endocrine problem in dogs. It can lead to weight gain (without an increase in eating), poor coat, loss of coat, skin problems, and even aggression. If your poodle suffers from any of these symptoms, have your veterinarian draw some blood for a full thyroid panel.

Autoimmune thyroiditis, in which the thyroid is destroyed by the body's immune system, is genetic and is seen in all three varieties of poodles. Reputable breeders test their dogs for autoimmune thyroiditis before breeding them.

Alert!

If you have your poodle tested for a thyroid disorder, the vet may want to run just a test known as a T4. However, you should ask for a full panel, including a TgAA (thyroglobulin autoantibody) analysis, which will tell you if there's a genetic autoimmune component to the problem. If there is, you should inform your poodle's breeder.

Hypothyroidism is fairly easily treated through medication that supplies the hormone that the body cannot make. That medication is given twice daily for the rest of the dog's life.

Addison's Disease

Addison's disease, technically known as hypoadrenocorticism, is the result of poorly functioning adrenal glands. It occurs in all three poodle sizes but is most common in Standard Poodles. An untreated poodle with Addison's disease will be lethargic, eat poorly, and perhaps limp. He might be depressed, and have vomiting or diarrhea (though some prediagnosis Addisonian dogs are constipated). His coat might be bad. These symptoms will worsen under stress, as the adrenal glands can't put out extra cortisol under stress as they're supposed to. Diagnosing Addison's disease can be difficult. For one thing, the symptoms wax and wane inconsistently. Also, on blood work the disease can give results that look like kidney disease. Many affected dogs are promptly treated for kidney failure, which makes them feel better but doesn't help with the adrenal insufficiency. Red flags on blood work are high potassium and low sodium, or a sodium-to-potassium ratio of 26 or less. There's a definitive test for Addison's disease, called the ACTH stimulation test. It requires drawing blood from your dog, injecting a form of the pituitary hormone called ACTH, which should stimulate the body to create cortisol, then drawing blood in an hour to see if the dog responded by making cortisol.

Some dogs have atypical Addison's disease, which means that their sodium and potassium aren't affected. This makes diagnosis even more difficult, though it can be detected through an ACTH stimulation test. These dogs are treated with only one of the two medications that dogs with primary Addison's get.

Fact

If your poodle is diagnosed with Addison's disease, you'll be able to learn much from other owners of Addisonian dogs. One place to meet them is through the Web site *www.addisondogs.com*.

Left untreated, Addison's is deadly. But once diagnosed, the dog can be treated with daily or monthly medication to replace the hormones that the adrenal glands can't produce. A poodle that continues to take these hormones can live a long life, though he'll always be extra sensitive to stress.

Idiopathic Epilepsy

Poodles are prone to idiopathic epilepsy, a disease that can be distressing for both dog and owner. If your poodle suffers from seizures, you'll want to take him to a veterinarian for a complete neurological work-up to try to find a cause for the seizures (like a metabolic disorder, tumor, trauma to the head, infectious disease affecting the central nervous system, or poisoning). If no cause is found, the diagnosis will be idiopathic epilepsy (epilepsy of no known cause).

While the exact mode of inheritance isn't known, researchers are working on identifying the genetic component of epilepsy in poodles. Be sure to let your breeder know about your poodle's epilepsy. This will help her with breeding decisions. Also, if your poodle is diagnosed with epilepsy, you can help others by participating in one or both of the poodle-epilepsy research projects currently underway at Florida State University and the University of California, Davis.

Alert!

If your poodle has a seizure that lasts longer than five to ten minutes, or has three or more seizures in a single day, seek veterinary assistance immediately. This condition can be life threatening.

Treatment for epilepsy usually involves giving the dog a lifetime treatment of either phenobarbitol or potassium bromide. Since these drugs can have long-term side effects, veterinarians don't rush to start dogs on either one. They first monitor to make sure seizures are regular and severe enough to warrant treatment.

Acupuncture can sometimes help control seizures. If it works with your epileptic poodle, you can take it a step further and have gold beads implanted in your poodle at acupuncture points, to provide a sort of permanent acupuncture. Some owners of epileptic dogs have had success controlling seizures with gold bead implants, rather than drugs. Dr. Terry Durkes, DVM, of Marion, Indiana, is the pioneer in this field.

Essential

Dr. Barbara Licht of the Florida State University is doing research into idiopathic epilepsy in poodles. She welcomes contact from owners of poodles who have had seizures or are diagnosed with epilepsy. Contact her at (850) 644-6272 or *blicht@psy.fsu.edu* for advice on testing and treatment options and to learn how to participate in her research.

Eye Problems

The bad news is that there are more than twenty eye diseases that poodles can inherit. The good news is that there is a DNA test for one of them, the progressive rod-cone degeneration (*prcd*) form of progressive retinal atrophy (PRA). Breeders of Toy and Miniature Poodles can test their dogs before breeding and make informed decisions about which dogs to breed in order to avoid producing puppies with PRA.

Progressive Retinal Atrophy

The cluster of diseases known as progressive retinal atrophy, in which the retina gradually deteriorates, causes blindness in all affected dogs. Each parent must be a carrier or be affected in order to produce an affected dog, but if only one parent is a carrier, some of the puppies will be carriers.

PRA typically first shows up as night blindness when the poodle is three to five years old. His pupils will stay dilated (in an effort to get enough light in to see), and the eyes will shine. The dog then will gradually become completely blind. PRA can be diagnosed with an ophthalmologic examination.

If your poodle has PRA, keep lights on for him or use night-lights to help with the night blindness. After his vision is gone, take care not to change the layout of furniture or leave obstacles in his path. Thanks to the amazing adaptability of dogs, if you keep his environment consistent and use toys with bells or squeakers, you may notice little change in your poodle's demeanor, even after he has lost his sight.

Fact

Standard Poodles are not exempt from PRA. Though the eye disease is less prevalent in standards, and a genetic test has not been developed for it, it does occur in that variety.

Juvenile Cataracts

Cataracts cause the lens of the eyes to cloud over, blocking light to the retina and affecting the vision. Severe cases lead to blindness. Cataracts that are inherited are called juvenile cataracts. Poodles are among the breeds that pass on this disease.

If you see signs of vision impairment in your poodle (bumping into things, hesitancy to jump onto or off of furniture) and/or the characteristic bluish-white cloudiness over the eye, take him to see your veterinarian. If your poodle's cataracts are inherited, they might be able to be removed surgically. A cataract can also occur secondary to another condition (like diabetes), so it is also important to catch them early and address any other related conditions.

Other Eye Diseases

In addition to PRA and juvenile cataracts, there are some twenty other eye diseases that poodles can inherit. Dogs with inherited eye problems should not be bred. Responsible breeders have the eyes of the dogs they breed screened each and every year and register the results with the Canine Eye Registry Foundation (CERF). If your poodle develops an inherited eye problem, be sure to inform your breeder.

Juvenile Renal Disease

The kidneys perform a very important function—they filter waste and maintain the appropriate amount of water in the body. When the kidneys fail, a dog (like a person) becomes very ill.

Chronic kidney failure is typically a disease of older dogs—their kidneys just wear out. But dogs with juvenile renal disease (JRD) lose kidney function very early, often when they're less than a year old. Early signs include increased thirst, urination, and leaking urine, as well as weight loss. Because of the increased urination, puppies with JRD are difficult to housetrain.

JRD is an inherited condition seen in Standard Poodles. There is no cure—the kidneys of a dog with JRD will inevitably fail. But the earlier it is caught, the more there is that can be done to slow the decline, primarily through diet, medication, and fluids, as needed.

Alert!

If your poodle is diagnosed with any heritable disease, be sure to let your breeder know. Don't feel like you're pointing fingers; this might be the only way she can find out that her dogs are carrying the disease. If your breeder ignores your communication, it's a sign that perhaps she isn't a reputable breeder after all.

Orthopedic Problems

Problems with your poodle's bones can be tragic because they cause pain to your beloved dog. Poodles of all sizes are susceptible to hip dysplasia, while Miniatures and Toys are also susceptible to Legg-Calve-Perthes disease and patellar luxation.

Hip Dysplasia

Hip dysplasia occurs when the femoral head (the ball part of the joint) doesn't fit properly in the hip socket. This causes looseness in the hip joints, which leads to damaged cartilage in the joint and painful arthritis.

Signs of hip dysplasia include decreased activity, stiffness, lameness, bunny-hopping (running with both hind legs moving at the same time), a swaggering gait, muscle wasting in the thighs, unwillingness to jump or stand on the hind legs, and soreness after lying down.

Treatment often includes surgery, though a nonsurgical approach involving anti-inflammatory medication or supplementation, moderate exercise, and weight loss is often tried first. Early detection is important if surgery is to be avoided. It's also important to keep your dog's weight to a healthy low level to help alleviate pressure on the hips.

Since hip dysplasia is hereditary, all breeding dogs should have their hips x-rayed, and those with poor hip ratings should not be bred.

Fact

Diet and supplementation are important considerations in preventing hip dysplasia. Puppies that are kept lean in their first year have a reduced risk of developing hip dysplasia later. A supplement called Glycoflex that comes from the Perna mussel can be helpful, as can glucosamine and chondroitin.

Legg-Calve-Perthes Disease

Legg-Calve-Perthes disease (also known as LCP, Legg-Perthes, or avascular necrosis) is a painful hip disease in which the cap of the femur bone in the hip joint suffers a loss of blood supply. This leads to deterioration of the femoral head, with the result that eventually, it no longer fits properly in the socket. As this is painful, the dog becomes lame on that leg.

Dogs usually start showing early symptoms of LCP—limping, favoring one leg, or walking with a strange gait—when they're under a year old, though sometimes symptoms show as early as four months. If your dog is diagnosed with LCP (which is done by x-ray), your veterinarian might want you to put him on anti-inflammatory drugs for a month to see if that improves the condition. If it doesn't, or if the condition is advanced by the time of diagnosis, surgery will probably be recommended. During surgery, the femoral head and neck are removed, eliminating the painful rubbing-together of bones. The body can then create a new false joint out of muscle and tissue, allowing your dog a full recovery.

While the mode of inheritance is unknown, LCP is suspected to be hereditary. Hip x-rays to rule out hip dysplasia and LCP are among the health screens that breeders should do before breeding a dog.

Luxating Patella

With a luxating patella, the kneecap (or patella, located at the joint of the hind leg) pops out of place. It can occur in one or both knees and can show up in Toy or Miniature Poodle puppies as young as eight weeks, though the problem can also occur later in life. A poodle with luxating patellas will stand funny, like he's bow-legged. He might cry out—because of the pain of his kneecap having popped out—and straighten his leg in an effort to put it back in place, or he might hold it up for the same reason. He might walk with a hitch in his gait.

A veterinarian can feel a luxating patella on examination, but x-rays are required to determine the development of the condition. Depending on the severity of the luxation and the age of the dog, surgery may be required. The earlier it's caught, the better the prognosis.

Sebaceous Adenitis

One of the things most poodle-lovers like about the breed is the luxurious, curly coat. But those poor poodles afflicted with sebaceous adenitis (SA), an inherited skin disease, lose their coats after the sebaceous glands become inflamed and are eventually destroyed. It's seen in all three poodle sizes, though it is seen more commonly in Standard Poodles. All colors are affected. Both parents must be carriers of SA or affected to produce affected puppies.

Poodles with SA develop excessive silvery dandruff that clings to the remaining hair. It can be accompanied by a musty odor and might cause secondary skin infections. Their skin thickens, and they eventually have patchy hair loss. Clinical SA can start showing symptoms when the dog is as young as eighteen months or as old as nine years.

Veterinarians diagnose SA with a skin biopsy. After the dog gets a local anesthetic, a biopsy punch removes two or more small cylinders of tissue to be examined.

Unfortunately, statistics show that perhaps as many as 50 percent of all Standard Poodles are carriers or affected. Some Standard

Poodles are affected subclinically and show no outward signs of the disease. Therefore, punch biopsies should be done annually on all poodles that are potential breeding prospects.

Essential

Some owners of SA poodles use weekly oil baths. They mix an inexpensive bath oil with water, spray it onto the dog, and rub it into the skin. After soaking for an hour, the dog is put back in the tub for three shampoo latherings. Before the final lathering, the skin is scrubbed with a soft brush. In some cases, dogs will regrow hair after this treatment.

There is no cure for SA. Antibiotics might be required for secondary skin infections. Most SA-affected dogs are bathed frequently with a hypoallergenic dog shampoo, which helps get rid of the dandruff and makes the poodle more comfortable.

Chapter 14

What Every Good Dog Should Know

TRAINING YOUR POODLE is not only a joy, it's a necessity. If you take the time and effort to go through training with your poodle, a number of things will happen. You'll have a canine companion that will listen to you, because you've taught her that good things come when she does. You'll have a common language. Your bond will grow deeper and broader. And your training will be a springboard for further fun things you can do together.

Why Every Poodle Needs Training

Poodles are smart, very smart. And they're highly trainable. So you're really missing out if you forgo training with your poodle. As long as the training is positive (that is, it teaches through rewarding desirable behavior) rather than punitive, training classes are a great opportunity to spend some high-quality, enjoyable time with your poodle. During training you're focusing on your dog, and she will revel in the attention. At the same time, you're teaching your poodle to do what you ask and become an exemplary citizen, whether you're at home or out and about.

Should You Enroll in Training Classes?

Training your poodle on your own is certainly possible. You can pick up a good training book, go through the exercises outlined, and at the end, you'll have a trained poodle. If you make sure you go with a program that uses training based on positive reinforcement, you really can't screw up.

Question?

When should I start training my poodle?
Start training the moment your poodle enters your life. It's never too early—or too late—to start. If you begin instilling good manners in your poodle from the moment he joins your family, training will be a breeze.

However, going through a group training class with a professional trainer has a number of advantages:

- You'll have a professional guiding you and offering feedback on your particular training style.
- Your poodle will learn how to behave around other dogs.
- You'll be motivated to practice your training because you'll be held accountable at each class.
- You'll get to meet other dog lovers.
- Your dog gets to meet other dogs (and other dog lovers).
- You can ask questions of an expert and get immediate answers.
- You can enjoy having the smartest dog in class!

There are many types of classes to choose from, from puppy kindergarten and manners classes for beginners, all the way up to advanced obedience classes. If you find a great trainer, and your poodle loves learning, you may decide to take class after class.

Finding the Right Trainer

When it comes to training, you already have an advantage: You have a poodle. She'll probably take to training like a fish to water.

Look for a positive trainer and a class whose participants are enjoying themselves. Don't accept harsh training techniques—the whole point is to have fun!

Narrowing Down the Choices

You can start your search for a trainer by observing the people and dogs around you. Watch for those who seem to have a particularly close relationship—owners who aren't yelling at their dogs and seem to have no problems with them. Ask those folks if they've been to training class and, if so, where. With any luck, you'll hear the same name over and over.

Alert!

Beware of trainers who refer to themselves as "balanced" trainers. That's a euphemism for trainers who use corrections in their training. They may use some positive reinforcement, but by using the term "balanced," they're saying that they also believe in training with punishment.

Selecting a Trainer

Once you find a trainer or two in your local area who you think might be appropriate for you, call and ask if you can observe a class (without your dog and at no charge). If the trainer says no, cross him or her off your list.

When you observe a class, take a close look at the attitudes of the students—both the people and the dogs. You're looking for an upbeat, fun atmosphere. Look at the collars the dogs in the class are wearing. If it's truly a class based on positive reinforcement techniques, you won't see any choke chains or pinch collars. Rather, the dogs should be wearing flat collars, or perhaps head harnesses (similar to a horse's halter).

Close your eyes and listen to the class. Do you hear lots of sweet-talking and encouragement? Or do you hear anger and frustration and dogs being told "No!"? You definitely want to hear the former. This class should sound as fun as a children's playground.

Watch how the trainer interacts with both the humans and the dogs in class. A good teacher uses positive reinforcement on the humans as well as the dogs.

Essential

If you see anything in the class you don't like, or if your gut tells you that this isn't the right class for you and your dog, don't enroll. Teaching your dog on your own using an excellent book is preferable to enrolling in a class that will make your dog dislike training.

Reward, Don't Punish

When you're interacting with your poodle, whether you're formally training her or just living life with her, you're well advised to follow the principles of the most progressive training experts. That is, catch your dog doing something right, and reward her. When your poodle does something you don't like, don't punish her. Instead, either ignore the behavior (if it's not dangerous), or distract her. Then get her to do something you like and reward her for that.

This positive approach is in stark contrast to traditional training methods (and, sadly, to human nature most of the time), in which you ignore your dog when she's behaving herself and yell at her when she does something you don't want.

Positive training operates under the theory that dogs (and all other beings) repeat behaviors for which they're rewarded. If you've ever taught a dog to sit using treats, you probably noticed that the dog sits the moment you ask her to. She quickly learns that she gets a treat when she sits, and soon she's sitting just to ask for a treat!

Focusing on positive interactions with your dog can require a fundamental change in the way you think. Instead of thinking about what you don't want your dog to do, you have to think about what you want her to do. If she's jumping on you, for example, don't think in terms of "don't jump." Instead, think about what you'd like her to be doing when she greets you. Sitting works well. So if your dog jumps on you, turn your back (so her jumping isn't being rewarded by your attention), and when she puts all four feet on the floor, ask her to sit. Then reward the sit.

Fact

Most poodles respond just as well to a gentle "no" as a harsh reprimand. Next time you see your poodle doing something you don't like (chewing on your slippers, for example), try a gentle admonishment as you take the slipper away and substitute a chew toy. Chances are that this correction will be as effective as shrieking at your dog, and less stressful for both of you.

Poodles tend to be so sensitive that yelling at them or giving them collar corrections might make them shut down or hate training. Stick to positive training—clicker training in particular—and you'll have a poodle that adores training and fulfills your expectations of a well-behaved dog.

Using a Clicker

Clicker training is not only fun and positive, it's highly effective. When your poodle sees that clicker brought out, she's bound to get very excited and practically beg for a training session.

What is a clicker? It's simply a small plastic box with a piece of flexible metal in it that makes a distinctive clicking sound when it's pressed. Doesn't sound so magical, does it? The power comes when you pair that distinctive click with a food reward. Soon your dog learns that the sound of the click means that food will be coming. She then grows to understand that whatever she's doing when she hears the click is what she's being rewarded for.

Therein lies the power of the click. Because dogs tend to repeat behaviors for which they're rewarded, your dog will likely repeat what she was doing when you clicked. You can use that tendency to shape new behaviors. A clicker is an extremely precise and effective way to communicate with your dog. Once you've taught a behavior, you'll be able to fade the clicker. But you'll probably always want to keep one around for training new behaviors.

▲ No puppy is too young to learn the basics, and games make learning fun.

If you feel you're not coordinated enough to handle the clicker and the treats together (and sometimes a leash too), or simply don't want to use one, you can use a bridge word, like "Yes!" in place of a click. A spoken reinforcer has a distinct advantage, as your voice is always with you. (But remember, you must pair the bridge with a treat.) A disadvantage to using a word over a click is that it's much less precise, so it's harder to pinpoint an exact behavior.

Essential

Always pair a click with a treat. This is imperative. Your clicker will lose its power if it's not followed by a treat. So don't click if you don't have a treat nearby.

Training Your Poodle to Sit

Teaching a dog to sit is such an easy thing to do. It requires no force. And it really comes in handy, because there are many things you might not want your poodle to do (for example, jumping up on you as a greeting) that he can't do while seated.

Teaching the Sit

One of the easiest ways to start teaching your poodle to sit is to grab a clicker and some treats, take a seat, and wait. Don't say a word. Your poodle will be nearby—after all, you are holding treats—and eventually he'll sit down. When he does, click (or say "Yes!") and toss a treat. He'll have to get up to go get it. Then wait for another sit and click it.

Fact

Positive trainers encourage the use of the word "cue" in place of "command." It better indicates the nature of the relationship between human and dog in a positive training scenario. You're letting your dog know what you want him to do, rather than ordering him to do something.

A more active, and equally effective, way to teach "Sit" is to hold a treat at chest level and wait for your dog to sit. He'll stare at it and maybe whimper and whine, but you should do nothing until he sits. If he tries to jump on you to get the treat, just get it out of his sight and turn your back. Don't look at him or say anything. When he sits, which he eventually will, click and treat.

Adding the Cue

No matter which method you use, before too long your poodle will catch on to the fact that you're clicking (and treating) because she's sitting. And by sitting, she figures, she can make you click. Then you've got her. She'll start sitting for you willy-nilly. After she's sitting reliably for a treat, add the word "Sit" just as her butt hits the ground. After a few rounds of that, add the cue just before she sits. Voilà! There you have it, a poodle that sits on cue. Doesn't that sound more pleasant than pushing your poodle's butt to the ground or lifting his chin to force a sit?

Fading the Lure

You want your poodle to sit when you ask, even if you don't have a treat in your hand, right? That's easy to accomplish, once she's learned what "Sit" means. Just put the treat behind your back and say, "Sit." If she knows what the cue actually means, she'll sit for you. Then give her the treat. If she doesn't sit when you ask, she hasn't learned the behavior yet. Put the treat in front of you again, and ask her to sit. Once she sits without the temptation of a treat in plain sight, you'll be in a position to ask for a sit without giving a treat. Remember, if she doesn't sit when she hears the cue, she's not being disobedient; she just hasn't learned what the cue means.

Teaching "Down"

Lying down is not quite as natural a behavior to most dogs as sitting. Lying down can be troubling to dogs because it places them in a subordinate position. But by using a clicker to train the down, you are helping your dog to think of it as her choice. She lies down in order to get you to click.

Capturing the Down

You can try capturing the down by simply clicking and treating when your dog lies down on her own accord. If you keep a clicker and treat handy, you can do it anytime. Or you can make it part of a more formal training session. Just sit or stand there silently and wait for your dog to lie down (out of boredom, if nothing else). Then click and treat. When she starts offering you a down in order to get the click and treat, then start adding the cue. This approach might take longer than a more active luring of a down.

Essential

Keep your training sessions short. Particularly if your poodle is a puppy, you don't need these sessions to be more than a minute or two. You want to keep it fun, and you don't want to overload your poodle's brain. Remember to end on a high note.

Luring the Down

To lure the down, have your poodle sit, put a treat in front of her nose, and make a direct path to the floor. Your poodle might just flop down. If she does, click and treat. If she doesn't follow the treat down to the floor, or if she stands up to try to get the treat, take it more gradually, moving the treat just a few inches toward the floor and clicking when your dog follows it. Increase the distance the treat travels by a few inches each try, until your poodle is following the treat to the floor. If she stands up instead of going down, ignore it (or if you just can't ignore it, cheerfully say "Ooops!"). Then move to another spot and try again.

For the dog that's having a hard time following the treat into a down, you might have to break the behavior into the tiniest possible increments. If she follows the treat to the floor with her nose but doesn't lie down, move the treat on the floor toward you, away from her nose, so that she'll stretch into a down eventually. Once she's actually lying down, click and give her a jackpot!

Fact

When your dog does something really great, or when he finally catches on to what you want for the first time, give him a jackpot. A jackpot can be a bunch of treats, rather than one, or it can be a particularly delicious treat. The jackpot is fun (for both giver and receiver) and sends a strong, "You've got it!" message to your dog.

Adding the Cue

To add the cue, as with the sit, say the word "Down" just as he's lying down. Then start saying it just before he's lying down. If you think he's got it, try saying "Down" with the treat behind your back (or making the luring motion without a treat in your hand). If he lies down, have a party with jackpots! If he doesn't, just put the treat in front of his nose and lure him down. Then click and treat. Keep working on it until he learns the cue.

Teaching Your Poodle to Come

Coming when called, which trainers call a "recall," is one of the most important skills your dog will learn. A dog with a reliable recall can enjoy much more freedom than a dog that ignores his owner. Training your poodle to come is all about making yourself more attractive than whatever else your poodle is doing. And the way you do that (naturally) is with food!

Laying the Groundwork

When you're teaching something this important, it's worthwhile to go slowly and do it right. Start in your living room. Working with a partner (or partners), stand just six feet apart, with one of you holding on to your poodle. Call your poodle's name, followed by a bright and enthusiastic "Come!" The person holding the poodle should let go and ignore the dog. Whether your poodle runs to you or just looks in your direction when you say her name, click for any kind of acknowledgment. Let her come to you for the treat.

Essential

Treats are an essential component to positive training. Just as you go to work every day for your paycheck, your dog does what you ask because of what he receives in return, not out of some instinct to please you. So think of treats as your dog's paycheck for a job well done.

If you're the caller and get absolutely no reaction from your poodle, walk up to her, show her the treats, walk back, and try again. Bend down to encourage her to come. Still no reaction? Get out a smellier treat. Walk up to her, show her the treat and walk just a short distance away. If necessary, keep shortening the distance between you until you get a reaction you can reward. (Most dogs will come to you from the outset.)

Now the other person should call the poodle by name and click and treat when she reacts. If you have more than one helper, take turns calling the dog among all of you. Make this lots of fun, gradually increasing the distance between you.

After your poodle is doing well with this exercise, have the person who is holding her try to distract her from the recall after he lets go. He can talk to her or even squeak toys. If your training foundation is strong, your poodle will ignore those distractions and come to you anyway for the delicious treat she knows you'll give her.

If you don't have a helper, don't despair. Just walk a few feet away from your poodle and say, "[Fill in the name], Come!" When she looks up at you, run backward a few steps. When she starts to move toward you, click. When she nears you, stop running. And when she reaches you, dole out the treats. Gradually increase the distance and the distractions, as above.

Alert!

Never, ever call your poodle to you and then yell at him when he arrives. Even if it took him ten minutes to come, give him a token treat. Don't call him to come for something unpleasant (like toenail clipping). You should always make coming to you a source of pleasure for your poodle.

The Next Step

Teaching your dog to come into the house is one thing. But getting her to come when you're outdoors, with all its temptations, is quite another. That's why laying the groundwork is so important.

After she's coming consistently into the house, start working with her outdoors in a safely fenced area or on leash. Don't let her off the leash in an unfenced area until her recall is rock solid. Start doing the exercises that you did in the house, starting at a shorter distance than you've ended up with in the house. Increase the distance, as well as the distractions that the holding person creates.

If you don't have a secure area in which to practice the recall, or if you want to practice in a new area that's not fenced (and it's a very good idea to practice in all different types of environments), you'll need to use a long line. It can be a retractable leash or a simple cotton web or nylon lead. (A hint: cotton is easier on your hands.) Don't use the lead to correct your dog or force her to come. Simply use it to keep her from running off—and being rewarded by the fun of running free.

When training the recall, increase the difficulty in very small increments. Use the word "Come!" only once—you don't want your poodle to learn that she can wait until the third "Come" before responding. And always, especially during training, give your dog a food reward when she comes on cue.

Fact

You can strengthen your poodle's recall and make it easier to train by selecting an especially delicious treat that you use only when you ask him to come. That way, he'll really be motivated to come when you call.

When Your Dog Won't Come

What do you do if your dog turns a deaf ear to you when you ask her to come? You show her that there are consequences to ignoring you. No, you're not going to get physical or angry with her. Instead, make her wish she had listened by excitedly giving the treats to another dog (if one is available) or, barring that, eating them yourself. (There are lots of treats, like cheese, cereal, and meat, that you can eat, too.) Be very dramatic about what your dog is missing. When your poodle sees that by not coming she's missing out on the good stuff, she should think again about ignoring the recall.

Teaching "Stay"

If your poodle knows to stay on cue, your life will be easier. You'll avoid worrying about her rushing out the door or jumping out of the car before you're ready, and you'll have a poodle that will stay out of the way on request.

The First D: Duration

To teach your poodle to stay using positive methods, start by asking her to sit, so that she is facing you. Keep a treat in your hand so that she can see it, and give it to her after one second, while she stays seated. Then use a release word of your choice, like "Break," "All done," "Free," or "Okay." If she doesn't get up at that point, encourage her to do so, but don't give her a treat. You're rewarding the stay, not the release.

Ask her to sit again, this time waiting several seconds before you give her the treat. Once she can sit there, treat in sight, for three or four seconds without getting up, add the cue "Stay."

Continue slowly adding to the duration—staying right in front of your dog—until your poodle is staying for twenty seconds. You can reward her during the stay, but add the "Stay" cue after each treat so she doesn't think she's free to go.

The Second D: Distraction

Now add a distraction, but make the duration short. Take a step to one side. Hop up and down. Dance a little jig. After each distraction, click and treat the stay. If your poodle breaks the stay any time during this process, move the treat out of her sight. Don't say anything about the break. Calmly ask her to sit, and try again, taking it back a step or two in duration or distraction. Training a stay positively means your poodle stays put of her own volition, rather than out of fear of getting in trouble.

Gradually add to the distractions—you can get creative about how you distract her—always setting your dog up for success. Only add further distractions after she's solid on the ones you've tried.

Alert!

Don't make the cue "Stay" sound like a threat. Make it an upbeat word, which will remind your poodle that "Stay" is a behavior for which he gets rewarded, rather than something you want to intimidate him into doing.

The Third D: Distance

Now that you've mastered two of the three D's (duration and distraction), it's time to add the third: distance. Again, make it easy by eliminating the distractions and lowering duration at first. Have your poodle sit, and start by taking one step back. If she doesn't take a step toward you, immediately click and return to her to give her the treat. Then use your release word to end the stay. Do it again, each time increasing the distance slightly. Always return to your dog to treat and release her, rather than calling her to you.

When you've worked yourself to about six feet away, you can add duration and distraction, one at a time, and gradually.

Teaching "Walk Nicely on Leash"

It's no fun having a dog that pulls. Even if your dog is so small his pulling isn't a hardship, it's still much nicer to have a dog that walks with a slack leash. Luckily, all it takes to train your dog to walk nicely on leash is a little time and patience. You can do it without aversive equipment like pinch collars and no-pull halters.

It's not hard to do. Simply reward your dog for walking on a loose leash, and don't reward her for pulling. If she pulls, you stop. ("Be a tree," trainers suggest.) When she turns to see what's up and puts some slack in the leash, click. She should return to you for the treat that inevitably follows the click, and you can encourage her to walk by your side, clicking and treating when she keeps the leash loose. If she pulls, become a tree again.

At first it might seem like you're getting nowhere, and walks will seem to take forever. But before long, you'll be able to just give your poodle an occasional treat for walking nicely. Just remember always to reward a slack leash, and don't reward a taut one. And remember that if your dog wants to pull, when you allow her to pull, she's being rewarded. (E)

CHAPTER 15

Teaching Manners

EVERYONE WHO WANTS TO ENJOY living with a dog needs to teach her some basic manners. Not unlike children, dogs need to have limits set and need to be taught what behavior is acceptable and what is not. Poodles crave human companionship, so they're always around, which gives you continual opportunities to teach manners. Remember to keep your relationship with your poodle positive and to treat her with respect. Soon you'll have a perfectly companionable canine family member.

Taking Charge

Dogs' wild relatives live with some strict rules. Their pack has a leader, and each dog knows his place in the pack and follows the rules the social structure demands.

For your dog, your family is the pack. And you need to be the leader of that pack if you want to live peaceably with your dog. That doesn't mean you have to physically dominate your poodle. It does mean that you control the resources. That is, you're the one who gives her food and treats, decides when she goes out, and so forth.

Reinforcing Your Role as Leader

Use your everyday dealings with your poodle to reinforce your role as his leader. Ask him to sit before putting his food bowl down or before you give him a treat. (Think of it as teaching a child to say "please.") Take away the toy he's playing with every now and then, and replace it with another one. This teaches him that you control his toys as well.

In your effort to establish yourself as the leader, you need to call the shots. If your poodle demands your attention, for example, turn the tables so you're in control. If you don't have time or inclination to lavish attention at the moment, ignore your poodle's prodding. If you don't mind giving him attention at that moment, ask him to do something, and use the attention as a reward. If your demanding poodle gets underfoot while you're trying to accomplish things around the house, put him in his crate for a couple of hours (and give him something to do in there).

Alert!

Leadership isn't necessarily going to be an issue between you and your poodle. Some dogs are born leaders and need more reminding than others that you're actually in charge. Others are happy to take a more subservient role. Whatever type of poodle you have, she'll benefit from your consistent show of benevolent leadership.

Forget about Alpha Wolf

Bear in mind that the old-fashioned notion of dominance when it comes to the relationship between people and dogs is falling out of favor with progressively minded behaviorists and trainers. That theory, popularly espoused in training books by the monks of New Skete, among others, would have you physically roll your dog onto his back in what's known as an "alpha roll." The theory behind this practice is flawed for a number of reasons. It's dangerous, for one. (You put your face in very close proximity to the face of the dog.) It's not even sound theory, since wolf experts report that alpha wolves don't actually do this to their subordinates. (Rather, it's the wolves that are trying to work their way up the pack hierarchy that practice this behavior.) Finally, it feels really bad to do this to your dog.

Scruff shakes (where you grab your dog by the fur on either side of his neck and shake him), another method encouraged by those who feel that you have to physically show your dog you're the boss, are also unpleasant and unnecessary.

Setting Rules

If you don't want your poodle running amok in the house, doing anything and everything his little heart desires, you'll have to set some rules about acceptable behavior. It doesn't matter what size your poodle is, though rule-setting might seem more urgent the larger the poodle is (and the more damage he can do). All dogs, no matter how small, take comfort in having limits set for them and having those limits reinforced.

What Should the Rules Be?

You don't need to adhere to some preset list of rules that someone provides for you. The rules you set for your poodle are entirely up to you and should be based on your lifestyle, your dog, and your personal preferences. If your poodle is doing something that doesn't bother you, let him do it as long as he's not hurting himself or someone else. For example, your Toy Poodle might like to sleep on your head at night. As long as that doesn't bother you or anyone else in your bed—and as long as he doesn't start growling at you when you ask him to move—there's no need to set a rule against that particular behavior.

Enforcing the Rules

Once you decide what the rules are, you need to enforce them. Treats can be a huge help in enforcing the rules. Remember, dogs repeat activities that are rewarding to them. Instead of punishing your dog for breaking a rule, if you redirect him to a desirable behavior, and then reinforce that behavior with a treat, he's apt to repeat the good behavior. This is more effective (and enjoyable) than punishment.

Remember, every interaction with your dog is a training opportunity, so use treats to your advantage. If he does something you'd like him to do again, give him a treat for it. Some people may think of that as bribery. Instead, think it of as an easy, stress-free way to demonstrate your leadership.

Fact

If you have leadership issues with your poodle, ask her to wait before each doorway to reinforce your role as a leader. You should go through the doorway first, then call your poodle to follow. If you don't have leadership issues, this isn't necessary.

No Jumping on People

Most dogs don't mean ill when they jump on people. Dogs often greet one another by touching noses. So it's perfectly natural for your dog to want to get as close as possible to the face of the person he's greeting. However, most people don't like dogs jumping on them. Even a Toy Poodle can run stockings or leave dirty paw prints on nice clothes. Standard Poodles can cause physical injury with an enthusiastic greeting. That's why one of the most important manners to teach your dog is proper greeting behavior.

Greeting You Properly

The way to solve this good-natured, if annoying, problem is to teach your dog to greet people by doing something incompatible with jumping up, like sitting. You can also satisfy your dog's desire to get to your face by crouching to the floor when you and your dog greet each other. Again, dogs repeat behavior that is rewarded. So if you want to teach your dog not to jump on people, don't reward the jumping behavior. Instead, reward the desired behavior, in this case, sitting.

Question?

Is it okay if my puppy jumps upon me?
Don't let your puppy do anything now that you don't want her to do as an adult. It might be endearing when your little Standard Poodle puppy jumps on you, but it won't be quite as cute when she weighs more than fifty pounds.

If your dog jumps on you, remove all your attention. Even negative attention, like yelling at him, can be rewarding for your dog. Silently turn your back on your poodle when he jumps on you. Wait for the sound of his front feet hitting the floor, turn around, and ask him to sit. When he does, give him a treat. (It's important to keep treats in your pocket or near the door to teach proper greeting behavior.) Then, while he's sitting, greet him by crouching down so he can get in your face.

If you say "Off" when he jumps, then reward him after he sits, he'll soon learn that "Off" means he should have all four feet on the floor. Before long, you might get a nice automatic sit when your poodle greets you, and you won't even need to say "Off."

Greeting Visitors Properly

It's even more important that your poodle not jump on visitors. When you answer the door, put him on leash. (You can keep a leash near the door just for this purpose.) Since you have your dog's leash in your hand, you're able to stop your poodle from making contact if he tries to jump. Ask your poodle to sit. You can ask your visitor to crouch down to greet your poodle, if he or she is so inclined. Either give a treat to your visitor to give your dog, or give it to him yourself, depending on how enthusiastic you want your poodle to be about visitors.

Don't let visitors undermine your training efforts by giving your dog attention when she jumps on them. These folks mean well—they may not mind the jumping, particularly if the dog is small. But you need to be careful that your dog's jumping isn't reinforced, so instruct visitors to turn their back if your poodle jumps.

Essential

Don't resort to old-fashioned techniques to try to teach your dog not to jump on people. These include grabbing her front paws until he's uncomfortable (some people suggest squeezing the paws so it hurts) or kneeing her in the chest. These punitive methods don't have a long-lasting effect, whereas teaching your dog to sit in greeting does.

Jumping Up on Cue

If you don't mind your poodle jumping on you, but don't want him to jump on others, you can train him to jump on cue. When you see that he's about to jump, pat your belly (or knee, depending on the size of your poodle) and say "Up" or "Hugs" or whatever cue you choose. Then reward him jumping on you by giving him a hug or petting him. When he jumps on you when you don't request it—this is important—turn your back and walk away. He should not be rewarded for jumping unless you gave him the cue. At some point, he should jump only when asked.

Off the Furniture

You might not mind if your poodle goes on the furniture. Or you might have some pieces of furniture he's allowed on and others he isn't. Whatever your personal rules are, it's a good idea to know how to teach your dog to stay off furniture, if for no other reason than you might visit a place together where the rules are different.

There are several approaches you can take to teach your dog to stay off furniture. One is management—simply don't give him the chance to get on the forbidden furniture. Do that by keeping the door to that room closed, or by crating your poodle (or putting him in an ex-pen) when he's in that room.

▲ It's okay for your poodle to go on the furniture—as long he'll get down when you ask him to.

Another way to handle it is to wait for him to clamber up on the furniture. When he does, gently tell him "No" and gesture for him to get off. If he doesn't immediately hop off, toss a treat onto the floor. He'll probably jump down to get the treat. If he tries to climb on again, be there to tell him no and block his ability to get on. Then redirect him elsewhere, perhaps to his own bed. Give him something else to do, like working on a chew toy.

Go to Your Bed/Place

It's great to be able to send your poodle to her crate or mat when you need her to get out from underfoot. Luckily, it's not a hard thing to train. Start by teaching her to go into her crate. Walk over to the crate, excitedly talking with her so she goes with you. Say "Go to bed" (or whatever cue you want to put on it), and gesture toward her crate. If she goes into it, give her a treat. If she doesn't, toss a treat into the crate to get her to go inside. Tell her she's wonderful, and when she turns around in the crate to face you, give her another treat. Every single time you have your poodle go in her crate, give her the cue and give her a treat. Soon she'll be going into the crate to ask for a treat!

Alert!

If your poodle growls at you when you ask her to get off the furniture, you have a leadership problem. Until you have that under control, restrict access to the furniture and bed. Reinforce your role as her leader by making her earn all privileges. If you think she might bite you, call in a professional.

You can teach your poodle a different cue for telling her to go to her dog bed (instead of her crate). Perhaps "Go lie down" will work for you. Give her the cue, toss a treat onto the bed, then ask her to lie down after she goes to the bed to pick it up. Treat her again for the down. If you've taught her to stay, you can put her on a down/stay if you want her to stay there. But don't forget to release her from it! Use the stay judiciously; if the bed is comfy or you give her a chew toy, your poodle might want to stay without being told. But if you ask her to stay every time she goes to the bed when you ask, she might be less inclined to enjoy her bed.

Leave It/Drop It

Since dogs can't always be trusted to use common sense when it comes to what they put into their mouths, teaching them to drop something—or (better yet) not to pick things up when you ask—can be invaluable.

Teaching Leave It

You can start teaching "Leave it" by putting a treat in your hand. Close your fingers around it to make a fist. Offer your fist, palm-side up, to your poodle. If the treat is smelly enough, he'll start sniffing and maybe even nibbling in an effort to get at the treat. Just ignore him and wait. Eventually, if only out of frustration, he'll remove his nose from your fist. At that point, click your clicker, then open your fist and give him the treat. Try again. He'll doubtless start sniffing again but will probably pull back more quickly. Again, click and give him the treat. Do a few more repetitions—you'll probably be surprised how quickly he gets to the point where he barely sniffs your fist before pulling back in anticipation of the treat. When that's happening, say, "Leave it" just before he pulls back, then click and treat. You've taught your dog an important command and done it very gently.

Essential

The best way to make sure your dog doesn't pick up something valuable or dangerous inside is not to leave things like that around the house. Put away anything that you think your dog might want to chew up. "Leave it" will still come in handy outside the house, however.

Now move the treat to the floor. When your poodle starts putting his nose toward it, gently say, "Leave it." Don't shout it or say it in a threatening manner. Cover the treat with your foot or hand if you have to. When he backs away from it, click and give him another treat (not the one on the floor—you don't want him to think it's okay to pick up something he's been asked to leave).

Now you can try "Leave it" under more natural circumstances. Try to always have a treat handy, in case you have the opportunity to practice. As your poodle shows an interest in something you think he might pick up (but that you don't want him to), say "Leave it." If he hesitates to pick it up, or better yet, looks at you, click and shower treats on him. Especially at the beginning, you need to make whatever treat you use to reward him better than the thing he's giving up.

Teaching Drop It

The key to teaching your dog to drop something when you really need him to (like when he's picked up a decaying carcass in the park) is to lay the groundwork at home. If your poodle has a long history of being rewarded for dropping something on request, he might come through for you when it really counts. If not, you'll probably be forced to play tug-of-war with him over that carcass.

Start at home by handing your poodle a toy. Don't make it a favorite toy. Make it something that he feels pretty ho-hum about. Brightly say, "Take it!" Play with it a little, if necessary, until he takes it in his mouth. Then offer him a treat. As he drops the toy to take the treat, say, "Drop it!" Let him nibble on the treat while you casually remove the toy. After he's eaten the treat, hand him an even better toy, and do the same thing all over. He'll soon figure out that dropping the toy gets him something great. Keep doing this, upping the ante by using toys that are more prized. This should be a fun game for your poodle that results in his rapid-fire response to the cue "Drop it."

Chapter 16

Socializing Your Poodle

PROBABLY THE MOST IMPORTANT THING you can do for your poodle puppy is to expose him to all manner of people, places, and things while he's young. This socialization plays a big role in shaping his personality and temperament—it allows him to be all that he can be without being encumbered by fear. And it will give him the confidence to encounter new things with ease.

In Your Home

The moment your poodle sets paw into your house, he starts learning. You and your family members should spend plenty of time indoors interacting with the puppy. He should be included in the daily routine of the house. Even while you're housetraining (see Chapter 7), don't isolate him in his crate in another room too often. Putting an ex-pen in the room where the family spends the greatest amount of time is a great way to involve the puppy without having to worry that he will get into trouble.

Make a special effort to expose your puppy to all sorts of sounds in the house, from the vacuum cleaner, to the television and stereo, to pots and pans clanging around. He should hear the lawn mower, the garbage disposal or trash compactor, and the various sounds the dishwasher and washing machine make. Basically, you should try to expose him as a puppy to anything he might encounter as an adult.

If your poodle startles at a new sound or sight, reassure him ("That's just the dryer"), perhaps patting the object or repeating the sound, but don't coddle him. Be upbeat and nonchalant about the thing that's scaring him. And make sure he hears it again.

Out in the World

Taking your poodle for regular walks in your neighborhood has numerous benefits. One, of course, is exercise. Another is the opportunity to teach her things like walking nicely on leash and sitting at the curb. But when she's a puppy, perhaps the most important aspect of outdoor excursions is socialization. She'll see lots of things that she's not exposed to in the house, like bicycles, birds, wildlife, strange dogs and cats, and kids on skateboards.

When you're walking your pup, let her go up to and sniff new things, like bushes, trash cans, even litter. She should be allowed to smell everything that's safe for her to smell.

Meeting the Neighbors

Encourage neighbors to greet your dog. Keep treats on hand so they can give her one and teach her how nice strangers can be.

Alert!

Even if your puppy has been vaccinated, she might be susceptible to infectious disease due to maternal immunity (as described in Chapter 8). However, isolating your puppy will cause her to miss valuable socialization opportunities. Always weigh the risks and benefits of each situation. Go ahead and take your poodle to places that are relatively safe, like play dates with dogs you know aren't ill.

When you encounter new people and dogs when you're out and about, be sure you communicate to your puppy that there's nothing to fear. Don't tug on her leash or hold it tight—that telegraphs fear. Greet people warmly and make friendly overtures when asking if they'll help you socialize your poodle.

Seeking Out the Hustle and Bustle

If you live in a tranquil rural or suburban neighborhood, try to take your poodle someplace where you can expose her to the sounds of traffic and large numbers of people. It's safest to carry her if the sidewalks are crowded and if you're concerned she's not been fully vaccinated. Let her see people of all different ethnicities and all different clothing styles. It's great if you encounter people using wheelchairs or crutches.

An urban park is a terrific place to go. Stuff your pockets with treats, and take your puppy to see the in-line skaters, joggers, walkers, maybe even soccer or softball games. If you sit down on a park bench with your puppy, you'll probably have people flocking to you asking to pet her. Take advantage of this golden opportunity for her to meet so many people! Ask folks to give her treats as well as talk to and pet her.

Preventing Separation Anxiety

All the attention you give your poodle in your effort to socialize him can backfire if he becomes so attached to you that he can't be comfortable when you're not around. You need to teach him that being alone is okay.

When you first bring your poodle puppy home, it's a great idea if you can take some time off work so that he doesn't have to spend long stretches of time alone, particularly when you're house-training him. However, make sure you give your poodle some time alone those first few weeks.

You can leave for a very short period of time at first. Just brightly say goodbye, put your poodle in his crate or long-term confinement area with a treat and a stuffed Kong and leave. (Don't smother him with kisses and hugs, or he'll miss you all the more.) Come back in ten minutes that first time and see if there's any evidence that he was stressed by your absence.

Essential

If you're not sure how your puppy reacts to being alone, you can leave a voice-activated tape recorder running while you're gone to see if he was barking. Or leave a video camera running for a real-time view of how he reacted to your leaving.

Increase the length of your trips outside the home, so that by the time you go back to work you're comfortable he's not going to carry on all day. When you get to the point where you're leaving your poodle four hours a day or more, give him plenty of exercise before you leave the house so that he'll snooze much of the time you're gone. Also make sure he has plenty to do while you're gone.

Socializing an Adult Poodle

If you adopt an adult poodle, rather than a puppy, socialization is still important. With any luck, your poodle will have been well socialized as a pup. But if you don't know whether that was the case, get her out and about and expose her to new things, just like you would if she were a puppy.

If your poodle is scared by some of the new experiences, do everything you can to make them positive. Make sure lots of treats are rained upon her in new situations. But don't ask more of her than she can handle. Stay upbeat, and be patient.

Helping the Shy Poodle

If your poodle is the shy and fearful sort, socializing her is doubly important. But it has to be done more carefully and slowly. If you properly socialize your shy dog from the moment she comes to live with you, she'll be able to approach new people and situations with more confidence.

Start by introducing your poodle to a trusted friend. Arrange this in advance, telling your friend to let the poodle approach him at her own pace. Your friend shouldn't reach out to the poodle or look her directly in the eye. Have your friend sit on the floor with a treat in his open palm and wait for the poodle to approach. When she does, she should be given the treat. If your poodle is so shy she won't approach to take the treat, your friend can gently lob treats in your poodle's direction, gradually letting them land closer and closer to him. After your poodle is willing to walk up to the friend (and this might not happen in the first session), he might be able to scratch her under the chin.

With introductions between all new people and your shy poodle, instruct them not to look her in the eye or reach for her. Let the dog come to the person. Control all introductions until your poodle becomes more confident. Rather than trying to correct any fearful behavior, it is better to ignore it.

Fact

Play dates should be fun for you, too. You get to watch your puppy play—what's more fun than that? And you get to make friends with other dog owners. If your poodle becomes especially close to another dog, and if you trust that dog's owner, you might be able to swap pet-care services when you need to travel without your poodle.

Play Dates

Arranging play dates for your poodle gives him great exercise, it's mentally stimulating, and it provides valuable opportunities for socialization with his own kind. If you do this when he's a puppy, he'll learn important lessons while he's wrestling and playing (reinforcing the lessons he learned from his littermates).

Try to expose your poodle to lots of types of dogs. Big dogs are fine for him to play with, as long as they are gentle. Small dogs are great too. The more types of dogs he's exposed to at a young age, the easier life will be when he encounters strange dogs later on. If your poodle isn't entirely comfortable with other dogs, choose playmates you know are friendly and gentle at first. After these successful interactions have given him new confidence around dogs, start increasing his circle of friends.

▲ Play time is important for keeping poodles healthy and fit.

Dog Park Etiquette

If you're lucky enough to live in an area that has a dog park, where dogs are allowed to run and play off-leash in a secure area, by all means take advantage of it. Before you go, you should know some basic rules that all dog-park attendees should follow:

- Bring your poodle only after you're confident she'll be friendly with other dogs.
- Always pick up after your dog and dispose of the waste properly.

- Don't bring out treats around a group of dogs.
- Always ask permission of the owner before giving another dog a treat.
- Apologize if your dog behaves inappropriately—don't get defensive.
- Offer to pay any vet bills if your dog injures another.

Dog parks can be overwhelming to some dogs. If your poodle doesn't enjoy the attention of the dogs there or seems overly stressed at the dog park, take a step back. Get her more comfortable through play dates, then take her back to the park.

Alert!

Calmly leash up your dog and leave if there's another dog at the dog park that you (or your poodle) are uncomfortable with. In order to avoid an injury to your dog, trust your instincts. Watch your poodle closely for clues as to how he feels about the other dogs at the park.

Riding in Cars

If you socialize and train your poodle, you'll want to take her everywhere with you. That'll be hard to do if she hates riding in the car! Start taking your poodle on short car rides as soon as she joins your family. Go on short trips to nowhere—don't make every trip end at the park (to keep her from getting overly excited by car rides) or the veterinarian's office (so she doesn't develop negative associations with the car, although if you socialize her properly to the vet that shouldn't be the case).

Be sure to keep your poodle safe in the car. Either put her in a crate that's affixed to the car, or restrain her with a seat belt harness designed for dogs. If your car has airbags, don't let your poodle ride in the front seat. She could be seriously injured or killed if the airbag deployed.

Overcoming Fear of the Car

If your poodle is afraid of the car, don't reprimand the fear-based behavior. Instead, use a clicker to help change her associations with it. Start by walking toward the car, clicking and treating for calm behavior. Stop when she reaches the point of stressing about her proximity to the car. The next day, see if you can get closer, increasing your distance gradually until she's actually sitting in the car, all the while clicking for calm behavior and ignoring stressed behavior. At that point, turn on the car's engine. The next day, see if you can turn on the engine and back down the driveway, or drive the distance of a few houses. Each day increase how far you go, rewarding calm behavior, until your poodle's associations with the car have changed. You might try using an extra-special treat that she gets only in the car.

Keeping Calm

If your poodle barks or carries on in the car, start by making sure she's securely restrained. She shouldn't be allowed to run from window to window. If you think the source of behavior is anxiety about the car ride, follow the instructions for fear of cars, above. If she hops into the car gladly, you can start from the point when she's already belted or crated in the car. If she's overstimulated by things outside the car, consider crating her and putting a sheet over the crate, like a bird cage. Just make sure she gets sufficient ventilation.

Becoming Accustomed to New Situations

A well-socialized poodle should be able to handle new situations without any problem. But certain situations that crop up in the lives of many dogs are worthy of special mention.

Meeting a New Baby

As soon as you find out that a new baby is going to be joining your family, you can start preparing your poodle. If you're going to have to change some of the house rules—for example, you might not want your poodle jumping on your lap if there's a baby in it—start teaching the new rules right away. Be gentle and patient with your poodle. Consistency is important to dogs, and changing the rules can be stressful for her.

Before you bring the baby home from the hospital, bring home a blanket the baby has slept on. Let your poodle smell this to her heart's content. Then, once the baby's home, his smell will be familiar.

Fact

If you haven't obedience-trained your poodle yet, now's the time. It's essential that your poodle be able to sit, lie down, stay, and come when you ask him to. He should be taught not to jump on you. This will give you much more control after the baby comes home.

When you bring the baby home from the hospital, have Dad hold the infant while Mom greets the poodle. After a warm greeting, leash up your dog and let her check out the baby under carefully controlled circumstances. If your poodle is totally jazzed up about your homecoming, keep the baby away until she's calmed down.

Reward your poodle for calm and gentle behavior around the baby. Be ready to divert her if she tries to lick or put her mouth on the baby (unless you don't mind the licking). If your poodle is afraid of the baby, keep them apart until she is more comfortable. Don't force the baby on the fearful poodle.

After the baby's arrival, do everything you can (even if it means enlisting the help of friends) to maintain your poodle's feeding and exercise schedules. It's up to you to make sure your poodle doesn't feel neglected. If behavior problems spring up, be patient and recognize them as symptoms of the disruptions to your poodle's life. If necessary, work with a behaviorist or trainer.

Moving to a New House

Moving can be very stressful for your poodle. Think how stressful it is for you! Do what you can to minimize the stress by being organized and packing as calmly as possible. On moving day, keep your poodle safe by taking her to a friend's house or day-care facility. This way, you alleviate the risk of her escaping through a propped-open door.

Alert!

Never leave your poodle alone with your baby, toddler, or child. All interaction should be supervised, no matter how gentle your poodle is. If a little finger is suddenly stuck in his eye, your poodle could bite, with tragic results.

Put your poodle's favorite stuff (her bowl, bed, and favorite toys) in a box that you take with you in the car, so that you can unpack it immediately. If possible, move your furniture in and arrange it before you bring your poodle in. That will make the new home seem more familiar.

Don't be surprised if your poodle shows the stress of the move by marking indoors or being destructive. Be patient. Give her lots of attention and exercise, and soon she should get used to her new surroundings. If her housetraining lapses entirely, however, take her to the vet to be checked out, in case there's a medical reason for it.

CHAPTER 17

Behavior Challenges

IF YOU FOLLOW THE ADVICE in Chapter 16 and do a great job of socializing your poodle, you may never deal with behavior problems. However, when your poodle is going through the rebellious teenage months, he might try to test the limits, just as human adolescents do (the exact age of this rebellion can vary). It's helpful to know about potential behavior problems to watch for and to know what you can do if they should arise.

Basic Tenets of Problem Solving

A well-socialized, properly brought up poodle knows you're the leader. He looks to you for guidance about what and what not to do. However, no matter how nice your poodle is, at some point or another you'll probably be faced with behavior you just don't like. When it comes to addressing behavior challenges presented by your poodle, keep some important things in mind:

- Dogs (and all other beings) repeat behaviors that are rewarded.
- Sometimes the best solution is to prevent the problem from happening.
- Some problems (like excessive barking) are symptoms of a larger problem.
- Your poodle doesn't misbehave to spite you.
- When in doubt, seek professional help.

If you keep these basic tenets in mind, you can figure out the motivation for problem behavior, take away the rewarding aspect of the behavior, and replace it with a desirable behavior you can reward.

Setting Your Poodle Up for Success

One key to dealing with problem behavior is management. That is, don't give your poodle the chance to misbehave. If you don't want your puppy chewing up your shoes, keep your shoes out of his reach, and give him something appropriate to chew on. If he has a propensity to get into the trash, put it in a cupboard or empty it every morning before you leave the house.

Fact

Some people advocate preventing scavenging by booby-trapping the trash or putting electrically charged mats on the counter. This can work, but why introduce this punishment into your poodle's life? You can manage the situation by simply not allowing her to find a tasty something that rewards her for her behavior.

If you eliminate opportunities for misbehavior, you set your poodle up for success. You don't spend your time being frustrated by his behavior, and he doesn't suffer your frustration. It's a win-win situation.

Redirecting Improper Behavior

If your poodle is highly rewarded by a behavior, he'll repeat it. By recognizing what your poodle sees as a reward, and removing the opportunity for him to be rewarded for problem behavior, you'll be on your way to ending those behaviors. If you face a problem behavior with your poodle, figure out how it is rewarding to him. Then figure out an incompatible, more acceptable, behavior you can reward him for doing instead.

While you're solving the problem, be patient with your dog. Don't punish him. Punishment is not very effective, and it's particularly unfair if you don't catch him in the act of doing something wrong. Always remember to reward the behavior you like!

Dealing with Specific Behavior Problems

Depending on your poodle's individual personality, how well socialized he is, and how well you manage his environment to prevent behavior problems, there are several types of challenges you might encounter. Many of these are entirely preventable. Others may require a little work on your part to solve.

Aggressive Behavior

Poodles aren't known as an aggressive breed, either with people or with other dogs. But every dog is an individual, and problems with aggression do sometimes occur. Having a dog that is aggressive toward humans is not only dangerous for the humans around you, it's dangerous for your dog. If you think you're facing an aggression problem with people—that is, if you're afraid your dog will hurt you or another person—seek professional help immediately. Until a solution is found, don't let him come into contact with people out in public. Muzzle him if necessary.

Essential

If your normally docile poodle suddenly becomes aggressive, take her to the veterinarian to see if there's a medical cause for the problem. She could be in pain, or she could be suffering from a neurological or even a thyroid problem.

If your poodle is aggressive toward other dogs, resist the urge to put him in doggie isolation. Try instead to find a solution to the problem. A behaviorist can help, as can classes intended for aggressive dogs. In these classes, sometimes dubbed "Feisty Fido" or "Growl" classes, safety precautions are taken to see that no dogs hurt one another. Look for one that uses positive methods like classical conditioning (in which the dogs' associations with other dogs are changed from negative to positive) and operant conditioning (in which dogs are rewarded for good behavior around other dogs).

Whatever you do, don't get aggressive with your poodle when he acts aggressively. Violence begets violence, and you could endanger yourself. If your poodle is dog-aggressive, punishing him around other dogs will only give him more reason to think ill of them.

Fact

Neutered male dogs are less likely to be aggressive than intact males. If your intact male is lashing out against other dogs, neutering him might help solve the problem. It might not be that simple—working with a trainer to counter-condition and desensitize your dog to other dogs may be in order as well. But neutering is a good first step.

Constant Barking

If your poodle is annoying you and the neighbors by barking at everything in the yard, refrain from putting him outside without supervision until he learns how to be quiet. When he's in the yard, you should be there with him. As soon as he starts barking, figure out what he's barking at, acknowledge his cleverness at letting you know, then try to divert him with a rewarding behavior, like throwing a ball for him or practicing obedience commands. Or just go back inside the house together.

If it's indoor barking that's bothering you (or your neighbors, if you share walls), try to take away the stimulus. If you're not home when the barking occurs, close the blinds on the window that lets your dog see things that make him bark. If it's noises that make your poodle bark, try leaving the radio on to drown them out. You might also confine him to an area of the house where he can't hear noise from the street.

Alert!

If your neighbors complain about your dog's barking, don't ignore them. Not only is excessive barking bad for neighbor relations, it can be a sign of unhappiness in your poodle. Either she's bored, lonely, overstimulated, or upset by something. Figure out the reason she's barking, and address it.

If your poodle is barking while you're home, perhaps when the mail carrier arrives or when other dogs walk by the house, don't shout at him. Instead, enthusiastically call his name. If he stops barking even for a moment, click and treat him. Acknowledge the reason for the barking, then divert him from the situation. Getting him away from the stimulus should stop the barking.

Barking is a very natural behavior for your dog. It should be okay for your poodle to bark at perceived threats. But if your dog is barking for hours on end, look at it as a symptom of a bigger problem. And try to address that problem. Don't ever punish your poodle with anti-bark collars that shock him. If barking is a critical issue–you're going to be evicted if your dog doesn't stop barking–consider an anti-bark collar that sprays a blast of citronella when your poodle barks. It doesn't address the source of the problem, but it's less cruel than some alternatives.

Begging for Food

If a meal at your home isn't complete without a poodle giving you sad eyes or putting his paws on your leg to ask for a morsel of food, you pretty much have only yourself to blame.

If your poodle was never rewarded for this behavior, he wouldn't repeat it.

So what if the damage has already been done, and you want your poodle to stop begging? Stop rewarding the behavior. Never, ever give him food from the table, and don't allow anyone else to do it, either. Ignore his begging completely—even (especially) if he gets noisy about it. After a few minutes, you can hope that he'll give up and go lie down (though some dogs are more persistent than others).

Essential

If you don't mind sharing your food with your dog, go right ahead. Some might call it rewarding the begging. But if it doesn't bother you, it can be a nice ritual—assuming that you eat healthily. When you have guests, however, you might need to confine your poodle away from the dining room.

A more proactive approach is to give your poodle something delicious of his own to chew on while you eat (like a stuffed Kong toy or a raw bone) and to put him in his crate or on a down/stay on his bed to enjoy it. Do this right before you sit down to eat, and he'll be too busy to pester you.

Inappropriate Chewing

Dogs chew for the fun of it. Young dogs need to chew. If your poodle is chewing things you don't want him to, there are two things you can do. Supply better chew toys, and prevent him from getting to things you don't want him to chew.

If your poodle picks up something to chew on that he shouldn't, take it away from him while offering something more appropriate. A rubber Kong stuffed with something delicious, like cream cheese or peanut butter, will deliver more satisfaction to your dog than any shoe can! Be careful not to leave things where your poodle can get to them, particularly when you're not home to replace them with chew toys.

Alert!

If you leave chew toys for your poodle to work on unsupervised, be sure they're safe. Watch your dog when she's chewing on a new toy to make sure she can't break off any pieces that are big enough to choke on.

Prevent your poodle from chewing on dangerous items, like toxic plants, by keeping them out of reach. Electrical cords can be covered to prevent electrocution from chewing.

If your poodle is chewing furniture, he's not ready for access to the house. Confine him in a furniture-free safe area with appropriate chew toys. Gradually give him access to more of the house, under your supervision, until you can trust him to only chew his own toys.

Digging Holes

Digging holes in your yard shouldn't be a problem if you're in the yard with your dog. If you catch him starting to dig, interrupt him and divert his energy elsewhere. Let him know, gently, that digging in that area is not appropriate. If it's happening when you're not out in the yard with him, stop letting him out in the yard unsupervised until he understands that he shouldn't dig. He should be in the house with you, or snoozing in comfort when you're not home, and not out in the yard excavating!

Poodles don't have an inbred need to dig, but some will dig to amuse themselves. If your poodle derives great pleasure from digging, you can make a pit for him where he is allowed to dig to his heart's content.

Spice the digging pit up with some favorite toys for your poodle to discover—this will reward him for using the sanctioned pit. When you first introduce it, praise him for going in the pit and digging, so he knows it's okay. If he digs in other parts of the yard, redirect him to the digging pit.

Fact

To make a digging pit for your poodle, dig up an area of ground and frame it with two-by-fours, as if you were making a child's sandbox. Or you can use a plastic wading pool, with some holes cut in the bottom for drainage, and fill it with sand, dirt, or rodent bedding.

Mouthing and Nipping

It's perfectly natural for your poodle puppy to mouth at you and nip you. That's one of the things puppies do (and one of the reasons some people prefer to adopt adult dogs!). A puppy's mother and littermates help teach her about bite inhibition—they yelp and stop playing when nipped too hard.

If your puppy mouths at you in play and it hurts, you need to continue the lessons of bite inhibition. Your poodle needs to learn that his teeth cause pain. Sit down and play with him. If he mouths you, say "Ouch!" and stop playing. After about a minute, go back to playing. If he mouths you for a second time, say "Ouch!" again, and actually walk away from him for several minutes. (Make sure he's in a safe area where it's okay to leave him alone.) After a few minutes have gone by, go back and start again.

Even if your puppy's mouthing doesn't really hurt, he needs to be taught not to apply pressure with his teeth. Continue to yelp and walk away whenever he mouths you, gradually decreasing the amount of pressure needed to get a reaction out of you, until he learns that important lesson and doesn't mouth you at all. Remember to praise and treat him for appropriate playing.

Separation Anxiety

Separation anxiety, in which the dog becomes very anxious when his human is away, can be a very serious problem. The best course of action is to prevent the problem by gradually leaving your dog alone and making sure he is occupied, as described in Chapter 16. But if you're faced with a poodle that suffers when you're gone, you'll need to take action to solve the problem. In most cases, you'll need to call in a professional behavior specialist. (Your vet might be able to recommend one.) Through a program of behavior modification and counter-conditioning, the specialist can help your poodle become accustomed to your absence without an anxious response.

Essential

If you make sure your poodle gets plenty of exercise before you leave her in the morning, she may fall asleep before she can get too anxious about your departure. Regular exercise, as part of a routine—dogs thrive on routine—might lick mild separation anxiety.

It can take a while for such a program to work. In the meantime, you have to keep your poodle (and your home) safe. If possible, take him to doggie day care or to a friend's house where someone is home during the day. (A retired neighbor might be a great asset here.) If your poodle has a close dog friend, see if that friend can come over during the day. If so, leave them alone together for a short while and see how they do. The company may be enough to ward off the anxiety.

Your veterinarian may want to prescribe a drug called Clomicalm to help with the separation anxiety. If you choose to go this route, do it in conjunction with a program of behavior modification and counter-conditioning so that your dog doesn't have to stay on the drug for the rest of his life.

▲ Poodles enjoy living with canine companions—especially other poodles.

Thunder and Fireworks Phobia

If your poodle is afraid of loud sounds, like thunder and fireworks, it can be stressful for both of you. Recognize that this kind of behavior isn't really within your dog's control, so there's no point in getting angry over any destruction that happens during a storm.

It's also counterproductive to soothe and coddle your poodle when he's afraid of noises. That can reward and encourage his fearful behavior. Instead, be upbeat and adopt an attitude that communicates there's really nothing to be afraid of. You can even try to distract him during a storm by throwing a ball or working on some obedience exercises or tricks. Make sure he has access to her crate or other place of refuge.

Some safe over-the-counter preparations that might help your poodle stay calm during storms and fireworks include the Bach flower remedy Mimulus (available at health-food stores) and the amino acid l-theanine (available from *www.painstresscenter.com*). Give a few drops of flower remedy or a single capsule of l-theanine at the beginning of a thunderstorm and repeat after a couple of hours, if necessary.

In extreme cases, your veterinarian can supply a pharmaceutical, like Prozac or Valium, that might help your dog's noise phobia. Don't try just sharing your own prescription, however; your veterinarian needs to decide whether your dog is a good candidate for this kind of medication and what the dosage should be.

Fact

It may sound odd, but putting a T-shirt on your poodle during a thunderstorm or fireworks display can provide a sense of security. Put it on your poodle with the tag at her throat. Then cinch it up and tie the excess fabric in a knot at your poodle's waist (or use a hair scrunchie to hold it in place). It may just calm her down.

Crying or Whining

Dogs whine to get attention. Whining can be really annoying, particularly if it goes on for any length of time. The key to curbing the whining is not to reward it. Just ignore it. Don't give your dog any attention if he's whining. None. By no means should you let him out of her crate while he's whining. Wait until there's a moment of quiet before you open the door.

The worst thing you can do is to give in and give your dog attention (this even includes yelling at him to stop) after he has been whining for some time. That just teaches him that if he whines long enough, he'll achieve his goal. If you don't want him to whine, don't reward whining. It's really that simple.

Working with a Behaviorist

If you're experiencing a serious problem, like aggression or separation anxiety, it can be worth the time, effort, and money to work with a behaviorist. This might be a veterinarian who has done advanced work in behavior. You might also happen upon someone with a Ph.D. who has studied behavior and received certification through the Applied Animal Behavior Society. A very experienced, highly recommended trainer can also help you with complex issues.

Essential

Try to follow the treatment plan prescribed by your behaviorist to the best of your ability. However, if any expert asks you to do something to your dog that you're uncomfortable with, don't do it without questioning it first. Follow your gut, and look elsewhere if you feel the behaviorist's recommendations are inappropriate for you and your dog.

Look for a behaviorist who doesn't use outdated methods like the alpha roll. Rather, find someone who uses behavior modification techniques based on positive reinforcement and negative punishment (stopping behavior by taking away something rewarding). The behaviorist will likely observe your poodle and ask you a lot of questions about his behavior and lifestyle. Be open and honest so that you can get an accurate diagnosis, and the behaviorist can work up an appropriate treatment plan.

CHAPTER 18

Competitive Obedience

POODLES ARE SO SMART AND FUN to train that they're naturals for obedience competitions. Go to any competition, and you'll see poodles of all sizes excelling. There are now two styles of competitive obedience from which to choose: traditional obedience, which has been around since the 1930s, and rally obedience, a new and less formal sport created to attract the types of dogs and owners who have started choosing agility competitions over traditional obedience.

About Traditional Obedience Trials

The American Kennel Club offers the most obedience competitions throughout the United States. The obedience requirements mentioned in this chapter refer to AKC competition. (The United Kennel Club and Canadian Kennel Club also offer obedience competitions.)

At AKC obedience trials, there are three levels that you and your poodle can work through, each one more difficult than the last: novice, open, and utility.

What Is an Obedience Competition?

An obedience trial involves a prescribed set of exercises you put your dog through, with each level of competition involving different exercises. A judge scores your dog's performance, with a total possible score of 200. If your dog earns at least half of the possible score in each individual exercise, and if she has a cumulative score of 170 or higher (known as a qualifying score), she earns a "leg" toward a title in that level. Once she gets three legs, she achieves the obedience title of that level of competition and is eligible to advance to the next level. At the novice level, the dog earns a Companion Dog (CD) title. At the open level, it's Companion Dog Excellent (CDX), and at the utility level, it's Utility Dog (UD).

Fact

Once you've achieved titles in all three AKC levels, you can work toward the Utility Dog Excellent (UDX) title, and then toward Obedience Trial Championship (OTCh), sometimes called a Ph.D. for dogs. The highest AKC obedience honor is National Obedience Champion (NOC), awarded to the winning dog at the National Obedience Invitational.

Obedience trials are often held in conjunction with conformation shows. If you're active with a local obedience school or club, you'll be able to find out about nearby trials and fun matches. Or you can check with the AKC for a schedule of competitions.

Any poodle can compete in AKC obedience competitions. If your poodle isn't AKC registered, you can apply for an indefinite listing privilege (ILP) number (by filling out an application and submitting a picture), which indicates that your dog has been recognized as a purebred poodle. Spayed and neutered dogs are eligible to compete.

Training for Obedience

Most communities have training classes for people interested in obedience competitions. The basic classes provide the groundwork in obedience, and these are recommended for all dogs, whether or not you're interested in competing. If you think you might enjoy competing in obedience with your poodle, you can sign up for novice classes and work your way up in classes as you train the skills for each level of competition. See Chapter 14 for more information about choosing the right class and trainer.

Essential

Nonconformation performance events don't adhere to the restrictions of the breed standard the way the conformation events do. So in obedience (as well as any other AKC event except conformation) any poodle hairstyle is welcome. Particolored poodles, phantoms, and poodles with unusual markings can compete as well.

Novice Competition

At the novice level of competition, your dog must display the skills of any excellent companion: heeling both on and off leash, coming when called, staying calmly, and standing for examination. Of course, he's expected to do it with a lot more precision than you might require at home.

In the obedience ring, you and your poodle are expected to be a smoothly functioning team, performing each exercise as flawlessly as possible. You can give him verbal cues, and cues in the form of hand signals but you can't talk to or otherwise communicate with your dog. (Clickers, for instance, are not allowed.)

There are two classes in novice obedience: Novice A and Novice B. While the dog that competes in either novice class is by definition a beginner, the handler in Novice A must also be a true beginner. Handlers who have titled a dog in obedience in the past must compete in Novice B. This is the class in which professional handlers and trainers compete as well. Both classes have the same exercises, described below.

Heel on Lead and Figure Eight

In the heel-on-lead exercise, your dog walks at your left side, in heel position (his head level with your left knee). Your dog walks on a loose lead—if you tighten or jerk on the leash, you're penalized. While you're heeling, the judge will ask you to change speeds, turn left or right, do an about-turn, and halt. Your poodle should stay in heel position while you do these things. He should automatically sit when you halt.

To do the figure eights, you and your dog walk in a figure-eight pattern between and around two show stewards, who are standing eight feet apart from each other.

Alert!

While you can use a clicker and treats to teach your dog obedience skills, you may not take them into the formal obedience ring. Nor may you use verbal encouragement or head halters. It's truly "traditional" obedience!

Stand for Examination

Next, your poodle is expected to stand still while the judge puts his hands on her. The exercise is done off leash. You remove the leash and hand it to the judge, put your dog in a stand, ask her to stay, then walk six feet away and turn and face your dog. The judge approaches your poodle from the front and touches her head, body, and hindquarters.

The key here is that your dog is not supposed to show any resentment about being touched by a stranger. (Poodles tend to have an advantage in this exercise, since they're groomed so often they're used to being touched all over.) The judge asks you to return to your poodle, who is supposed to continue standing still until the judge says "Exercise finished."

Heel Free and Recall

The heel-free exercise is performed like the on-leash heeling exercise, except, of course, there's no leash. The recall exercise demonstrates your poodle's ability to stay in place while you walk away from her, as well as her willingness to come to you when you call. On the judge's signal, you ask your poodle to stay, then walk to the other end of the ring, and call her to come. She should come quickly. (The AKC regulations state, "The dog must come directly, at a brisk trot or gallop.") When she gets to you, she should sit directly in front of you, facing you. When the judge instructs you to, you then ask your poodle to finish, which means she goes into a heel position and sits.

Fact

When performing a finish, a dog can walk behind the handler to sit at heel position. He can also move to his right from his seated position in front of you, then pivot left and sit at heel position. A flashy variation of this finish is when he jumps up, and pivots in mid-air to land sitting at heel.

Novice Group Exercises

During group exercises, all dogs in the competing class perform together. They're asked to go into either a sit or a down and to hold the position for a designated time. The handlers space themselves and their dogs along one side of the ring, put their dogs in position, instruct them to stay, then walk to the opposite end of the ring and face their dogs. After one minute for the sit and three minutes for the stay, on the judge's instruction, the handlers return to their dogs, walk around behind them, and stop when the dog is at heel position. The dogs must stay still until the exercise is finished.

If a dog gets up or starts to interfere with another dog, the judge will ask the handler to remove the dog.

The Open Level of Competition

The open level of competition builds on the skills established at the novice level. As in novice, there are two classes in open: Open A (for people who have put a CD, but not a CDX—the open title—on a dog) and Open B (for more experienced handlers). The exercises are the same in both, though in Open B the order of the exercises might change.

Heel Free and Figure Eight

Several of the exercises in the open level are similar to those used during novice competitions, only slightly more advanced. For example, the heel and figure-eight exercise is conducted in the same manner as at the novice level, except the dog and handler are now working together without a leash.

Drop on Recall

The drop-on-recall exercise is handled like the novice recall exercise, with an important addition. During the recall, when the dog is partway to her handler, she must immediately drop into a down position when asked and stay there until told to continue with the recall. The judge tells the handler when to signal the dog to drop.

Alert!

If you're at all tempted to participate in obedience with your poodle, attend a trial and check out the relationship between dog and handler. Seeing these teams working together at the top levels of obedience is a beautiful thing. The communication and bond between the two can be practically tangible.

Retrieve on Flat and over High Jump

In the retrieve-on-flat exercise, the dog begins by sitting at heel position. The handler tells her to stay, tosses a dumbbell at least twenty feet away, then asks the dog to retrieve it. The dog should briskly run to it and bring it directly back, then sit in front of the handler, facing him. When the judge says, "Take it," the handler removes the dumbbell from the dog's mouth. The dog must give it up readily.

The retrieve-over-high-jump is a similar exercise, except that the dumbbell is thrown over a high jump, which the dog must jump over going for the dumbbell and when returning. The jump's height is set according to a formula so that it is at an appropriate height for the dog. The minimum jump height is eight inches.

Broad Jump

In the next exercise, the dog jumps over a broad jump at the request of the handler, then returns to the handler and sits in front of him. The jump is twice as broad as it is high, but the actual height and breadth will vary according to the size of the dog.

◀ The elegant exterior of the poodle can hide a fun-loving personality that is eager to work!

Open Group Exercises

The long sits and downs in the group exercises are performed much as they are at the novice level. In open competition, however, after leaving their dogs, the handlers file out of the room, so that they're completely out of sight of their dogs. The dogs must hold their stays for three minutes and their downs for five. At the judge's request, the handlers return in the reverse order and line up opposite their dogs, then cross the ring and return to them. All dogs then return to the heel position.

Utility Competition

As the highest level of competition, utility offers more complex exercises. Again, there are two classes of competition: Utility A and Utility B, depending on the handler's experience.

Signal Exercise

The signal exercise is similar to the novice exercise heel free and recall. However, there's an important difference between the novice and utility versions. At the utility level, the handler and judge use only signals—the exercise must be done without verbal communication. While the dog and handler are heeling at a normal pace, the judge adds an additional order, and it's a complex one. He first signals the handler to "Stand your dog." The team stops and the dog remains standing. When the judge signals, "Leave your dog," the handler signals the dog to stay, walks to the opposite end of the ring, turns and faces the dog and, at the judge's indication, signals the dog to down, sit, come, and finish.

Retrieving Exercises

There are two scent-discrimination exercises, one with metal dumbbells and one with leather. In each, a group of five dumbbells is put into the ring. One of the five has the handler's scent on it. The dog is asked to select the dumbbell with the handler's scent and return with it, then sit in front of the handler.

In the directed retrieve, the judge puts out three white-cotton work gloves, spaced apart at one end of the ring. He tells the handler which of the three gloves to have the dog retrieve, and the handler sends the dog, signaling which glove she should select and bring back.

Moving Stand and Examination

The utility level examination is similar to the stand-for-examination exercise in novice competition, except that the exercise starts with the dog and handler heeling. At the judge's direction, the handler signals the dog to stay, then keeps walking. The dog stays at a stand. She shows no shyness or resentment when the judge examines her as he would in a dog show (though the teeth and testicles may not be touched). When told to, the handler calls the dog to the heel position.

Essential

No matter what type of obedience competition you choose to do, or what level you achieve, training your dog should be fun for both of you. It should bring you closer together. Seek a training class that both of you enjoy. And never do anything to your dog in the name of training that makes you feel bad.

Directed Jumping

For directed jumping, two jumps (one a bar jump, the other a high jump) are set up at right angles to the side of the ring, about eighteen feet apart from each other. The handler, who stays put, sends the dog between the jumps to the opposite side of the ring, about twenty feet past the jumps, and asks the dog to sit. The judge designates one of the jumps, and the handler has the dog return to him, jumping over that jump, and ending at heel position. The exercise is then repeated over the other jump.

Rally Obedience

Agility is the fast-paced sport in which dogs negotiate obstacle courses at the direction of their handlers. Noticing that agility competition was becoming increasingly popular, while the number of participants in traditional obedience dropped off, Charles "Bud"

Kramer invented rally obedience, a new and different way to approach obedience competition.

In rally obedience, called both "Rally-O" and "Rally" for short, handlers are allowed to talk to their dogs. Enthusiasm and fun is encouraged, and any harshness is a big no-no. Rally is all about promoting a great dog/handler relationship. If working with your poodle in obedience is appealing to you, but traditional obedience seems too formal, Rally-O might be the sport for you!

The AKC offers rally obedience as a nonregular class, which means that titles are not yet awarded. You cannot use food in the ring, but you can use your voice. You may not touch or correct your dog.

Fact

The Association of Pet Dog Trainers (APDT) also offers rally obedience competitions and titles. In APDT Rally, food rewards are allowed after each exercise, but food may not be used as a lure during the exercise.

In Rally, judges set up courses, each with between ten and fifteen "stations" (or more, depending on the level at which you're working). Each station has a sign, posted at ground level, that specifies a Rally exercise. The judge has thirty-one exercises to choose from when setting up the course for the novice level, an additional fourteen for the advanced level, and a total of fifty exercises for the excellent level.

Unlike traditional obedience, the judge doesn't tell you what to do next. You and your dog go from station to numbered station, in order, and perform the exercises listed on each sign. The exercises range from about-turns to spiraling or weaving around cones.

Your dog is on leash in the novice class and off-leash in the advanced and excellent classes. She walks at your left side but does not have to be in perfect heel position. You and your dog are judged on your continuous performance as you go through each station.

The Canine Good Citizen Test

The Canine Good Citizen (CGC) test, offered by the American Kennel Club to all dogs, purebred or not, isn't really a competition. It's just a way to tell the world that your poodle possesses the skills that all good dogs should have. Each dog taking the CGC is asked to perform ten simple tests to prove that he's a good citizen. Those tests are the following:

1. Accepting a Friendly Stranger
2. Sitting Politely for Petting
3. Appearance and Grooming
4. Walking on a Loose Lead
5. Walking Through a Crowd
6. Sit and Down on Command—Staying in Place
7. Coming When Called
8. Reaction to Another Dog
9. Reaction to Distraction
10. Supervised Separation

Official CGC tests can be conducted only by evaluators who have been approved and registered by the AKC, and they are often offered by training clubs or at dog-related events. Treats are not allowed during the test itself (though you can certainly use them when training for it!).

Question?

What happens if my dog doesn't pass the CGC?
While it is a serious evaluation of your dog, the CGC test is typically an upbeat procedure. If you don't make it through all ten exercises, you can take the test again (and again) at another time, so the pressure shouldn't be too high.

If your dog passes the CGC test, the AKC gives you a nice certificate you can display in your home. Your dog's name is also recorded in the AKC Canine Good Citizen Archive. A CGC award can come in handy if you're looking for rental housing. Some therapy groups even make it a prerequisite.

If you're concerned that your dog might not be able to pass all ten of the exercises—if she fails even one, she doesn't get the CGC award—you can take a preparatory class. These classes can be fun, teach your dog some basic skills (or remind her about skills she's already learned), and give you the chance to interact with other dogs and owners.

CHAPTER 19

Other Sports for Poodles

PARTICIPATING WITH YOUR POODLE in some kind of sport, competitive or otherwise, can be fun for both of you. It provides you with quality time together and keeps your minds and bodies exercised. There are many activities to choose from. In addition to competitive obedience, you and your poodle might compete in dog shows, agility matches, hunting, even dancing. With the versatile poodle, you can do anything!

Conformation Shows

Conformation competition, one of the most familiar dog-related activities, refers to the dog shows in which dogs are judged on how well they conform to the written breed standard. In these competitions, it is the dog's looks, structure, and movement that are taken into account.

Fact

Because conformation shows were originally conceived as a way to judge whether dogs were fit for breeding, all dogs shown in conformation must be intact. Spayed and neutered dogs are not allowed in the show ring, though they're allowed to compete in most other sports.

For some short-haired breeds that don't need much grooming, the decision to show a dog in conformation can be relatively spontaneous. But that's not the case for poodles. Because the breed standard calls for certain hairstyles that can take a while to achieve, you must plan ahead to show your dog in conformation.

Grooming Considerations

Show poodles are extremely glamorous. The clips required for adult poodles in the show ring, the Continental and the English Saddle, are works of art in and of themselves. The dreadlock-style cords that are allowed as an alternative to curls also make a dramatic statement. (See Chapter 10 for descriptions of these clips.)

However, all that glamour takes a lot of effort. Achieving and maintaining a show coat can become a central concern in caring for your poodle. From the time your poodle is a puppy, his coat has to be grown out and cared for. You must be careful that the coat is never damaged. It mustn't be brushed when dry—you have to brush it with moisturizer so as not to damage the hairs—and you can't use a slicker brush.

Alert!

If you decide you'd like to show your poodle in conformation, try to find a mentor who can show you the ropes in terms of grooming and coat care (and everything else). An insider's knowledge of the tricks of the trade could be very helpful.

Not only is grooming right before the show a time-consuming experience, caring for the coat between shows requires work. Show poodles are bathed every week or so, brushed every few days (though that's a good idea for all poodles) and usually clipped once a week. The topknot and ear hair are conditioned and wrapped in plastic or paper every day to prevent damage. After the dog is bathed, a mixture of oil and moisturizer is applied and left in the coat to protect it (and washed out before showing). The show dog looks great in the ring, but a little odd at home—though you can certainly get used to seeing a poodle with his ear hair wrapped in plastic.

It's clear that the decision to show your poodle isn't one that should be made lightly.

Achieving the Championship

When you decide to show your poodle in conformation, you'll work to achieve his championship. Dogs earn points toward championships at all-breed dog shows or single-breed specialty shows. To become a champion, a dog must earn fifteen points under three different judges.

At any given show, a dog can earn from one to five points, depending on the number of dogs he beats. In general, the more dogs are entered in the class, the more points are offered for the win, though the number of dogs required for points varies according to geography and gender. Only one male and one female dog of each breed or variety can win points at a show.

A win that earns three, four, or five points is called a major. Two of the wins that count toward those fifteen champion-qualifying points must be majors, and both majors must be from different judges.

AKC shows are divided into five classes within each breed or variety: puppy class (usually subdivided into a six- to nine-month class and a nine- to twelve-month class), twelve- to eighteen-month class; novice, bred-by-exhibitor, American-bred, and open. Not all shows offer all classes, however. Male dogs (referred to as dogs) compete in each class against other dogs. Female dogs (called bitches) compete against other bitches.

There are several prizes that are awarded at each show. The winners of each class compete against one another to be awarded Winners Dog and Winners Bitch, who receive points and compete against each other for Best of Winners. Then these two are joined in the ring by any dog that has already achieved his or her championship. From this group, the judge names a single dog or bitch

Best of Variety. The best-of-variety winner goes on to compete in the group ring for the Best in Group award. (There are seven groups: Hound, Sporting, Working, Non-Sporting, Herding, Toy, Terrier.) The seven group winners then come together, and the judge selects one to be Best in Show.

Essential

Since the poodle is considered a single breed with three varieties (Toy, Miniature, and Standard), a poodle wins best of variety, not best of breed. Each of the variety winners competes against other best of breed or variety winners in the group ring (the Non-Sporting Group for Miniatures and Standards, and the Toy Group for Toys).

Specialty Shows

At specialty shows, dogs of only one breed compete. At the Poodle Club of America National Specialty, you'll see poodles of all three sizes and all colors competing in conformation, agility, obedience, and hunting. Conformation tends to take center stage at the national specialty. The poodle that wins best in breed there is considered the top poodle in the country—a coveted title.

Attending a specialty show, whether or not you're there competing with your poodle, will give you the unique opportunity to be among a large number of accomplished, delightful poodles. It's an experience you'll not soon forget. See the Poodle Club of America's Web site (*www.poodleclubofamerica.org*) for the location of the next specialties. (There are regional specialties, as well as national.)

Deciding on a Handler

Some owners choose to handle their own poodles in the show ring. This can be a great experience that can help build a very close relationship between you and your poodle. The pride you'll feel in handling your dog to his championship will be tremendous.

But giving your dog a show career and handling him yourself also requires a great deal of work (and skill in negotiating the politics that surround all dog shows). It's not for the faint of heart.

Because preparing a poodle for the show ring can be such an arduous task, many owners choose to hire a professional handler. These people make their living showing dogs in conformation competition. A dog with particularly good prospects might live with the handler and travel to various shows as he is "campaigned." If you decide to show your poodle but don't want to handle him yourself, select a professional handler carefully. Not only do you want to make sure that the handler is someone you'll want your poodle to live and travel with, you want to know that your poodle is a priority for the handler, who probably will handle multiple dogs at any show. Follow your gut instincts when selecting a handler, and don't go with anyone who makes you feel uncomfortable for any reason.

Fact

Versatility in Poodles, Inc., was founded to improve the health and promote the many talents of poodles. The group issues a Versatility Certificate to well-rounded poodles. Their Web site, *www.vipoodle.org*, is chock-full of information about things you can do with your poodle. They also offer printed educational materials at a very slight fee, as well as a newsletter and e-mail list for members.

Agility Events

Poodles are agile dogs and great candidates for agility, a fast-paced dog sport in which dogs negotiate an obstacle course. The obstacles include tunnels, jumps, an A-Frame, a see-saw, a balance-beam, weave poles, and a tire your dog jumps through. At competitions, you're racing against the clock. While the dog is doing the obstacles, he's relying on the handler's direction (since the order of obstacles selected by the judge is different at each trial and isn't known in advance). Agility is truly a team sport, and you and your dog are the team. Agility is lots of fun to train for, and the competitions are even more fun.

All three sizes of poodles can be great agility competitors. The breed is agile, there's no doubt about that. And poodles are smart. They are closely connected to their people, and they take direction well. Unlike conformation, a poodle can wear any type of haircut in the agility ring.

▲ **This poodle is negotiating the weave poles—one of the more challenging obstacles in agility.**

Before you start training in agility, your poodle will need to know some basic skills. He'll need to walk on a loose leash, come when called, and stay when instructed. You can start your puppy doing agility from the very beginning, though Standard Poodle pups are better off not doing any high jumping until they're through growing, for fear of orthopedic damage.

Because agility is so popular, it's usually not difficult to find an agility class for you and your poodle. Look for one that emphasizes positive methods and no force. If you force your poodle to do an obstacle that frightens him, you might make him fear that obstacle for life. Take it slow and easy; keep it fun and positive.

Alert!

Different agility organizations have different rules. Competitions and titles are offered by the AKC, the United States Dog Agility Association (USDAA), the United Kennel Club (UKC), the Canadian Kennel Club (CKC), and the North American Dog Agility Council (NADAC). Be sure to read each group's regulations carefully before entering.

Field Work

As you learned in Chapter 1, Standard Poodles were originally bred to help humans hunt game. You can tap into your poodle's innate retrieving instincts by participating in hunting events sponsored by the AKC, UKC, PCA, or the North American Hunting Retriever Association.

In 1988, the AKC voted to allow Standard Poodles to participate in retriever hunt tests. (Miniature and Toy Poodles are not allowed to participate in AKC hunt tests, although some lobbying is afoot to admit Minis.) These are noncompetitive tests that measure the dog's ability to perform against established standards (as opposed to competing against other dogs). The tests replicate real hunting situations. A hunter shoots a bird, and the dog retrieves it, relying on his senses of sight and smell to find the felled bird.

In the AKC, dogs that earn qualifying scores can achieve three levels of titles: Junior Hunter (JH), Senior Hunter (SH), and Master Hunter (MH). Dogs that are Master Hunters and that pass five master hunter tests in a single year are eligible to test at the Master National Hunting Test.

The Poodle Club of America (PCA) has a Working Certificate (WC) and Working Certificate Excellent (WCX) program for poodles.

These titles are awarded to poodles for passing scores attained at any recognized retriever working test or hunt test.

Fact

Many retrieving clubs or hunt clubs will allow poodles to participate in their tests. Because of the size of the birds that are retrieved, tests are usually limited to Standards or Miniatures. The PCA also offers a WC/WCX trial at their national specialty.

Freestyle Routines

In canine freestyle, dogs and handlers perform choreographed routines set to music. Poodles are naturals for this. They're elegant and look wonderful on the center stage. They're smart and move beautifully. And they're natural performers—performing is part of the poodle's heritage, after all.

Heeling forms the basis for freestyle—heeling to music, that is. More difficult moves are added, like spinning while heeling, sidestepping, bowing, and weaving through the handler's legs, until a complete routine is created. The selection of music is an important part of creating a routine. (Remember, if you're going to be performing a routine in public or on video, you must get permission to use the music.)

Training a dog for freestyle should be fun and use positive techniques. Freestyle classes and workshops are starting to crop up around the country. Videos are also available.

Freestyle titles are offered by the World Canine Freestyle Organization and the Canine Freestyle Federation, each of which has titles at varying levels of difficulty.

One of the great things about freestyle is that your participation can extend beyond competing and earning titles. People love to watch it, so you and your poodle can perform at nursing homes, hospitals, schools, and fundraisers. You can use costumes and collar adornments to enhance your performance (though the two titling organizations have different regulations about costumes). Like all dog sports, it's a great way to build your bond with your poodle.

Other Activities

The list of sports you and your poodle can participate in together doesn't stop with the activities outlined above. There are a number of other fun activities at which your smart and quick poodle can excel.

Tracking Events

In tracking, dogs use their noses to follow the scent track laid by a person. Any dog that is particularly scent-oriented can enjoy tracking. The AKC offers tracking titles that poodles are eligible to qualify for: Tracking Dog (TD), Tracking Dog Excellent (TDX), and Variable Surface Tracking (VST). In the latter, as its name implies, dogs track on both grassy and paved surfaces. In tracking, the dog is tested against an established standard, rather than competing against other dogs.

Alert!

Tracking is done outdoors, under all types of weather conditions. Your poodle's Velcro-like coat might pick up burrs, seeds, or other natural detritus, including dangerous foxtails. You can put your poodle in a special jumpsuit (like the K9 Top Coat) to practice, though she's not allowed to wear it during the tracking test.

Flyball and Scent Hurdling

In the fast-paced sport of flyball, dogs run a relay race in teams of four. One dog from each team runs down a straight course, jumps over four hurdles, and touches a flyball box to release a tennis ball. He grabs the ball and runs back with it over the four hurdles. When he reaches the starting line, the next dog on his team is allowed to take his turn. The fastest team wins.

The North American Flyball Association offers three titles: Flyball Dog (FD), Flyball Dog Excellent (FDX), and Flyball Dog Champion (FDCh). The AKC does not have a flyball program.

Scent-hurdle racing is similar to flyball, except that rather than retrieving a ball released by a flyball box after jumping four hurdles, the dog retrieves a scent article, choosing the one from among four that was touched by her handler.

While titles aren't available yet in the United States, the Canadian Kennel Club and the Canadian Scent Hurdle Racing Association award titles at three levels: Scent Hurdle Dog (SHD), Scent Hurdle Dog Excellent (SDHX), and Scent Hurdle Dog Champion (CHSHD). In the United States, some local groups put on scent-hurdle races.

Question?

Where can I go to try out different sports?
A dog camp can be a great place to try out new activities. A number of weeklong camps that you attend with your dog are offered nationwide, and they all offer a variety of dog sports. See Appendix B for information on some of them.

Herding Tests

While poodles don't belong to the Herding Group, many demonstrate an ability to herd, and they can pass a herding instinct test. In this test, the dog keeps the livestock grouped together and moves them toward (or ahead of) the handler. A dog that passes is awarded the Herding Instinct Certified (HIC) title. These tests are primarily offered by herding clubs.

The AKC does not recognize the HIC title for poodles, or allow them to be part of its herding programs; however, any poodle registered with the Canadian Kennel Club may participate in its herding program. Poodles can also participate in American Herding Breed Association (AHBA) trials, where they can earn any of six titles that culminate in the Herding Trial Champion title.

Fact

A great activity for poodles with a strong prey drive is lure coursing. This involves chasing an ersatz "bunny" (usually just a couple of white plastic bags) as it is pulled around a track by cables. While only sight hounds and Rhodesian Ridgebacks can officially compete, you might be able to find a sight-hound club that will let your poodle practice with them.

Special Considerations for Canine Athletes

If you participate in athletic events with your poodle, it's up to you to keep him safe. Your dog might enjoy the activity so much that he doesn't know when to slow down. Exercise caution in allowing your poodle to do anything that might injure him.

While poodles are pretty light on their feet, they can still become injured in hunt tests, on the agility course, or in any other sport. Be sure to keep a first-aid kit in your car when you travel to a competition or practice with your poodle. And know how to use it.

A specific problem to watch out for, especially during the summer, is heatstroke. Keep a close eye on your poodle, and stop all activity at the first signs of heatstroke: rapid panting, a bright-red tongue, and thick saliva. Make plenty of water available to your poodle when you're at an event. Don't count on it being available at the show site—play it safe, and bring a bottle and bowl with you. See Chapter 12 for more information about first aid for heatstroke and other issues.

Essential

Exercise extreme caution when leaving your dog in the car. If the day is at all warm or sunny, don't leave your poodle in a car without air conditioning for any length of time, even with the windows cracked. A car can heat up to the point where it causes heatstroke in just minutes.

Finally, be sure your dog gets proper nutrition. Canine athletes need more calories than couch potatoes. To keep their bodies running well, be sure to feed high-quality food, with plenty of protein from a very good source. Your poodle will run his little heart out for you. You need to supply him with the best fuel you can.

CHAPTER 20

Traveling with Your Poodle

YOU AND YOUR POODLE undoubtedly have a very close bond, and when you go on family vacations, you'll want to bring her along. A well-trained and socialized poodle will make a perfect traveling companion. As long as you plan ahead and do your research in advance, traveling with even the largest Standard Poodle can be a breeze. On the other hand, you should also know how to find someone trustworthy to watch your poodle on occasions when she will need to stay behind.

The Importance of Identification

Properly identifying your poodle is never more important than when you're traveling. The idea of losing your dog when you're in unfamiliar territory is almost too awful to contemplate. But think about it you must, so that you can plan ahead and do everything in your power to make sure your poodle isn't lost while you travel. If you identify her properly, you'll have more hope if the worst does occur.

Your poodle should always wear a collar while traveling, with a tag that lists your current contact information. Obviously, your home number won't do any good if you're traveling. Rather, your dog's travel tag should have your cellular phone number (if you have one), as well as an emergency number in case your cell phone isn't working properly. You might use the number of a trusted friend or relative who will have your itinerary and know how to contact you. If you don't have a cell phone, the tag should give the phone number of the hotel where you're staying. This might mean a new tag every day, but that's easy to accomplish if you pack extra paper tags and a permanent marker.

Staying in a Hotel

Finding a place to stay overnight where your dog will be welcome is luckily not as difficult as it once was. If you plan ahead, you can find a hotel or bed and breakfast that will accommodate you and your poodle. When you stay at the hotel with your dog, remember that you should both be on your best behavior so the hotel has no reason to question its dog-friendly policy.

Essential

Don't sneak your dog into the hotel. You might be able to smuggle a small dog in unnoticed, but you'll worry about every peep he makes. That's stressful for you and for your poodle. It's much better to call ahead and make a reservation, explaining that you are traveling with your dog.

Finding Accommodations

The Internet can help you locate dog-friendly hotels, motels, and bed-and-breakfasts, and you can find several good sites in Appendix B. The American Automobile Association (AAA) notes in its TourBooks the hotels that are pet-friendly and even periodically publishes a book of pet-friendly accommodations called *Traveling with Your Pet: The AAA PetBook*. Since hotels sometimes change their policies, a telephone call to confirm their pet-friendly status is always in order.

Some hotel companies—like Loews and Starwood, which owns the Westin, Sheraton, and W hotel chains—are bending over backward to accommodate people and their pets. They even offer a special room service menu for dogs, as well as comfy canine beds.

When you make your reservation, explain that you're traveling with your poodle. Some hotels automatically put pets in smoking rooms. If that is not satisfactory to you (why should nonsmoking pet owners have to stay in smelly rooms, anyway?), explain to the hotel that your poodle shouldn't cause problems with future guests who are allergic to dogs. If the hotel won't budge, and you don't want to stay in a smoking room, just seek out another hotel.

Hotel Etiquette

When you stay in a hotel, keep the other guests in mind. Don't leave your poodle alone in the room if she's going to bark. If you know you can leave her alone and she'll remain quiet, it's a good idea to crate her when you're away from the room, in case a hotel employee enters the room. You don't want your poodle to scare the employee, and you don't want the employee accidentally letting your dog out the door.

If your poodle sleeps on the bed, bring along a sheet from home she can lie on. Even though she won't leave behind dog hair, she could mar a spread with dirty paws. Always, always, always clean up after your dog eliminates outdoors, and be sure to find out from hotel personnel where to deposit her poop.

Car Travel

Safety should be your primary concern when it comes to car travel. Don't let your poodle ride in the front seat if you have passenger-side airbags. If the airbags inflate, they could seriously injure or suffocate him—no matter which variety he is. And certainly don't let your poodle ride in your lap while you drive! No matter what size your poodle is, he should be restrained in your car. You can do that with a crate, a carrier that's belted in with the car's shoulder belt, or a seat belt harness.

Alert!

It's not safe to let your poodle hang his head out the open window when the car's moving. A pebble could hit him in the eye. No matter how much he loves it, keep those windows closed enough to make it impossible or buy specially made goggles (called Doggles) that will protect his eyes.

Crates and Carriers

The safest way you can transport your poodle in the car is in a hard-sided crate that is affixed to the car's interior. A plastic airline-style crate is useful for all three sizes of poodles. This will protect your dog from being thrown around inside the car, in the event of a traffic accident, and also protect her from being crushed. And your dog will be contained if rescue workers must come to your car after an accident.

It can be a challenge to secure crates in the car. If your crate is small and has a handle on top, you can thread the seat belt through the handle. The Kennel Cab, from PetMate, features a seat-belt slot in the roof to help secure it. It comes in sizes suitable for Toys and Miniatures. For a larger crate, try threading the seat belt through the wire in the side or side grate. If you have a sports utility vehicle, you can use bungee cords to affix the crate, since most SUVs have cargo hooks or other places to anchor a cord.

Seat Belt Harnesses

If your car is too small to hold a crate for your poodle, or she simply cannot stand to be crated, a seatbelt harness can provide some security. There are several types on the market, but each type puts a secure line between your dog and the car's seat belt. These belts provide security in the event of an accident (the seat belt freezes when the brakes are applied suddenly) but allow the dog some mobility when the car is moving normally.

Look for a belt that doesn't rely on plastic quick-release buckles to stay fastened in the event of an accident. Metal is much stronger. One especially sturdy harness is the Champion Canine Seat Belt System sold at *www.canineauto.com.*

Essential

When you travel with your poodle, you should make sure that you and your dog are exemplary guests. The restrictions that are placed on dogs are often the result of poor behavior on the part of prior canine and human visitors. Do your part for all canine travelers, and let your poodle be an ambassador for her species.

Your poodle might get twisted in the seat belt harness initially, but don't let this make you give up on it. She should quickly get the hang of moving around without getting tangled. Even if you have to keep pulling over in the beginning to untangle her, in the long run it's worth the trouble to keep her safe!

Booster Seats

If your small poodle likes to look out the window but can't because she's too low in the seat, you can purchase a booster seat for her to sit in. This fleece-lined seat is secured by a seat belt and also has a safety strap that attaches to your dog's harness. This option isn't as protective as a hard-sided crate, but it might make travel more enjoyable for your little poodle.

Rest Areas

Rest areas can pose a special challenge when you're traveling alone with dogs. If it's warm out, you don't want to leave your poodle in the car. Yet most rest areas forbid pets from entering the building.

If your poodle is a Toy or small Mini, and you have a soft-sided carrier that looks like an ordinary duffle, you can try bringing your dog with you into the restroom. Probably no one will even notice you have a dog with you. Larger dogs are trickier, though. You may have no choice but to leave her in the car while you race in and use the facilities. Blast the air conditioning as you pull in, and try to park in the shade. Do your business quickly, then race back to the car to give your poodle her turn.

Alert!

Don't leave your poodle in the car with the engine running. It might be too tempting for a would-be thief who may not be deterred by your poodle. It would be terrible to have your car stolen—but think how much worse it would be if your dog were in it!

Dealing with a Car-Sick Dog

Some dogs, particularly puppies, get nauseous in the car, which can put a damper on car travel. If your poodle gets motion sickness or overanxious and needs a little help feeling well in the car, opening your windows a crack to let some fresh air in might make her feel better. Don't open them far enough for her to stick her head out, though! You can also try some ground ginger (either in capsules from the health-food store or in tasty ginger snaps), or the Bach flower remedy called Rescue Remedy, which is calming. In severe cases, your veterinarian might want to prescribe a tranquilizer.

If you think your dog may get sick, feed a smaller-than-normal meal before embarking on a trip. Cover your seats with towels to make potential cleanup easier. It's a good idea to keep paper towels, plastic bags, odor-eliminating cleaner, and some paper plates (which make good scoops) in the trunk of your car for emergency cleanups.

If you have a dog prone to motion sickness and you're preparing to take a long trip, try taking her on short trips in advance to acclimate her to the motion. If you increase the length of your trip gradually, she'll be more likely to be more comfortable on your trip, which will be more pleasant for all concerned.

Essential

Motion sickness is a disturbance in your dog's balance center. It's not uncommon for puppies, in particular, to start salivating, then throw up when the car is in motion. The good news is that most pups eventually grow out of it. So if your puppy vomits in the car, don't minimize car rides his whole life.

Leaving on a Jet Plane

Flying with your poodle is much easier if your poodle is small enough to fit in a carrier in the seat in front of you. If you have a Standard Poodle, she'll have to fly in the cargo hold of the plane. Both modes of doggie travel require you to make reservations in advance. Some airlines may not allow dogs on their planes at all, so it's important to double-check the airline's policy before buying your tickets.

Flying in the Cabin

If you're going to take your small poodle in the cabin with you, you must make a reservation for her. Airlines limit the number of pets they allow in the cabin on any given flight. They also charge a fee for carrying a pet on the plane, though they don't charge for other types of carryons.

When you call to make the reservation, find out exactly what kind of documentation might be needed at check-in. Sometimes the airlines don't ask for the documentation, but if you are asked and don't have it, you and your poodle could be turned away. Typically, you need to have a veterinary exam and a letter from your vet stating that your dog is healthy enough to travel.

Fact

An airline called Companion Air is being established specifically to cater to pet owners. The planes hold six people and up to twelve pets, and part of the cabin accommodates crates for the pets, who are allowed to visit with their owners one at a time during the flight. It can be pricey, but it's definitely a cut above the noisy cargo hold.

Flying as Checked Baggage

Your poodle can fly in the cargo hold with the luggage on your flight. Be sure to check with the airline in advance about their individual regulations. Tell the representative that you're traveling with a dog when you make the reservation. And call twenty-four to forty-eight hours before the flight to confirm—pets are prohibited when temperatures are extreme, so it's wise to check close to the flight to make sure your dog will be allowed.

Put a big sign on your poodle's crate saying that there's an animal inside. Make the sign a bright color so that you will easily be able to identify the crate from a distance. List all your contact information, including a cell number (if you have one) and a phone number at your destination. And put your dog's name on the crate—it will help him to be viewed as an individual, not baggage.

Question?

Should I tranquilize my dog before he gets on the plane?
No. The airlines discourage it, and a recent study has shown that tranquilizers don't help calm a stressed dog in flight. And on top of that, half of all flying-related deaths are attributed to sedation and its effect on respiration and the ability to regulate body temperature.

In the gate area, watch out the window for the crate to be loaded onto the plane. Seeing it being loaded even before you board the plane will be reassuring. If you don't happen to see the crate being put on the plane, after you board you can notify the flight attendant that your dog is in the baggage hold and ask her to make sure the dog is on board before the plane takes off.

Traveling Abroad

If your poodle is small enough to travel in the airplane cabin with you, she might make a delightful companion for traveling to other countries. Assuming she is able to sit still in her carrier under the seat in front of you for the duration of the trip and is not stressed by traveling, your poodle may really enjoy the freedom that she'll find in some foreign destinations.

◀ **Poodles make excellent (and eye-catching) traveling companions.**

In France, for example, dogs are welcome in many restaurants and hotels and on public transportation. It is not unusual to see a well-behaved poodle (or other dog) sitting under her owner's chair in a restaurant, or even on the chair next to him!

If you're going to take your poodle abroad, make sure she's well trained and well behaved. You and she will be acting as ambassadors for American dogs and owners. Your poodle should be able to remain quiet in public, shouldn't growl or bark at strangers (unless provoked, of course), and should know her basic manners.

Before you travel to a foreign country with your poodle, check out the entry requirements. Some countries require vaccinations or titers within a certain time period prior to entry. Do your research so that you know the most current regulations for the countries you're planning to visit.

Fact

Unfortunately, it can be hard to find ways besides cars and planes to travel with your dog. Amtrak doesn't allow dogs on board their trains, though some commuter lines do. Greyhound buses only allow service dogs. Some ocean liners will accept dogs, but they might require them to be confined for the whole journey.

Leaving Your Poodle Behind

If your poodle is a large Miniature or a Standard, you might think twice before checking her as baggage for a long flight or series of flights. While she'd doubtless rather be with you when you travel, she might be better off staying at home with a pet sitter or going to a boarding kennel.

Boarding Kennels

If you must travel but can't take your poodle with you, one option is to leave her at a boarding kennel. How do you find a good one? Word of mouth is a good start. Ask your dog-loving friends where they take their pets when they're out of town. Then go visit the kennel. Use your eyes and nose to investigate how clean the kennel is. Find out how much exercise the dogs are given. Ask about emergency procedures and whether the building is equipped with a sprinkler system in case of fire. Be very selective—your poodle will doubtless miss you, and you want her to be as comfortable as possible in your absence. Now is not the time to be a bargain hunter.

Ask the kennel whether you can bring your own food in, so that your dog doesn't have to have a change in diet. Find out whether you can bring favorite toys and your poodle's bed to the kennel. It's also nice to bring a worn T-shirt or other garment that smells like you.

Pet Sitters

You may choose to have someone come stay in your home or care for your poodle in her own home while you're away. Pet sitters have several advantages over kennels. They give truly personalized attention to your dog. Your dog can stay home (or at least in a home environment, if she stays with the sitter). There's usually less stress because there are usually fewer strange dogs to contend with. And they don't require annual vaccinations as many boarding kennels do.

You're obviously entrusting this person with something very important: your canine family member and (perhaps) the key to your house. Unless your dog stays with a close friend you already know and trust, interview any potential pet sitters in person, preferably with your dog present so you can gauge how the pet sitter interacts with your dog (and how your dog reacts to the sitter). Ask about the sitter's emergency procedures. Ask for references and call them. Go with a pet sitter who has many satisfied, repeat customers.

CHAPTER 21

The Senior Poodle

WITHOUT A DOUBT THE HARDEST part of sharing your life with a dog is that you will almost certainly outlive him. Losing a poodle is like losing a little piece of your heart. But if you give your poodle great care, with any luck he'll grow to a ripe old age. That's what every poodle owner wants, although the senior years provide some new challenges for both you and your dog.

What Is Old?

It used to be you'd figure out a dog's "real" age by multiplying the number of years he'd lived by seven. The result was supposedly the human equivalent of his doggie age. A seven-year-old dog, for example, was middle-aged, like a forty-nine-year-old human. But it's really more complicated than that. Dogs, small dogs, in particular, can live to be quite old. A twenty-year-old Toy Poodle isn't unheard of. But a 140-year-old human certainly is!

As in humans, each dog's individual health, genetics, and spirit affect how old he seems. A ten-year-old Miniature Poodle with health concerns can seem older than the thirteen-year-old active Miniature Poodle down the street. With that in mind, some generalizations can be made.

The size of your poodle is the main factor in determining "old age." In general, owners of Miniature and Toy Poodles can expect their dogs to live fifteen to eighteen years. At about the age of twelve, these dogs are considered senior citizens. Standard Poodles don't live as long. Their life span is approximately ten to twelve years, and they can achieve geriatric status starting at about the age of eight.

Essential

Listen to your internal voice if you feel that something is up with your senior poodle's health. You know your dog better than anyone and if you sense that something is wrong, take him to the vet for an examination and blood work.

The Senior Health Exam

Ask your veterinarian when he considers your individual dog a senior citizen, for the purposes of his veterinary care. Right at the very beginning of that stage you should have blood work done to provide a baseline for comparison.

You should have the blood and urine of an elderly poodle drawn and analyzed twice a year. Problems like potential kidney failure can be caught early this way and addressed nutritionally long before your poodle would have shown symptoms. A holistic vet might use blood test results to prescribe nutritional supplements to address deficiencies.

Your vet will also give your poodle a physical exam, looking at his teeth, eyes, and ears, and checking for signs of arthritis and unusual lumps or bumps.

Think long and hard before vaccinating your older dog. He's probably received ample vaccinations in his lifetime, and giving him more might unnecessarily tax his immune system. Talk with your veterinarian about it. If she's of the opinion that your dog needs shots, ask if she'll draw blood for a titer first. If the titer tells you your dog is protected against the core diseases (except for rabies, which is required by law), you can skip the shot. Consider skipping vaccinations for the noncore diseases entirely.

▲ Caring for your poodle as he ages helps pay back the lifetime of love he gives you.

Nutrition for the Older Dog

Older dogs have a decreased ability to handle the same poor-quality foods they might have eaten happily when they were young. So if you haven't done so already, now might be the time to upgrade your poodle's food. Switch to a better brand of food or, better yet, start feeding a home-prepared diet made with high-quality ingredients. Whether or not you improve her diet, adding digestive enzymes can be beneficial (Prozyme is one popular brand). They'll help your poodle digest her food more thoroughly.

It might be harder to keep weight off your poodle as she ages. A dog's metabolism slows down with age, and her energy level might decrease as well. If you continue feeding her the same quantity of food she's always eaten, her weight will go up. Obesity is unhealthy for your dog: it can lead to serious health problems, heart disease, joint problems, diabetes, even cancer. So do her a favor and keep her trim. (See Chapter 8 for tips on helping an overweight poodle.)

Alert!

Make dietary changes slowly if your dog is older. His system might not be able to handle a sudden change in diet. To minimize digestive difficulties, transition from one food to another over the course of several weeks.

You might notice that your poodle is less enthusiastic about her food as she gets older. If you don't feed a variety of food, she might be just plain sick of it, in which case a gradual shift to different food might help. More likely, however, her senses have diminished, so the food doesn't smell as good to her. You can help make her food more enticing by topping it with fresh food (if you feed commercial food). Or add some liver powder to it. Another possibility is that her mouth hurts, so she doesn't want to chew. In that case, feed her softer food (and see your veterinarian about her dental health).

Question?

If I just wait him out, won't my poodle eat eventually?
Maybe, but don't starve your elderly poodle into eating. That's not fair or kind. Instead, do what you can to make his food more enticing.

If your poodle has a sudden and drastic loss of appetite, or if she is losing weight even though she's eating, take her to the veterinarian. These could be signs of serious illness.

Problems of Aging

Veterinary care is more important than ever as your dog ages. Don't chalk up every health change in your senior poodle to "old age." Rather, get symptoms checked out—they might indicate a condition that can be treated (or at least the symptom itself can be dealt with).

Degenerative Joint Disease

Degenerative joint disease, also known as arthritis, occurs when the cartilage that cushions the bones in the joints deteriorates. Then bone rubs painfully against bone. This can happen just through ordinary wear, even if there isn't an injury. If your poodle becomes stiff, starts limping, or has difficulty lying down or getting up, arthritis may be the culprit. Take him to the veterinarian for a checkup.

Alert!

Don't give your poodle any over-the-counter nonsteroidal inflammatory drugs (NSAIDs) like aspirin, acetaminophen (Tylenol), or ibuprofen (Advil) without first talking with your veterinarian. Such drugs can help humans with arthritis, but may not be good for your dog. Ibuprofen, in particular, is toxic to dogs.

Your poodle doesn't need to live in pain. A number of "nutraceuticals," like glucosamine and chondroitin combinations, as well as anti-inflammatory supplements made from sea animals, can help rebuild the cartilage and reduce the pain associated with arthritis. Their proponents even say that these nutraceuticals can reverse the cartilage damage. Treating with nutraceuticals early in the degenerative process can be particularly helpful. These treatments haven't been shown to have side effects, though it can take a while for your dog to show signs that the nutraceuticals are helping.

If the arthritis doesn't respond to the more benign support of nutraceuticals, there are a number of anti-inflammatory drugs on the market for dogs. Rimadyl, Duramaxx, and Etogesic are all drugs that can help ease the pain of arthritis. These drugs all have side effects, however, and some of them are serious. Ask for blood tests to ensure that your poodle isn't suffering from any liver or kidney problems—which can be exacerbated by these drugs—before giving these medications to your dog. If you choose to start using them, be sure to monitor his blood work to see that his internal organs aren't being damaged.

Canine Cancer

While certainly not all old dogs develop cancer, it is a major cause of death for geriatric dogs and accounts for over 50 percent of canine deaths per year. Depending on the type, a diagnosis of cancer is not necessarily a death sentence. More and more treatments for cancer in dogs are becoming available, including surgery, chemotherapy, radiation, and alternative therapies.

Making a decision on how to treat cancer in your dog can be very difficult, particularly when your dog is older. But one thing is certain. The earlier the cancer is diagnosed, the more options you will have.

Here are ten common signs of cancer, according to the American Veterinary Medical Association:

- Abnormal swellings that persist or grow
- Sores that don't heal
- Weight loss
- Loss of appetite
- Bleeding or discharge from any body opening
- Offensive odor
- Difficulty eating or swallowing
- Hesitation to exercise or loss of stamina
- Persistent lameness or stiffness
- Difficulty breathing, urinating, or defecating

If you see any of these signs, take your dog to the veterinarian. As scary as a potential diagnosis of cancer is, delaying a vet visit out of fear can only make matters worse.

If your poodle is diagnosed with cancer, talk with your veterinarian about the best diet for him. Research done by Greg Ogilvie, DVM, of Colorado State University's Animal Cancer Center indicates that minimizing simple carbohydrates (starches and sugars); providing high-quality protein, and soluble and insoluble fiber; and increasing omega-3 fatty acids and antioxidants is beneficial for cancer patients.

Fact

A number of e-mail lists have been formed to provide information and support for people whose dogs have been diagnosed with cancer. If you're facing cancer in your poodle, look for these lists at *www.yahoogroups.com*: CanineCancer, CanineswithCancer, and CanineCancerComfort.

Cognitive Dysfunction

Cognitive dysfunction (CD), also known as canine senility or "doggie Alzheimer's," is defined as any decline in mental function that can't be attributed to another factor. A poodle that suffers from cognitive dysfunction might seem disoriented or confused. He might wander in the house aimlessly or even seem to be lost in familiar surroundings. He might not get involved in what's going on around him and not respond to you like he used to. He might even lose bladder or bowel control.

A drug called deprenyl (brand name Anipryl) can reverse these signs of aging and help your poodle gain back his quality of life. About a third of the dogs that took deprenyl for their cognitive dysfunction responded extremely well. (An additional third responded reasonably well to the drug, and the final third did not respond at all.)

Other research suggests that giving your aged poodle antioxidant supplements, like vitamin E, might help repair her cognitive dysfunction. Talk with your veterinarian about supplements and dosages.

Diabetes

Diabetes occurs when the pancreas stops making sufficient insulin, which helps regulate blood sugar. It's not an uncommon ailment in older poodles. Signs that your poodle may be diabetic include increased thirst and urination, increased appetite, recurrent urinary tract infections, weakness, and fatigue.

Alert!

Diabetes occurs in one out of every 400 to 500 dogs and cats. Unspayed females are more prone to diabetes than males or spayed females. Poodles are among the breeds that might have a higher prevalence of the disease. Obese dogs are at a higher risk of developing diabetes.

Diagnosis is made with a blood test. Treatment includes twice-daily injections of insulin. As tough as that might sound, once you get into a routine of giving your dog shots, it should be easy to manage. Talk to your veterinarian about your poodle's diet and how much exercise he should get, since strenuous exercise has an effect on blood sugar. Ask your vet how to recognize signs of low blood sugar, and find out what to do if they occur.

Hearing Loss

Your poodle's hearing may deteriorate with age. Dogs are so adaptable that it might actually take you some time to notice there's a problem. As soon as you see signs of hearing loss (or even before), you can teach your dog to recognize basic sign language. Since dogs are so in tune with body language, it's sometimes easier for them to understand sign language than words. Create and teach simple signs for messages, like "Good boy!" "Watch me," and "Would you like a treat?" as well as cues for "Sit," "Come," "Down," and "Stay."

Essential

Living with a Deaf Dog, by Susan Cope Becker, can help you with any difficulties you might encounter due to your poodle's hearing loss, as can the excellent Web site hosted by the Deaf Dogs Education Action Fund (*www.deafdogs.com*). Both supply suggestions for signs you can use with your dog.

If your poodle starts to lose his hearing, be vigilant about his safety. Don't let him off-leash in an unsecured area. He might not hear oncoming traffic or other dangers, and he won't benefit from any verbal warning you give him.

Incontinence

If your poodle starts to leak urine in his sleep, or if he suddenly begins to poop in the house, you could be seeing the signs of several problems. A trip to the veterinarian is definitely in order. Increased urination could be something as simple as a urinary tract infection, but it can also be a sign of diabetes or a hormone-related problem.

Especially in an older dog, don't assume that incontinence is a behavioral problem. Don't yell at him, punish him, or banish him. Instead, have him checked out by your veterinarian. You should also give him more opportunities to go outside. He just may not be able to hold it as long as he could when he was younger.

Kidney Disease

The kidneys are very important organs, since they remove waste products from the body and regulate water and electrolytes.

They also assist in regulation of blood pressure and in the production of red blood cells. As a dog ages, his kidneys can show wear, and they may not function as well.

The main signs of kidney problems are increased thirst and urination and weight loss. Regular blood tests will help your veterinarian detect kidney problems even before symptoms start to show up.

Fact

A new urine test called early renal detection (ERD) detects small amounts of albumin, an indication of early kidney disease. This test can help your veterinarian identify kidney problems before they would show up on a blood test.

Nutrition is a key component of dealing with kidney problems. Acupuncture or other holistic modalities may be of great benefit as well.

Old-Age Vestibular Syndrome

One day your poodle might suddenly become very dizzy. He might start walking in circles, his head may tilt to one side, or he might not even be able to keep his balance well enough to stand up. His eyes might drift back and forth. One side of his face might become paralyzed, and he might seem to you like he's had a stroke. (Strokes in dogs are very uncommon.) Chances are that he has peripheral vestibular disease.

The condition is also called old-age vestibular syndrome because it most commonly appears in geriatric dogs. It seems to be caused by an inflammation of the nerve that connects the inner ear to the cerebellum.

If your dog begins to exhibit these symptoms, stay calm and call your veterinarian. In some cases, a veterinarian will be able to determine the cause of this inflammation, but it is not always obvious. If no cause is found that your vet can address with medication or other treatment, your vet will probably just ask you to wait for the symptoms to subside. If your poodle is so dizzy that he can't eat or drink, your vet might prescribe an antihistamine, like Benadryl, which helps with the nausea, or motion-sickness medication, like Antivert. Dogs with peripheral vestibular disease usually recover fully within two weeks, though sometimes a head tilt can linger.

Vision Loss

Your poodle might start losing his vision as he ages. As with hearing loss, he'll probably adapt readily, using his other senses to make up where his eyes fail.

Essential

You can help your poodle cope with vision loss by keeping the floor free of clutter and by not rearranging furniture. If you must move things around, carefully walk your poodle through the new arrangement to show him where he can now expect to find obstacles in his path.

If your poodle's vision loss is due to cataracts, ask your veterinarian about the feasibility of having the cataracts surgically removed. She may refer you to a veterinary ophthalmologist, who might recommend surgery. If successful, cataract surgery could restore much of your poodle's vision. Other forms of vision loss may be permanent.

Keeping Your Old Poodle Comfortable

In addition to providing regular veterinary care to address problems that might crop up, you can do your geriatric dog a big favor by making her as comfortable as possible. Give her an especially comfy bed to lie on, so that her sore joints are well cushioned.

Install ramps up to the couch or bed (assuming she's accustomed to lying there) so she doesn't have to jump on and off them.

Take her outside to go to the bathroom more often, since she may no longer have the bladder and bowel control of a young dog. Take her out for regular walks, even if they aren't as long as they used to be. Regular exercise is good for her, and getting out to see, sniff, and listen to the world is important. Don't ask her to exercise more than she's comfortable with, however.

When to Say Goodbye

Losing your beloved poodle can be extremely difficult. If you have to make the decision to euthanize your ailing dog, it can be even harder. But euthanasia is sometimes the last favor you can give your dog. It can be a real mercy that leaves you in peace. When you're faced with a decision about euthanasia, ask yourself a few questions:

- Is she eating and drinking?
- Is she getting pleasure out of her usual delights?
- Does she still have her dignity?
- Is there any hope for a rebound or recovery?
- Are you hesitating to euthanize for your sake or hers?

If the answer to any of the first four questions is "No," and you realize that it is you, not your dog, who is having trouble letting go, then euthanasia might be the best course of action, as hard as it is.

The Last Appointment

When you have your dog euthanized, try to do it under the best conditions for your dog. If your poodle is fearful of the veterinarian's office, you might see if your vet will make a house call. If you take your poodle to the vet for euthanasia, try to do it at a time when the clinic isn't too hectic.

If you can, be with your poodle during the procedure. Hold her close as she passes, and she'll have the comfort of your presence. Euthanasia is a painless procedure that should be peaceful. Ask your veterinarian to give your poodle a sedative with a subcutaneous injection before giving her the final injection into the vein. Because it can be difficult to find a vein, it's less stressful for your poodle (and you) if she's sedated first. Then she can just slip away after the lethal injection.

Fact

There are many types of creative tributes available for your poodle's cremated remains. In addition to buying a box or urn to store or bury them in, you can have wind chimes or a gas lamp or even a painting made using the ashes. Your poodle can live on in your life through her remains.

Remembering Your Poodle

Think in advance about what you'd like to have done with your poodle's remains, so that you don't have to make a difficult decision on the spot. Usually, you have one of these options: to get any remains back, to take your poodle's body home for burial, to have her remains cremated, or to have her remains cremated and packaged for you to take home. If your poodle is cremated—and if you want to make sure that the ashes you get back are from her—ask for a private cremation. This can be more expensive, but many people consider it well worth the expense. Whatever you do, remember always to cherish the memories of times you and your poodle shared, from the moment you chose her and welcomed her home, through all the new things you learned and experienced together. You'll never regret the time you devoted to spending with your poodle.

Appendix A

Organizations

American Animal Hospital Association
12575 W. Bayaud Ave.
Lakewood, CO 80228
(303) 986-2800
www.healthypet.com

American Kennel Club
5580 Centerview Dr.
Raleigh, NC 27606-3390
(919) 233-9767
www.akc.org

AKC Canine Health Foundation
P.O. Box 37941
Raleigh, NC 27627-7941
(919) 334-4010
www.akcchf.org

ASPCA Animal Poison Control Center
1717 S. Philo, Ste. 36
Urbana, IL 61802
(888) 426-4435 (to use a credit card)
(900) 443-0000 (to have fee charged to your phone bill)
www.napcc.aspca.org

Association of Pet Dog Trainers
17000 Commerce Pkwy., Ste. C
Mt. Laurel, NJ 08054
(800) 738-3647
www.apdt.com

Canadian Kennel Club
89 Skyway Avenue, Suite 100
Etobicoke, Ontario, Canada M9W 6R4
(416) 675-5511
www.ckc.ca

Canine Eye Registry Foundation
Purdue University
CERF/Lynn Hall
625 Harrison St.
West Lafayette, IN 47907-2026
(765) 494-8179
www.vmdb.org

Delta Society
580 Naches Avenue, SW, Suite 101
Renton, WA 98055-2297
(425) 226-7357
www.deltasociety.org

Foundation for Pet-Provided Therapy
P.O. Box 6308
Oceanside, CA 92058
(760) 740-2326
www.loveonaleash.org

Morris Animal Foundation
45 Inverness Dr. E.
Englewood, CO 80112-5480
(800) 243-2345
www.morrisanimalfoundation.org

National Association of Professional Pet Sitters
17000 Commerce Pkwy., Ste. C
Mt. Laurel, NJ 08054
(800) 296-7387
www.petsitters.org

North American Dog Agility Council
11522 South Hwy. 3
Cataldo, ID 83810
www.nadac.com

North American Flyball Association
1400 W. Devon Ave., #512
Chicago, IL 60600
(800) 318-6312
www.flyball.org

North American Hunting Retriever Association
P.O. Box 5159
Fredericksburg, VA 22403
(540) 899-7620
www.nahra.org

Orthopedic Foundation for Animals
2300 E. Nifong Blvd.
Columbia, MO 65201
(573) 442-0418
www.offa.org

PetCare Insurance
3315 E. Algonquin Rd., Ste. 450
Rolling Meadows, IL 60008
(866) 275-7387
www.petcareinsurance.com

Pet Sitters International
201 E. King St.
King, NC 27021-9161
(336) 983-9222
www.petsit.com

Poodle Club of America
Mrs. Helen Tomb-Taylor
Corresponding Secretary
2434 Ripplewood
Conroe, TX 77384
(936) 271-0397
www.poodleclubofamerica.org

Therapy Dogs, Inc.
P.O. Box 5868
Cheyenne, WY 82003
(877) 843-7364
www.therapydogs.com

Therapy Dogs International
88 Bartley Rd.
Flanders, NJ 07836
(973) 252-9800
www.tdi-dog.org

United Kennel Club
100 East Kilgore Rd.
Kalamazoo, MI 49002-5584
(269) 343-9020
www.ukcdogs.com

United States Dog Agility Association
P.O. Box 850955
Richardson, TX 75085-0955
(972) 487-2200
www.usdaa.com

Veterinary Pet Insurance
P.O. Box 2344
Brea, CA 92822-2344
www.petinsurance.com

World Canine Freestyle Organization
P.O. Box 350122
Brooklyn, NY 11235-2525
(718) 332-8336
www.worldcaninefreestyle.org

APPENDIX B

Books, Magazines, and Web Sites

Books

Activities

Bonham, Margaret H. *Introduction to Dog Agility.* (Barron's, 2000)

Bonham, Margaret H. *The Simple Guide to Getting Active with Your Dog.* (TFH Publications, 2002)

Burch, Mary R. *Wanted! Animal Volunteers.* (Howell Book House, 2002)

Coile, D. Caroline. *Beyond Fetch: Fun, Interactive Activities for You and Your Dog.* (Howell Book House, 2003)

Davis, Kathy Diamond. *Therapy Dogs: Training Your Dog to Reach Others.* (Dogwise, 2002)

Behavior and Training

Adams, Janine. *How to Say It to Your Dog.* (Prentice Hall Press, 2003)

Alexander, Melissa. *Click for Joy!* (Sunshine Books, 2003)

Arden, Andrea. *Dog-Friendly Dog Training.* (Howell Book House, 1999)

Book, Mandy, and Cheryl S. Smith. *Quick Clicks: 40 Fast and Fun Behaviors to Train with a Clicker.* (Hanalei Pets, 2001)

Cothier, Suzanne. *Bones Would Rain from the Sky: Deepening Our Relationships with Dogs.* (Warner Books, 2002)

Donaldson, Jean. *The Culture Clash.* (James and Kenneth, 1996)

Dunbar, Ian. *After You Get Your Puppy.* (James and Kenneth, 2001)

Dunbar, Ian. *Before You Get Your Puppy.* (James and Kenneth, 2001)

Dunbar, Ian. *Dog Behavior: A Guide to a Happy, Healthy Pet.* (Howell Book House, 1999)

Dunbar, Ian. *How To Teach a New Dog Old Tricks.* (James & Kenneth Publishers, 1998)

McConnell, Patricia. *The Other End of the Leash.* (Ballantine, 2002)

Miller, Pat. *Positive Perspectives: Love Your Dog, Train Your Dog.* (Dogwise, 2003)

Miller, Pat. *The Power of Positive Dog Training.* (Howell Book House, 2001)

Owens, Paul, with Norma Eckroate. *The Dog Whisperer: A Compassionate Approach to Non-Violent Training.* (Adams Media, 1999)

Pryor, Karen. *Getting Started: Clicker Training for Dogs.* (Sunshine Books, 2001)

Spector, Morgan. *Clicker Training for Obedience.* (Sunshine Books, 1998)

Tillman, Peggy. *Clicking with Your Dog: Step-by-Step in Pictures.* (Sunshine Books, 2001)

Wood, Deborah. *Help for Your Shy Dog.* (Howell Book House, 1999)

Wood, Deborah. *The Tao of Bow Wow.* (Dell, 1998)

Diet

Billinghurst, Ian. *The BARF Diet: Raw Feeding for Cats and Dogs Using Evolutionary Principles.* (Lithgow, N.S.W., 2001)

Lonsdale, Tom. *Raw Meaty Bones Promote Health.* (Revetco P/L, 2001)

Martin, Ann N. *Foods Pets Die For: Shocking Facts about Pet Food.* (NewSage Press, 1997)

Morgan, Diane. *Feeding Your Dog for Life.* (Doral, 2002)

Palika, Liz. *The Consumer's Guide to Dog Food.* (Howell Book House, 1996)

Schultze, Kymythy. *Natural Nutrition for Dogs and Cats: The Ultimate Diet.* (Hay House, 1998)

Segal, Monica. *K9Kitchen: Your Dogs' Diet: The Truth Behind the Hype.* (Doggie Diner, Inc., 2002)

Strombeck, Donald. *Home-Prepared Dog and Cat Diets: The Healthful Alternative.* (Iowa State University Press, 1999)

Health

Allegretti, Jan, and Katy Sommers, D.V.M. *The Complete Holistic Dog Book.* (Celestial Arts, 2003)

Copeland, Sue M., and John M. Hamil, D.V.M. *Hands-On Dog Care.* (Doral Publishing, 2000)

Diodati, Catherine J. M. *Vaccine Guide for Dogs and Cats: What Every Pet Lover Should Know.* (New Atlantean Press, 2003)

Flaim, Denise. *The Holistic Dog Book: Canine Care for the 21st Century.* (Howell Book House, 2003)

Goldstein, Martin. *The Nature of Animal Healing: The Definitive Holistic Medicine Guide for Caring for Your Dog and Cat.* (Ballantine Books, 2000)

Hamilton, Don. *Homeopathic Care for Dogs and Cats: Small Doses for Small Animals.* (North Atlantic Books, 1999)

Pitcairn, Richard, and Susan Hubble Pitcairn. *Dr. Pitcairn's Complete Guide to Natural Health for Dogs and Cats.* (Rodale, 1995)

Puotinen, C. J. *The Encyclopedia of Natural Pet Care.* (Keats Publishing, 1998)

Shojai, Amy. *First Aid Companion for Dogs and Cats.* (Rodale, 2001)

Siegal, Mordecai, ed. *UC Davis Book of Dogs.* (Harper Collins, 1995)

Magazines

AKC Family Dog
AKC Gazette
Animal Wellness Magazine
The Bark
Dog Fancy
Dogs USA
Dog World
Popular Dogs: Poodles
Whole Dog Journal

Web Sites

Books and Products

www.doggonegood.com
www.dogwise.com
www.friendlyfence.com
www.sitstay.com
www.petextras.com

Dog Camps

www.campgonetothedogs.com
www.campw.com
www.dogcamp.com
www.dogscouts.com
www.thedogscamp.com

Dog-Friendly Travel Sites

www.dogfriendly.com
www.petswelcome.com
www.takeyourpet.com

Health and Safety

www.altvetmed.org
www.canineauto.com
www.poodlehealthregistry.com
www.vetquest.com
www.wellpet.org

Poodle-Specific

www.poodleclubofamerica.org
www.poodlehistory.org
www.vipoodle.org

Raw-Food Manufacturers

www.barfworld.com
www.bravorawdiet.com
www.omaspride.com
www.raw4dogs.com
www.stevesrealfood.com

Training

www.apdt.com
www.clickertraining.com

Index

A

B

C

D

I

J

K

L

M

R

S

T

U

V

W

The Everything® Breed-Specific Series

With *The Everything® Dachshund Book,* you'll learn all there is to know about this social, friendly canine. From adopting the perfect addition to your family to keeping your dog in top shape, this user-friendly guide is filled with the breed-specific information you need to keep your dachshund happy and healthy for years to come.

Trade Paperback, $12.95
ISBN: 1-59337-316-3

The Everything® Yorkshire Terrier Book is the definitive guide to this popular dog. Pet expert Cheryl Smith explores not only the history of this personable breed, but also their mannerisms and necessary day-to-day care.

Trade Paperback, $12.95
ISBN: 1-59337-423-2

Available wherever books are sold!

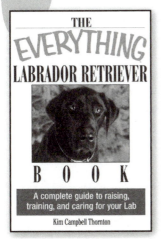

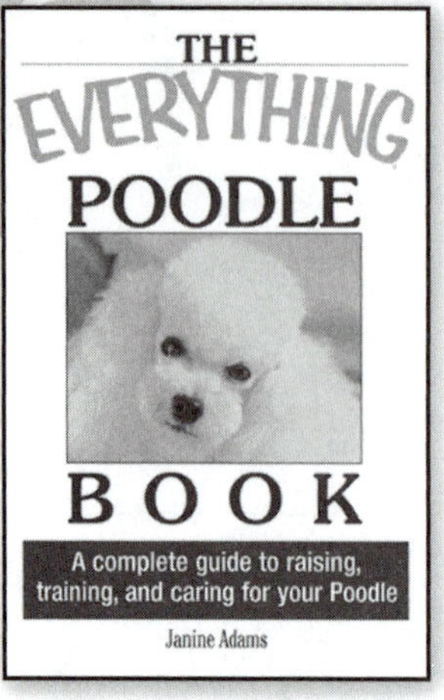

The Everything® Poodle Book is your definitive guide to learning how to care for your dog from puppyhood into adulthood. Complete with tips for training your dog to basic health care information, this book gives you all the essential facts you need to understand your pet's needs.

Trade Paperback, $12.95
ISBN: 1-59337-121-7

With *The Everything® Pug Book* you'll learn all there is to know about your best friend! From adoption methods and training techniques, to specific tips on diet, exercise, and basic care, you can anticipate your Pug's every need and be prepared for any situation.

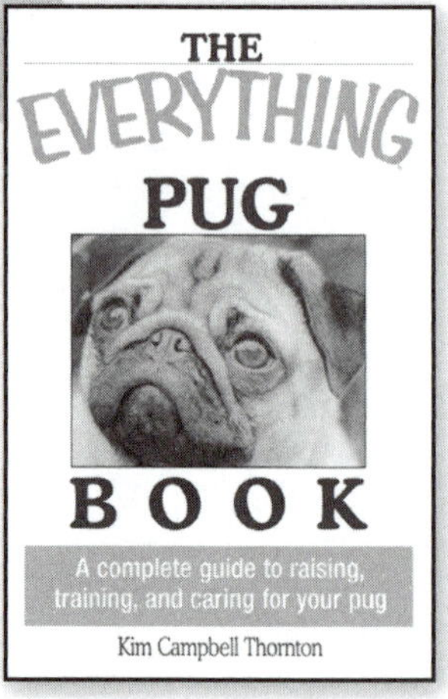

Trade Paperback, $12.95
ISBN: 1-59337-314-7

The Everything® Rottweiler Book tells you everything you need to know about making a rottweiler part of your life. This handy book is an all-inclusive work, covering all aspects of rottweiler care, so you know what to expect and can watch out for issues before they become serious problems.

Trade Paperback, $12.95
ISBN: 1-59337-122-5